Regulation and its Alternatives

Politics and Public Policy Series

Advisory Editor

Robert L. Peabody

Johns Hopkins University

Congressional Procedures and the Policy Process
Walter J. Oleszek

Interest Groups, Lobbying and Policymaking
Norman J. Ornstein
Shirley Elder

Mass Media and American Politics
Doris A. Graber

Financing Politics: Money, Elections and Political Reform, 2d ed.
Herbert E. Alexander

Invitation to Struggle: Congress, the President and Foreign Policy
Cecil V. Crabb, Jr.
Pat. M. Holt

Implementing Public Policy
George C. Edwards III

The Supreme Court
Lawrence Baum

Congress Reconsidered, 2d ed.
Lawrence C. Dodd
Bruce I. Oppenheimer, eds.

Energy, Politics and Public Policy
Walter A. Rosenbaum

The Politics of Federal Grants
George E. Hale
Marian Lief Palley

Congressional Elections
Barbara Hinckley

A Tide of Discontent: The 1980 Elections and Their Meaning
Ellis Sandoz
Cecil V. Crabb, Jr., eds.

The Politics of Shared Power: Congress and the Executive
Louis Fisher

Congress and Its Members
Roger H. Davidson
Walter J. Oleszek

Understanding Congressional Leadership
Frank H. Mackaman, ed.

Change and Continuity in the 1980 Elections
Paul R. Abramson
John H. Aldrich
David W. Rohde

Regulation and its Alternatives

Alan Stone
University of Houston

Congressional Quarterly Press
a division of
CONGRESSIONAL QUARTERLY INC.
1414 22nd Street N.W., Washington, D.C. 20037

David R. Tarr *Director, Book Department*
Joanne D. Daniels *Director, CQ Press*
Susan D. Sullivan *Developmental Editor, CQ Press*
Diane C. Hill *Project Editor*
Maceo Mayo *Production Supervisor*
Robert O. Redding *Cover Design*
Cheryl B. Rowe *Graphics*

Library of Congress Cataloging in Publication Data

Stone, Alan, 1931-
    Regulation and its alternatives.

    Bibliography: p.
    Includes index.
    1. Trade regulation—United States. I. Title.
KF1600.S69   343.73´08   81-22118
ISBN 0-87187-215-3   347.3038   AACR2

To my father

Foreword

When is it appropriate for the government to intervene in the relationships of two or more individuals or organizations? What are the criteria for determining when government regulation is efficient and equitable? These are the kinds of problems addressed by Professor Alan Stone of the University of Houston in his new book *Regulation and its Alternatives*. A former trial attorney with the Federal Trade Commission, Professor Stone has been teaching courses on law, politics, and economic regulation for more than a decade. This is his fifth book or collaborative work on such interdisciplinary subjects. A lawyer and political scientist by training, the author utilizes a law-and-economics approach to discuss government regulation.

One of the single most important influences on Professor Stone, as on almost all students of political economy, is Adam Smith's classic *An Inquiry into the Nature and Causes of the Wealth of Nations*, published on the eve of our own revolutionary war.[1] Perhaps Smith's greatest mark on the economics and history of the Western world was in setting forth the virtues of a market or free enterprise system, which he identified as

> free trade; noninterference of government in the individual's choice of occupation, residence, or investment; freedom for the individual to make his economic decisions of all kinds in response to the price movements of free and fully competitive markets—in short, of "economic liberalism" or "laissez-faire," as these terms were used in the nineteenth century....[2]

However, even Adam Smith was not an unqualified proponent of the freedom of landholders and businessmen to do whatever they wished. Smith recognized the need for government to engage in some forms of regulation, even two centuries ago. While placing great emphasis on the division of labor as a prerequisite for economic development, Smith also recognized its potential for the degradation of the individual worker. Moreover, he argued that government not only had a responsibility for educating the children of the poor but also for protecting against the creation of special privileges and the formation of legal monopolies for favored classes or groups. And Smith also conceded a need for government to establish standards that would prohibit some individuals from harming others through carelessness or lack of attention to other hazards that might jeopardize life or limb. Smith also conceded as proper roles of government the defense of the state against foreign aggressors and the right to raise taxes in order to finance such endeavors.

One can only conjecture what Adam Smith might think about contemporary relations between business, labor, and the state were he suddenly to be transported into the last quarter of the 20th century. Initially, he probably would be appalled to view the degree to which his free enterprise system has vanished. One likes to think that given Smith's interest in economic relationships and statistics he would have immediately plunged into collecting materials for a revised *Wealth of Nations*.

Lacking a visit from Adam Smith, we are indeed fortunate to have Professor Stone's interpretation of modern government regulation. Stone defines regulation as "a *state-imposed limitation on the discretion that may be exercised by individuals or organizations, which is supported by the threat of sanction.*" (p. 10) After discussing the alternatives posed by the marketplace as described by Smith and other economists, Stone outlines the advantages and disadvantages of various forms of government intervention.

Stone sets forth three criteria for evaluating regulatory activities: efficiency (Chapter 3), externalities (Chapter 4), and equity (Chapter 5). These chapters are noteworthy for their incisive reviews of what economists, political scientists, legal scholars, and historians have had to say about such critieria; and they provide a framework for determining when regulation appears to be justified and when it remains questionable or unwarranted. All of the chapters of the book are highlighted by theoretical and actual applications that help the reader to better understand the problems posed by regulation and other policy techniques.

Regulation and its Alternatives is not only informative and comprehensive but is also timely. We live in an era where the scope of government regulation has come into question once again, and properly so. *The Reagan Presidency: A Review of the First Year* reported that in 1981 the number of new pages in the *Federal Register* was down one-third from the previous year. During the first 10 months of 1980, the *Register* contained 73,061 pages, compared with 51,412 pages for the same period in 1981—21,649 fewer pages. Moreover, according to this same report, new rules or regulations had been reduced to one-half of the previous year's total.[3]

Professor Stone's arguments and careful reasoning throughout this book remind one that the mere reduction of pages in the *Federal Register* or the reduction of rules is not enough. The more important questions about government regulation remain: who is being protected, who is being deprived, and whose rights need to be restored, both immediately and in the long run.

NOTES

1. Adam Smith's work, first published in London in 1776, has been reissued in numerous editions; for example, as part of the *Harvard Classics,* ed. C. J. Bullock (New York: P. F. Collier & Son, 1909).
2. Jacob Viner, "Smith, Adam," in *International Encyclopedia of the Social Sciences 14* (New York: Free Press, 1968), pp. 322-328 at 328.
3. *The Reagan Presidency: A Review of the First Year, 1981* (Washington, D.C.: White House Office of Public Affairs, 1982), p. 3.

Robert L. Peabody

Preface

Most social scientists probably would rank Adam Smith's *Wealth of Nations* as one of the 10 greatest works of social science ever written. This judgment stands even though most of us would reject or modify many of that treatise's observations and conclusions. One of the principal reasons for Smith's continued high standing in the academic community is that he looked beyond the conventional learning of his time, incessantly returning to fundamental questions. What is an economic system supposed to accomplish? What are the alternatives to current economic and social arrangements? How should we evaluate these alternatives? By asking and attempting to answer these basic questions, Smith formulated novel and revolutionary doctrines.

The temper of the 1980s in the United States and Western Europe has led many scholars and political actors as well as the attentive public to imitate Smith's probing style of analysis. Conventional learning in areas such as the economy, crime, and education no longer seems reliable given the failures of policies based on that thinking. Newer solutions are diverse. In the realm of economic management policies, for example, there are new advocates of democratic socialism, indicative planning, and supply-side economics. But as conflicting as these solutions are, their advocates share a common intellectual quest. They seek to understand the failures of past policies and argue for the comparative superiority of their particular schemes.

This book attempts to return to first principles in the realm of government regulation, an area that has been subject to considerable questioning, notably during the 1980 presidential election campaign. But while there have been many profound critiques and defenses of particular regulatory policies and processes, there have been few systematic attempts to determine whether regulation might be justified.

This book was written to provide a framework for this and related questions.

But while I hope my analysis will help the reader ask important questions about regulation and its alternatives, it does not provide categorical or final answers to these questions. Rather, the best (or better) solution to each problem raised by a regulatory proposal—whether it is in the area of air pollution abatement, motor carrier rates, or local cable television franchising—can only be found after examining specific facts. But at least we can frame the central issues more sharply, which is the major purpose of *Regulation and its Alternatives*.

I was struck by a curious phenomenon while writing the book. Numerous economists, political scientists, legal scholars, and historians have made important contributions to the literature on regulation, yet there has been very little dialogue across disciplinary lines. In my view, a study of regulation is made more valuable by incorporating and integrating the insights generated by each discipline. I have tried to do that here.

In this undertaking I have benefited considerably from the advice, suggestions, and critical reading of many people. Valuable efforts by colleagues in the political science, economics, and finance departments of the University of Houston have been especially important in this respect. In particular, I would like to thank Jim Anderson, Richard Barke, George Daly, Paul Horvitz, Peter Mieszkowski, Bruce Oppenheimer, and Darlene Walker for their exemplary collegiality. Perceptive reviews of the entire manuscript were undertaken by Mel Dubnick and Dave Welborn; I have learned much from them. Ted Lowi, Norman Ornstein, and Peter Woll provided valuable insights at the outset of the book's preparation. Barry Mitnick's efforts at that stage and in many discussions thereafter went far beyond the call of duty. I would also like to thank Robert L. Peabody, advisory editor of this series for Congressional Quarterly Press, for writing the foreword to the book.

Finally, three other persons to whom this book owes a great deal must be singled out. While I was "living" the book, my wife Celeste and I continually discussed the general issues as well as many specific events, such as the Love Canal incident, in the context of the book. She forced me to think through the issues, frequently compelling me to change my mind. Jean L. Woy and Diane C. Hill of Congressional Quarterly were remarkable; their substantive contributions as well as the normal editorial ones were extraordinary.

Alan Stone

Contents

FOREWORD   vii

PREFACE   xi

I   MARKETS AND REGULATION   1

  1 What is Regulation?   7

    The Plan of the Book   8

    Defining Regulation   10

    The Design of Regulation   13

    A Regulatory Statute: Form and Subject Matter   15

    Collection of Regulatory Information   20

    Regulatory Sanctions and Remedies   23

    Regulatory Procedure   27

    The Waves of Regulation   30

    Conclusion   33

  2 Competition and Regulation   35

    Performance and Policy   36

    Economic Performance Goals   37

    Social Performance Goals   40

    The Classic Argument for
      Unfettered Competition   44

    Competition and Economic Performance   48

    Competition and Social Performance   52

    Questions about Markets and Regulation   55

    Conclusion   59

II   REGULATORY JUSTIFICATIONS   61

  3 Efficiency   65

    The Concept of Efficiency   66

    Natural Monopoly Regulation   68

    Antitrust   74

    Coordination Regulation   78

    Promotional Regulation   83

    Conclusion   87

  4 Externalities   91

    The Love Canal Dump Site   92

    Defining Externality   93

Private Law 101
Taxes and Subsidies 104
A Market for Pollution? 110
Regulation: The Least Worse Alternative? 115
An Unhappy Ending 121

5 Equity 125
The Nature of Contract 127
Regulation and the Defects of Contract 133
Government Agreements 134
Discriminatory Contracts 139
Bargaining Power Disparity 146
Information Disparity 151
Conclusion 164

III THE POLITICS OF REGULATION 167

6 Regulatory Legislation 171
What is Different about Regulatory Legislation? 171
The Environment of Regulatory Legislation 177
The Environment of Legislative Motivation 184
Legislative Motivation 189
Conclusion 194

7 Regulatory Administration 197
The Regulatory System 198
Adjudication: The Federal Trade Commission 205
The Substantive Consequences of Procedure 212
Rulemaking: The Consumer
     Product Safety Commission 216
The Behavior of Regulators 222
Regulatory Politics 228
Conclusion 233

8 Regulatory Reform 237
Old and New Regulatory Reform 237
Major Reform Questions 243
A Typology of Regulatory Reformers 246
Deregulation 250
Overregulation 254
Cost-Benefit Analysis 257
Cost-Effectiveness and Procedural Reform 267
Nonconclusion 274

BIBLIOGRAPHIC NOTE AND RESEARCH GUIDE 279

INDEX 283

PART I

Markets
and Regulation

M odern states have a wide variety of public policy techniques that *may* promote the social and economic well-being of their citizens, including subsidies, loan guarantees, special tax provisions, public ownership, and regulation. Of course, policymakers may choose not to intervene in social and economic affairs, preferring to allow the natural operation of the market to promote well-being. Sometimes only one technique is reasonably applicable to a public problem, but at other times policymakers plausibly may consider several alternatives that include nonintervention—the free market.

Ideally those responsible for public policymaking in the modern state—as well as concerned citizens—will treat the various policy techniques rationally as the means to achieve certain performance goals, such as a clean environment, low prices, high productivity, and rapid technological progress. Which policy technique will most likely attain the hoped-for results, or is the free market the answer? Which technique will yield the highest net benefit relative to cost?

But while policymakers and others *should* look at regulation, other public policy techniques, and the free market in so rational a manner, they frequently (perhaps often) do not. Although a backlash has occurred recently in favor of free market solutions, the characteristic response of U.S. public policymakers, confronted by what loosely may be called "public" problems, has been to adopt regulatory solutions. Thus, what was perceived as bad performance by the stock market in the late 1920s and early 1930s led to the enactment of new regulatory statutes and the creation of a new regulatory agency, the Securities and Exchange Commission. Similarly, the environmental "crisis" that claimed widespread public attention in the 1960s resulted in major regulatory legislation and the Environmental Protection Agency.

In short, regulation has been a favored policy response to perceived public problems. The accumulation of numerous individual cases has formed a vast regulatory apparatus that engages the energies of thousands of civil servants, corporate employees, and private citizens.

But, as we noted, in recent times a fundamental questioning of regulation has begun to take place. Ordinary citizens bandy words and phrases such as "deregulation" and "cost-benefit analysis." Public officials and leaders of political parties call for replacing regulation with free markets or alternative policy techniques, asserting that regulation

3

often fails to achieve its intended results or that its undesirable effects outweigh the benefits.

These claims and the call for a fundamental examination of regulation provide the unifying thread of this book. We will look at what regulation is, when it is justified, and what the alternatives are, most importantly the free market. Sometimes it will be possible to reject some alternatives or claim superiority for others. At other times, since definitive answers are not available, we will be able to do no more than frame the issues with more precision than is customary.

This framework sets the agenda for the book, generally, and the first part, "Markets and Regulation," specifically. Our first task is to define regulation and compare it with other public policy techniques, then look at regulation in detail as the technique on which we will focus. We will dissect a regulatory statute—the foundation for the rulemaking, decisions, and numerous other activities undertaken by those involved in the regulatory process. It is important to realize that regulators cannot lawfully act in any arbitrary manner suiting their whims of a particular moment. They must show that their every action is permitted by their agencies' operating statutes. For this reason it is critical that we examine and understand the component parts of regulatory statutes.

The purpose of the first chapter, then, is to set forth some important points about regulation as a public policy technique. But regulation, like other governmental techniques and like the free market, *should not* be instituted solely for its own sake. Any political-economic arrangement should be put in place because it more closely achieves desired economic and social performance goals than other policy choices. In his classic *The Wealth of Nations,* Adam Smith sought to justify the free market under most circumstances not because he had an ideological predisposition toward it but rather because, in his judgment, it was more effective in attaining performance goals than alternative arrangements.

Our first task in the second chapter is to specify these performance goals. Then we will look at the questions that must be asked in evaluating available alternatives to achieve these goals. Keeping in mind performance goals and these key questions, Chapter 2 examines the free, unfettered market idea to see how it purports to attain these goals. (In later chapters we will see how regulation is expected by its advocates to remedy the market failures of the free market.)

A final word about my approach to discussing these issues is in order. It is called a "law-and-economics approach," but it is more than simply employing legal and economic principles to analyze policy problems. While a full-scale explication is inappropriate at this point— and many of these principles will be discussed and applied in the book—a brief description will be given here. The law-and-economics approach is based on the observation that such principles as justice, goodness, and fairness are neither susceptible to scientific discourse nor subject to quantification.

For example, consider the question of whether the graduated income tax is "fair" or "just." You may maintain it is, and I may believe otherwise. One person's notion of "fairness" or "justice" may be another's concept of "unfairness" or "injustice." This is not to suggest that such questions are unimportant or that we should hold no values; far from it. It only suggests that at some level in a discussion involving value-laden terms we will not be able to resolve our differences. But such an impasse does not mean that all discourse is fruitless, for we can make certain assumptions about our ends and scientifically investigate the alternative means that might bring about those desired results.

This is the starting point of the law-and-economics method, which in this respect is analogous to engineering. We will never decide whether it is "fairer" to use scarce available resources to build only one bridge in either the Boston, New York, or San Francisco area. But if we agreed on certain ends, such as building a bridge across the points that will maximize the value of additional commerce or minimize the extent of additional air pollution, we would be able to ascertain where our resources would best be applied.

Once we decide on the area where the new bridge will be constructed, an engineer's next step is to create a design that, according to certain principles, makes a trade-off between quality and cost. The engineer would not want to construct a bridge from rotted wood, even though it would be the cheapest available material; nor would he want to build the structure from an extremely costly exotic steel alloy, although it would produce the highest quality bridge.

The law-and-economics approach starts with given ends, such as the economic and social performance goals discussed in Chapter 2. It then uses the concept of efficiency, which we will examine in detail in the third chapter, to ask questions about: (1) the cheapest of the alternative means that can be employed to attain certain ends; (2) the trade-offs between costs and benefits; (3) the secondary results that flow from the various means available to achieve goals; and (4) similar issues that theoretically (although not always practically) are quantifiable.

Since law is the policy mechanism that is used to achieve the desired results—analogous to the materials that may be used in our bridge-building example—the law-and-economics method asks these questions in terms of legal alternatives. Are government-imposed design standards for pollution control equipment a less costly way to attain a designated level of air quality than a special tax on sources emitting pollutants? Is private litigation more effective in curbing fraudulent advertising than government regulation? In these and other issues raised throughout the book, the law-and-economics approach will be used to ask—but frequently will not be able to answer definitively— what legal arrangements can best attain optimum levels of economic and social performance and what the economic consequences of particular arrangements are or will be.

1

What is Regulation?

Virtually every business day, Americans are confronted with a vast array of new regulatory statutes, rules, decisions, and orders emanating from public agencies at all levels of government. Ordinary citizens tend to view as wasteful or unfair regulations limiting the rate of interest that may be paid to small depositors, for example, or restricting the commodities that truckers may transport. Other regulations, such as those proposed by the Federal Trade Commission to ban the advertising of certain products aimed at small children, are considered insulting or dangerous. Sometimes regulation is perceived as being too zealous, as in many rulings entered by the Occupational Safety and Health Administration, yet at other times it is perceived as being too lax, as in some regulations adopted by the Nuclear Regulatory Commission and the Federal Aviation Administration. The Food and Drug Administration has been accused of both sins.

Although public opinion is notoriously volatile on the subject, most Americans generally believe the costs of government regulation outweigh the benefits.[1] But while a majority maintains that government regulation is, on balance, harmful, Americans also—and apparently inconsistently—believe that big business is greedy and indifferent, at best, to the rights of the public. Consequently, many opinion polls show majorities supporting a vast body of regulations.[2] Indeed, the public's fear is often justified. Consider a 1979 *New York Times* report that top managers of the Hooker Chemical Corporation knew and approved of a local plant manager's decision to discharge far more noxious emissions per day than permitted by law.[3]

The public is obviously in a quandary about regulation, rejecting both the extreme of doing away with all regulation in favor of the

7

unfettered market and the extreme of placing unqualified faith in the government as regulator. Important questions for the ordinary citizen, as well as for the student and the expert, are raised: What general principles should be employed to evaluate particular regulations? What criteria should we use to determine whether a specific regulation is appropriate or not? In short, any discussion of regulation must also consider an evaluation of its alternatives.

In this chapter, after briefly indicating the plan of the book, regulation will be defined and distinguished from other governmental techniques as well as from private action. It is important to remember in this section and throughout the book that discretion over particular policy decisions may be vested in both the public and private sectors, and there may be important substantive implications flowing from who in fact exercises that discretion. For example, should decisions regarding airline safety largely be made by a government agency, the airline firms, or some combination of both?

If the regulatory path is chosen, the agency charged with enforcement is faced with a paramount obligation in carrying out its mission. It must operate within the framework set forth in the relevant legislation enacted by Congress on the subject. As one might anticipate, those individuals and business firms adversely affected by regulatory actions often argue in courts and before the agencies themselves for different interpretations of statutory language than those proposed by agency staffs.

Obviously, understanding statutes is critical to understanding regulation. In this chapter, we will examine the elements of a regulatory statute, including the preamble, definitions, substantive provisions, exemptions and defenses, ways of obtaining information, procedural provisions, sanctions, and remedies. We also will briefly look at the history and development of federal regulation in the United States.

THE PLAN OF THE BOOK

Governments have devised numerous techniques designed to effect policy goals. For example, they have granted subsidies to private individuals and organizations to achieve goals. The great railroad building boom of the 19th century was facilitated by government subsidy policy. Some governments, notably those of the communist countries, own and operate economic enterprises that in the West are largely controlled by private owners and managers.

In the earlier era of mercantilism, the western nations exercised extremely tight regulatory control over economic activity, often restricting the carrying out of an enterprise to a single firm. Then Adam Smith in 1776 explicated the revolutionary idea that economic and social goals usually were best achieved when government minimized intervention in economic activities and permitted the free market to operate. Smith's idea of the power of the market to achieve the most effective results continued to exert a powerful influence on public affairs in the West long after his death. But since the latter part of the 19th century, government has eroded the unrestricted workings of the market through a variety of policy techniques of which regulation is one of the most important. This book will look at the uneasy coexistence of the market mechanism and regulation as well as other techniques that some observers allege achieve more efficient results.

Our starting point here in Chapter 1 is to define regulation. Then we will take a close look at regulatory statutes and briefly examine the growth of regulatory legislation in the United States. The second chapter serves two principal purposes. In order to evaluate the free market and regulation as well as other governmental techniques, we must first ask what objectives these techniques are intended to achieve. Then we will examine how the market system is supposed to operate to attain these goals and its underlying assumptions. The problems that suggest to some observers that market mechanisms sometimes fail to achieve their expected results will also be discussed.

The concept of market failure leads to three justifications for regulation: efficiency, externalities, and equity. Each of these justifications will be examined in the following three chapters. A word of caution is appropriate here. I use the phrase "regulatory justification" in the sense that regulation is a defensible public policy technique under certain circumstances. But it does not necessarily follow that because regulation is a defensible technique it is superior to the market mechanism or other governmental techniques.

In certain situations the market mechanism does have serious failings and regulation is justified. But despite its failings, the market (or some other governmental technique) might lead to better results than regulation. The heart of most serious controversies about particular policy problems is which technique or mechanism is, on balance, the "least worse." The reader should think of these questions in the framework of least worse (or better) solutions, not perfect ones, and not make the error of concluding that market failure always necessitates regulation.

Efficiency, as discussed in Chapter 3, simply means the maximum output per given input of resources. Several categories of efficiency are examined in which evidence or theory indicates that the market mechanism leads to less efficient results than would be obtained under regulatory or other arrangements. Chapter 4 looks at the problem of externalities, which is related in some respects to the problem of efficiency, but the type of market failure is different. Here the problem is that the costs engendered by a transaction are not borne entirely by the parties to that transaction. That is, if A purchases steel from B, noxious emissions from the steel mill can affect C, who is not a party to the sale. This is the problem of externalities, which many policy techniques, including regulation, are expected to solve.

While the emphasis of Chapter 4 is on the costs imposed upon those parties external to a transaction, the emphasis of Chapter 5—equity—is on problems raised by the very nature of transactions and contracts. Specifically, the free market system implies a legal structure in which people exchange goods, services, money, and promises under a system of free contract. The fifth chapter looks at the system of free contract, which some observers have found inadequate, leading them to propose regulation as the solution.

Regulation obviously involves more than just substantive questions related to performance goals. It also involves politics at both the legislative and administrative levels. To avoid a distorted view of regulation, both its theory and its politics must be considered. It is difficult to describe the behavior of political actors in regulatory processes, however, and facile overgeneralizations abound. The first step is to realize that political behavior in the legislative arena (discussed in Chapter 6) is different from politics in the administrative arena (Chapter 7). On both levels, the politics of regulation is rife with controversy.

Because virtually all solutions to the problems that regulation addresses are less than perfect, it should be no surprise that reform proposals are put forth continually. Some of the most important of these reforms, such as deregulation and cost-benefit analysis, will be examined in the final chapter. The reader should be apprised, however, that this book does not have a happy ending or a resolution. Regulation and its alternatives have been subjects of intense controversy for a long time, and we may be sure that each reform proposed and adopted will, like its predecessors, be less than perfect and subject to pleas for further change.

DEFINING REGULATION

Of course, regulation may be defined in various ways, each embracing a set of activities that virtually everyone agrees should appropriately be labeled "regulation." But for the purposes of this book and the examination it undertakes, regulation is best defined as *a state-imposed limitation on the discretion that may be exercised by individuals or organizations, which is supported by the threat of sanction.*

An example will serve to clarify this definition. Prior to the enactment of a law requiring automobile manufacturers to install safety belts in cars, manufacturers were free to exercise their discretion by either installing these devices, not doing so, or complying with an individual purchaser's requests. After the law became effective, however, a certain degree of discretion was taken away from the car makers; they were penalized if they failed to install safety belts in newly produced cars.

Private and Public Discretion

The first important facet of regulation follows from this definition. The term "regulation" is pertinent when decisionmaking in a branch of activity is apportioned between what may be termed the private and public spheres.

As private organizations, automobile manufacturers' discretion in decisions for the design, production, and marketing of cars has been reduced or limited in recent years. They may be required to install safety and emission devices in the automobiles they produce; they cannot falsely advertise the average mileage per gallon their cars obtain. But car makers nevertheless do retain control over a large number of business decisions. They may still decide to paint all their automobiles bright yellow or, more importantly, to redesign a forthcoming model-year's automobiles completely.

This dichotomy of the private and public spheres leads us to two of the most important questions we will examine in this book. First, why do we permit any activities that have an impact on others—such as the design of an automobile—to be undertaken in the private sphere without government regulation? Second, assuming there is sufficient justification for much unregulated activity in the private sphere that has a social impact, under what circumstances is regulation the preferred alternative?

Other Governmental Techniques

As we noted, activity with social impact may be private or public, but not all state activity or law is regulation. A great deal of state activity falls into other categories. Political scientist Theodore J. Lowi has proposed a threefold scheme of public policy techniques—distribution, redistribution, and regulation.[4]

Distributive policies are subsidies in which government transfers funds from the public Treasury to individuals or groups in the private sector. The U.S. maritime industry, for example, has been a substantial beneficiary of subsidies. Redistributive policies are employed by the government to affect the economy as a whole, such as policies involving the aggregate levels of spending and taxing—so-called fiscal policies.

In addition to Lowi's categories, governments engage in a wide variety of other policies, including the provision of information to farmers and consumers, loan guarantees, government purchases, public enterprise and management, and numerous tax incentive techniques. Nor does this list exhaust the vast amount of public law and rulemaking. A large body of law concerns procedural matters or the appropriate relationships between public officials and citizens. Each of these techniques may also be supported by regulations. One should also note that these are pure categories, and any particular statute may include elements of any of these governmental techniques.

Distinguishing regulation from other public policy techniques serves purposes other than simply clarifying the definition of our subject. Assuming for the moment that some form of public intervention is warranted in what was formerly an activity where decisions were made entirely in the private sphere, we must decide what form that intervention should take. Too often the choices about how to deal with a public problem are presented as either to regulate the activity or to retain virtually unlimited private discretion—as if these were necessarily the only possible alternatives. Yet it is entirely conceivable that there are other techniques that would yield "better" results. Policymakers must assess the relative merits and drawbacks of various alternatives according to the particular situation.

Political Considerations

Distinguishing regulation from other governmental techniques facilitates an examination of the relationship between regulation as a policy and its particular politics. Lowi has hypothesized that each of his policy categories develops its own specific political processes and interest group relations. He argues that the legislative battle over redistributive policies tends to reflect divisions among classes, while the legislative battle over regulatory matters reflects differences among interest groups such as the coal or natural gas industries. Economist Hendrik Houthhaker has argued that subsidy programs are particularly susceptible to legislative logrolling, since the natural response of one party to the subsidy proposal of another is to request its own subsidy benefit in exchange for support rather than oppose the first proposal. Something is better than nothing.[5]

Without endorsing either of these hypotheses, this idea that there may be a relationship between regulatory policies and their politics compels us to appreciate that—even if we can hypothesize situations in which regulation is justified—political considerations, rather than policy justifications, may in fact be responsible for a significant portion of the existing regulatory apparatus. Economic historian Gabriel Kolko, for example, has argued that much regulation was enacted in the United States not for the efficiency justifications set forth in Chapter 3, but rather: "Federal economic regulation was generally designed by the regulated interest to meet its own end, and not those of the public or the commonweal." [6]

Casting away the naive notion that legislators will necessarily enact regulatory statutes for the reasons that some analysts argue justify the technique, still another important question is raised. Even if one could show that a *specific* set of regulations is for some reason inappropriate or counterproductive, it does not necessarily follow that deregulation or another policy technique is the best alternative. That particular set of regulations may be the result of political considerations, and another set designed to take proper policy considerations into account may be the best alternative.

Airline deregulation, for example, might not be the best alternative to the foibles of airline economic regulation that resulted from the 1938 Civil Aeronautics Act. Indeed, most scholars have concluded that this statute was enacted at the behest of already-existing commercial air carriers in an attempt to exclude new competitors.[7] A different regulatory format for the airline industry might be superior to complete deregulation in this case. And even if a regulatory format were introduced for entirely justifiable motives, a more suitable one might still be available, for regulation does not imply a single inflexible policy response but rather a wide range of alternatives.

THE DESIGN OF REGULATION

When Congress debates new regulatory legislation, numerous proposals are likely to be advanced, each quite different from the others yet all intended to achieve the same basic goals. The most important judgmental differences concern two basic questions. First, are the proposed means and regulatory structure the most efficient way to achieve the given result? (Do they result in the lowest costs relative to other possible alternatives?) Second, assuming that the most efficient means to obtain a given result has been selected, what are its side-effects?

For example, a rapid trial before a police officer, devoid of procedural safeguards, might be the cheapest way to deal with persons accused of petty theft; it certainly is far cheaper than the current system. But to most of us this kind of curt procedure (aside from its constitutional objection) involves unacceptable side-effects since a police disposition offends basic values concerning the right to a fair trial. To take a more topical example, many persons who accept traditional civil rights regulation prohibiting discrimination based on race, color, religion, and sex object to affirmative action programs that require good-faith efforts to recruit disadvantaged groups on the ground that this procedure yields the unacceptable side-effect of a quota system.[8]

Economics, Values, and Predictions

The choices in designing regulation thus necessarily involve a mixture of economic judgment, value imposition, and prediction. Of course, sometimes one of these factors is more important than the others, but they are all usually present in any regulatory situation. This does not mean that scientific design of regulation is impossible. To the contrary, one can use the findings of economic theory to reject certain regulatory alternatives on that ground.

For example, an economist might reject minimum wage regulation on the ground that it would lead to a high rate of unemployment among the working poor whom it is intended to benefit. On the other hand, in a situation where a proposed course of action involved a trade-off between higher productivity and a cleaner environment, values would ultimately determine the choices made. At other times a novel course of regulatory action might involve insufficient information and experience upon which to base a highly confident prediction, as in the regulation of nuclear power generation.

In short, while economic science is certainly a factor in evaluating regulation, we should be aware of its limitations. We might be able to reject certain alternatives on the basis of scientific theory, but in many cases we would still be left with a number of other plausible policy choices.

Regulatory Decisionmaking

The difficulties in evaluting regulation are compounded when we realize that policy decisions are not made only once with respect to a particular policy problem. Rather, regulation usually involves three levels of decisionmaking.

The first level in the decisionmaking process is usually the legislative level. To illustrate, Congress in 1914 enacted the Federal Trade Commission Act charging the newly created agency with the responsibility of declaring unlawful "unfair methods of competition." At the middle level, agencies spell out their legislative mandate in more detail, either through a rule or a leading decision. To follow our example, the Federal Trade Commission (FTC) early in its career decided that false and deceptive advertising constituted an unfair method of competition. At the bottom level of decisionmaking, regulators apply these rules and decisions to a particular situation to ascertain whether it falls within or outside the prohibition. For example, does the offering of a product at a "special low price" for an extended period of time constitute false and misleading advertising? Although regulatory statutes have been written with such specificity that administrators are sometimes hardly more than robots, this decisionmaking structure is the typical situation.

It is easy to understand why regulation is an ongoing process. From the legislative perspective, it is extraordinarily difficult to draft legislation that will cover every situation. In our FTC example, the law makers debating the Federal Trade Commission Act considered it impossible to name every conceivable "unfair method of competition" of which businesses were capable. They were confident that businesses could devise other unfair business practices not contemplated at the time of the statute's enactment in 1914.

Not only is it extremely difficult to draft explicit language that will prevent the development of important loopholes in a law, but a third major problem presents itself. The noted social scientist Max Weber acutely warned:

> Those who continuously operate in the market have a far greater rational knowledge of the market and interest situation than the legislators and enforcement officers whose interest is only formal.[9]

It is virtually impossible for legislators, who must look at an enormous body of policy questions during every session of Congress, to develop anything like the expertise in a problem or an industry experienced by those who work with it on a daily basis. Intelligent caution, then, often leads legislators to provide little more than substantive general guidelines in regulatory statutes, leaving wide discretion to agency officials charged with implementing the law.

A REGULATORY STATUTE: FORM AND SUBJECT MATTER

The best way to understand a policy initiative is to examine carefully the documents pertaining to it. Too often, glib characterizations of what a particular policy is supposed to accomplish contrast sharply with the wording of the statute. It is important to remember that statutory language ultimately determines what an agency must, may, and may not do. The first two pages of a typical regulatory statute—in this case, the Commodity Futures Trading Commission Act—have been reproduced on pages 16 and 17.

Public Law 93-463
93rd Congress, H. R. 13113
October 23, 1974

An Act

88 STAT. 1389

To amend the Commodity Exchange Act to strengthen the regulation of futures
trading, to bring all agricultural and other commodities traded on exchanges
under regulation, and for other purposes.

*Be it enacted by the Senate and House of Representatives of the
United States of America in Congress assembled,* That this Act may
be cited as the "Commodity Futures Trading Commission Act of
1974".

Commodity
Futures Trad-
ing Commission
Act of 1974.
7 USC 4a note.

TITLE I—COMMODITY FUTURES TRADING COMMISSION

SEC. 101. (a) Section 2(a) of the Commodity Exchange Act, as
amended (7 U.S.C. 2, 4), is amended—

(1) By inserting "(1)" after the subsection designation.

(2) By striking the last sentence of section 2(a) and inserting in
lieu thereof the following new sentence: "The words 'the Commission'
shall mean the Commodity Futures Trading Commission established
under paragraph (2) of this subsection."

(3) By adding at the end thereof the following new paragraphs:

"(2) There is hereby established, as an independent agency of the
United States Government, a Commodity Futures Trading Commission. The Commission shall be composed of a Chairman and four other
Commissioners, who shall be appointed by the President, by and with
the advice and consent of the Senate. In nominating persons for
appointment, the President shall seek to establish and maintain a balanced Commission, including, but not limited to, persons of demonstrated knowledge in futures trading or its regulation and persons of
demonstrated knowledge in the production, merchandising, processing
or distribution of one or more of the commodities or other goods and
articles, services, rights and interests covered by this Act. Not more
than three of the members of the Commission shall be members of the
same political party. Each Commissioner shall hold office for a term of
five years and until his successor is appointed and has qualified,
except that he shall not so continue to serve beyond the expiration of
the next session of Congress subsequent to the expiration of said
fixed term of office, and except (A) any Commissioner appointed to
fill a vacancy occurring prior to the expiration of the term for which
his predecessor was appointed shall be appointed for the remainder
of such term, and (B) the terms of office of the Commissioners first
taking office after the enactment of this paragraph shall expire as
designated by the President at the time of nomination, one at the
end of one year, one at the end of two years, one at the end of three
years, one at the end of four years, and one at the end of five years.

"(3) A vacancy in the Commission shall not impair the right of the
remaining Commissioners to exercise all the powers of the Commission.

"(4) The Commission shall have a General Counsel, who shall be
appointed by the Commission and serve at the pleasure of the Commission. The General Counsel shall report directly to the Commission and serve as its legal advisor. The Commission shall appoint
such other attorneys as may be necessary, in the opinion of the Commission, to assist the General Counsel, represent the Commission in
all disciplinary proceedings pending before it, represent the Commission in courts of law whenever appropriate, assist the Department of Justice in handling litigation concerning the Commission in

Commodity
Futures Trad-
ing Commission,
establishment.
Chairman and
Commissioners.
7 USC 4a.

General Counsel.

courts of law, and perform such other legal duties and functions as the Commission may direct.

Executive Director.

"(5) The Commission shall have an Executive Director, who shall be appointed by the Commission, by and with the advice and consent of the Senate, and serve at the pleasure of the Commission. The Executive Director shall report directly to the Commission and perform such functions and duties as the Commission may prescribe.

Exercise of functions.

"(6)(A) Except as otherwise provided in this paragraph and in paragraphs (4) and (5) of this subsection, the executive and administrative functions of the Commission, including functions of the Commission with respect to the appointment and supervision of personnel employed under the Commission, the distribution of business among such personnel and among administrative units of the Commission, and the use and expenditure of funds, shall be exercised solely by the Chairman.

"(B) In carrying out any of his functions under the provisions of this paragraph, the Chairman shall be governed by general policies of the Commission and by such regulatory decisions, findings, and determinations as the Commission may by law be authorized to make.

"(C) The appointment by the Chairman of the heads of major administrative units under the Commission shall be subject to the approval of the Commission.

"(D) Personnel employed regularly and full time in the immediate offices of Commissioners other than the Chairman shall not be affected by the provisions of this paragraph.

"(E) There are hereby reserved to the Commission its functions with respect to revising budget estimates and with respect to determining the distribution of appropriated funds according to major programs and purposes.

"(F) The Chairman may from time to time make such provisions as he shall deem appropriate authorizing the performance by any officer, employee, or administrative unit under his jurisdiction of any functions of the Chairman under this paragraph.

Conflict of interests.

"(7) No Commissioner or employee of the Commission shall accept employment or compensation from any person, exchange, or clearinghouse subject to regulation by the Commission under this Act during his term of office, nor shall he participate, directly or indirectly, in any contract market operations or transactions of a character subject to regulation by the Commission.

Liaison with Agriculture Department.

"(8) The Commission shall, in cooperation with the Secretary of Agriculture, establish a separate office within the Department of Agriculture to be staffed with employees of the Commission for the purpose of maintaining a liaison between the Commission and the Department of Agriculture. The Secretary shall take such steps as may be necessary to enable the Commission to obtain information and utilize such services and facilities of the Department of Agriculture as may be necessary in order to maintain effectively such liaison. In addition, the Secretary shall appoint a liaison officer, who shall be an employee of the Office of the Secretary, for the purpose of maintaining a liaison between the Department of Agriculture and the Commission. The Commission shall furnish such liaison officer appropriate office space within the offices of the Commission and shall allow such liaison officer to attend and observe all deliberations and proceedings of the Commission.

Transmittal of budget requests and legislative recommendations to congressional committees.

"(9)(A) Whenever the Commission submits any budget estimate or request to the President or the Office of Management and Budget, it shall concurrently transmit copies of that estimate or request to the House and Senate Appropriations Committees and the House Com-

Preliminary Material

Regulatory statutes are all different, but there are certain elements common to most. A statute usually begins with a section defining some of the important words employed in the law. For example, a statute concerned with export trade would spell out the meaning of that phrase in exact terms. Second, a statute usually contains a paragraph that relates it to prior statutes covering approximately the same subject matter. Does the new statute overrule the older ones or is it to be reconciled with them? If the latter is the case, some framework of reconciliation is usually briefly detailed. For example, the statute might state that "nothing contained herein shall be construed to overrule the Export Trade Act."

The jurisdictional scope of the statute also is set forth. Does it cover foreign commerce? Is the statute operative within Puerto Rico or the Virgin Islands? Finally, most regulatory statutes indicate whether they are applicable to natural persons, artificial persons (corporations), or other forms of association. Further, the statute defines the groups within these larger categories to which the law applies. For example, the statute may apply to only export trade corporations, all corporations, or all corporations except those engaged in export trade. Sometimes a statute's application is based not on activity (e.g., export trade) but on size. For example, a statute may apply only to corporations with assets in excess of $1 million.

Substantive Requirements of a Regulatory Statute

The heart of a regulatory statute is the section that spells out the substantive obligations of the parties covered. This portion of the law is frequently negative in its terms, describing the area removed from the discretion of the subject groups involved. For example, all corporations subject to the jurisdiction of the Federal Trade Commission are prohibited from engaging in unfair methods of competition. This prohibitory language may be framed either in terms directed at the groups covered—all corporations subject to this act may not engage in unfair competition—or it simply sets forth the prohibition—every contract, combination, or conspiracy in restraint of trade is declared to be illegal. In the latter instance, the groups subject to the prohibition are listed in another part of the statute. In any event, the difference is merely stylistic.

Of greater consequence, the limitation on private discretion may also be drafted in affirmative or conditional terms. In the first case, a party subject to the statute is affirmatively required to do something. For example, the Textile Fibers Identification Act requires clothing manufacturers and others subject to the statute to attach a label to their products setting forth fiber content by generic name. The truth-in-lending statute requires credit providers to inform debtors of the annual rate of interest to be paid.

The limitation on discretion imposed by a statute may also be conditional. A party subject to a statute may not be required to undertake a particular action, but if it does certain limitations are imposed on that action. For example, railroads are not required by law to abandon service between two points. But if a railroad decides to do so, it must comply with Section 13A of the Interstate Commerce Act (49 U.S.C.A. 13A), which sets forth a number of actions that a carrier must undertake as well as the standard that the Interstate Commerce Commission must apply before the service abandonment may take place.

Conditional language is frequently employed when the activity in point is an unusual one in the party's business, as in the case of railroad abandonments. Affirmative language is used when the party would not ordinarily do something without regulation, such as providing extensive information about fiber content. Negative language usually is employed in circumstances where a party is likely to do something undesirable (such as falsely advertise) without regulation.

Exemptions and Defenses

Many regulatory statutes also spell out exemptions and defenses that excuse the failure of a party to comply with the regulatory obligations set forth in the law. While the distinction between an exemption and a defense is sometimes blurred in practice, there is a clear difference conceptually. An exemption refers to a group that is excluded from a statute's prohibitions because of the nature of its activities. For example, Section 22 of the Interstate Commerce Act excludes from the statute's rate-regulations those carriers shipping property of the United States, state or municipal governments, destitute people, or charities.

A defense—or more technically, an affirmative defense—is a statutory justification for conduct that has been shown to violate a statute's prohibitions. For example, the Robinson-Patman Act under some circumstances prohibits price discrimination between customers where the effect may be to injure competition. But even if the elements of a violation are shown, the charged party may escape liability by showing that the price difference was justified by cost differences in serving customers. Of course, an affirmative defense is not the same as simply showing that the elements necessary to indicate a violation have not been proved. In the affirmative defense, the elements of violation are proved, but the statute permits the accused to justify his conduct.

COLLECTION OF REGULATORY INFORMATION

One of the most difficult problems that regulators face is obtaining the information necessary to determine whether a violation has taken place. Obviously a violator will not often voluntarily provide the information that might result in penalties against it. Indeed, it is reasonable to assume that in many cases the violator's best interests are served in concealing damaging information. But even if a subject firm believes itself to be wholly innocent of any charges made against it, it may still be reluctant to spend the time and effort necessary to comply with a regulator's request.

For these reasons virtually every regulatory statute delineates methods through which the information necessary to determine a violation may compulsorily be obtained. In recent years, much criticism of regulation has centered on the large amount of information businesses are required to supply to regulators. Some defenders of these requirements suggest that the burden would not be so great now had business firms not been so skillful in evading the information-producing mechanisms contained in earlier statutes.

The Subpoena

The oldest device used to obtain information about possible wrongdoing is the subpoena. Failure to comply with a valid subpoena is usually punishable by contempt of court. The critical word here is "valid." An agency has the right (indeed, the obligation) to obtain the information necessary to discharge its duties, but other values weigh against an unlimited right to subpoena. These include the Fourth Amendment's prohibition of unreasonable searches and seizures and the Fifth Amendment's prohibition against compelling any person to be a witness against himself in criminal proceedings.

The courts have responded to this problem of balancing competing considerations with a three-part test. First, any request for information must fall within the substantive authority that Congress has granted to an agency. If an agency has authority to regulate pharmaceutical advertising, but not package labeling, it may not subpoena documents relating to an inquiry in the latter area. However, when it is not clear whether the information sought is pertinent to a proper subject of investigation, the courts will usually give the benefit of the doubt to the agency.[10] Second, the regulatory agency must show that it has explicit statutory authority to issue the type of subpoena in question.

The third requirement has proved to be the most vexing: the request for information must be reasonable or, as sometimes worded, "not unreasonable." This means that the information sought must be identified as specifically as possible. A sweeping request for information such as one covering "all advertisements" of a major corporation would be judged unreasonable, a so-called "fishing expedition." On the other hand, a request specifying "all advertisements regarding the sale of microwave ovens that mention cooking time" would be enforced since it is clearly related to an investigation of the accuracy of such claims.

Another dimension of the reasonableness criterion is that the request must not be oppressive relative to the need for the information. Here courts will enter orders based on the particular facts. To reduce the regulatory burden, sometimes the courts will reduce the number of documents demanded, while at others they will extend the time period during which a witness must comply.

Information Innovation and the FTC Act

The reasonableness criterion illustrates the principal limitation of the subpoena as a mechanism for obtaining information. In order to make a reasonable request, an agency must have already obtained information sufficient to frame that request. Consequently, agencies responsible for monitoring a broad range of activities in an increasingly complex business environment require other investigative tools to get information. They cannot depend on luck, accidental discovery, and the often unreliable information supplied by disgruntled informants (who often rely more on suspicion or rumor than hard data) to provide this information.

The provisions of the 1914 Federal Trade Commission Act revolutionized the manner by which regulatory agencies may obtain information and has provided the model for many subsequent statutes. First, the statute authorized the commission to direct corporations to furnish both specific and periodic reports or answers to specific questions. Second, the commission was authorized to inspect the files of corporations and copy their contents. Agencies may employ these powers not only to obtain information about possible wrongdoing but also to guide them in making new rules or policy, to propose new legislation to Congress, and to help them determine if their regulatory activities are satisfactory.

Of course, unless a party subject to possible investigation maintains the information and records that may be sought by a regulator, these powers can be easily defeated. Consequently, statutes enacted after the FTC Act often contain explicit record-keeping provisions. For example, Section 308A of the Water Pollution Control Act (33 U.S.C.A. 1318) permits the administrator of the Environmental Protection Agency to require the keeping of certain records and the submission of reports based on these records. In addition, the installation, use, and maintenance of monitoring equipment and the submission of periodic water samples may be required.

While these techniques are an improvement over the subpoena as devices to obtain information, four major problems remain. First, they may be subject to governmental abuse and serious incursions upon privacy. The Supreme Court has designed certain protections intended to prevent these problems. Generally an agency must obtain a search warrant showing reasonable cause for inspection if a party subject to the inspection refuses voluntary entry.[11]

Another problem is that control over the information is in the first instance under the domain of persons who might have a strong incentive to withhold or distort that information. An example from the beginning of this chapter comes more sharply into focus here. Notwithstanding the range of techniques for obtaining information with which the Environmental Protection Agency is provided, the Hooker Chemical Corporation allegedly was still able to pollute Florida's air with fluoride over a considerable period without detection.

Insofar as there are incentives to conceal or distort information, there is a danger that these information-gathering techniques may be defeated, which leads to a third difficulty. Too often these techniques are useful only *after* some harmful conduct already has taken place. For example, it is common in cases of alleged false and misleading advertising for the FTC to begin its investigation after the potentially harmful advertisement has been disseminated (sometimes long afterward). This leads directly to the fourth major difficulty: even after information is obtained—sometimes after a laborious process where data is supplied in an unorganized or complicated format—it must still be examined and evaluated, which can cause considerable delay. Efficient regulation may be impeded not only by resistance but also by cooperation.

Requiring Government Approval

An additional information technique, although not appropriate to every regulated activity, has been developed to cope with these problems. Agencies often require that information be supplied and approved *before* an activity may lawfully commence. Physicians, for example, may not lawfully practice medicine before passing various tests. Even as commonplace an activity as driving an automobile requires the provision of information obtained by testing. The Food and Drug Administration requires that a pharmaceutical manufacturer supply an enormous body of test information before it can market a new product.

But despite the obvious advantage of obtaining information in advance, many regulated activities do not lend themselves to this technique. For example, it would be cumbersome (at the least) if a regulatory agency had to approve every piece of advertising before publication.

Three variables are important in evaluating whether a particular activity is appropriate for the technique of prohibition prior to testing and agency approval. The first is a value judgment concerning the costs of not employing this technique. Driving automobiles and marketing drugs are perceived as so fraught with danger that policymakers are willing to incur the delay costs involved in the testing procedures. The second consideration is the number of units subject to the technique. Obviously, the fewer the number, the more likely that delay costs will be minimized. The third variable is the cost of the information requisite to the commencement of the activity. The lower the information costs, the more effective will be the technique.

But even the requirement of providing information before lawfully undertaking an activity may involve unacceptable costs or may not truly provide regulators with what they need to fulfill their missions effectively. No reader will be surprised to learn that the requirements of a driving test and license have not led to the elimination of unsafe automobile driving. Nor is there any assurance, except where the information sought is solely quantitative and precise monitoring devices are operative, that the information supplied will be complete and accurate.

REGULATORY SANCTIONS AND REMEDIES

Sanctions, another important component of all regulatory statutes, are intended to assure compliance with the informational and substantive requirements described above. A *sanction* is a penalty that may be imposed for disobeying the provisions of a statute, rule, or order. That a sanction merely exists does not indicate its effectiveness, however. For example, a $10 fine imposed on a corporation with annual profits in the hundreds of millions of dollars is patently not effective in deterring undesirable activity. Nevertheless, it is a sanction.

The sanction element of a regulatory statute must be analytically separate from the question of who enforces that sanction. For example, in certain cases the regulatory agency with substantive jurisdiction over a subject does not enforce the law. Instead, enforcement powers may be vested in another agency, usually the Department of Justice at the federal level. At other times, enforcement powers may be vested in private sector groups, such as parties injured by a practice. Some utility regulation statutes allow consumers to sue for overcharges, for example. It is also important to note that statutes often provide for a variety of sanctions, which may be imposed alternatively as well as cumulatively when a law or rule is disobeyed.

The sanction element of a statute must also be distinguished from the remedy element, since each raises different problems. A *remedy* is a directive ordering someone to engage in conduct that will correct and/or prevent the resumption of an undesirable act or condition. An order requiring a utility to reduce its rates and one forbidding a food manufacturer from further misrepresenting the nutritional value of its product are both remedies. As these examples illustrate, the directive may be either positive or negative in form: "do something" or "do not do something again."

The critical questions in assessing a remedy are: (1) Will it achieve the result desired by the regulator? and (2) Is it the best instrument to achieve that result among the remedies available? For example, in false and misleading advertising cases the Federal Trade Commission had traditionally ordered respondents not to engage in similar conduct again. But more recently the FTC has ordered respondents to engage affirmatively in advertising that corrects the false impressions created by the misleading advertising on the ground that this constitutes a more effective remedy. Like sanctions, remedies are not necessarily mutually exclusive.

Relationships Between Sanctions and Remedies

The relationships between sanctions and remedies should now be clear. Sanctions require that a party who violates a statute, rule, or order undertake (or not undertake) a certain action that the party might not do voluntarily, presumably because the perceived costs of obeying the regulator outweigh the benefits. The *threat* of a sanction is intended to compel the party to undertake what the regulator demands on the ground that its imposition would be more costly than the benefits that would be achieved by continuing the prohibited conduct. A fine, for example, should exceed the returns that a firm would obtain by continuing the unlawful conduct. Compliance should be perceived as a lesser evil than the penalties imposed by the sanction.

The sanction must not only be costly, however, but also be credible. Ironically, if the costs imposed by a sanction are too high, it might not be a credible threat. For example, the 1970 automobile emission law imposed a $10,000 fine for each car that did not meet the standards established by the legislation. But because the level of the fine was so high—far in excess of the price of most vehicles—this sanction was not credible. Its imposition would have shut down the U.S. automobile industry, an obviously unthinkable alternative to all but a few zealots. Accordingly, the high fine was more acceptable to automobile manufacturers than a lower, more realistic one.[12]

Although sanctions and remedies are distinct elements, they sometimes appear to merge into one. For example, in the automobile emission case the fine (a sanction) at first glance looks like it is also the remedy. But upon further reflection one sees that the remedy is simply stated in implied form. The function of the automobile emission statute was not to obtain funds for the government by fining car makers but rather to direct those firms to meet the statutory emission standards. Instead of being drafted in a directive form (a remedy), then, some statutes assert the conduct that is desired and in a different section specify the costs of not achieving that standard (a sanction).

And just as there are remedies not framed in the form of an order, there are orders that are not remedies. For example, if a motor carrier applies to the Interstate Commerce Commission for a rate increase or an applicant applies to the Federal Communications Commission for authority to operate a television station, the orders granting these requests are more benefits conferred than directives requiring a prohibition or change in conduct. Unlike those containing remedies, orders that grant permissions do not require a link with sanctions, although granting permission to one applicant implies the rejection of others, which may require the imposition of sanctions.

Categories of Remedies and Sanctions

Remedies, as noted earlier, are either negative or positive in form. They may be subdivided further into other categories, however. Thus, negative remedies include those that prohibit the repetition of the forbidden conduct as well as those that prohibit conduct different from that involved in the original transgression. An example of the latter category would include an unlawful acquisition of one company by another for which the remedy might be to not make any further acquisitions.

Far more flexible are positive remedies that include, first, those that require that the transgressor restore conditions existing prior to its unlawful conduct. For example, a remedy that has been used in cases involving unlawful mergers is to require the transgressor to divest itself of the company that it unlawfully acquired. Requiring the transgressor to create a set of new conditions is another type of affirmative remedy—corrective advertising or mandatory labeling of information not previously disclosed, for example. A third category requires the transgressor to withdraw entirely from the field of endeavor in question. Broadcast licensees who have abused the terms of their licenses are refused renewal by the Federal Communications Commission. Other remedies include the surrender of something valuable to the government and its correlate, government seizure of property.

Statutes usually provide remedies and sanctions not just for substantive transgressions but for every duty that they impose upon parties subject to them. Under environmental protection statutes, for example, remedies and sanctions are imposed not just for the substantive acts involved in polluting the environment but also for failing to maintain proper records or to maintain equipment in good working order.

Moreover, remedies are available not just at the conclusion of a proceeding but may be instituted even before a proceeding has formally begun. Under these circumstances, regulators usually must apply to the courts for a temporary injunction that will restrain an alleged transgressor from doing something, pending the outcome of a formal proceeding. While statutory standards for obtaining temporary injunctions are often vague, courts usually are loath to grant them unless the agency can show that irreparable harm will be done if the temporary injunction is not granted or that conditions will have changed by the time the proceeding terminates so as to make the proceeding useless.

Temporary injunctions as well as remedies granted at the termination of formal proceedings or for the violation of other imposed duties are associated with four types of sanctions. These sanctions may conveniently be labeled: (1) criminal, (2) civil, (3) equitable, and (4) informal. Criminal sanctions include the imposition of fines and jail sentences for violations. Such sanctions are intended both to punish transgressors and to deter others from engaging in similar conduct. For an offense to be considered criminal, the standard of conduct required must be set forth clearly and explicitly, and the offender must have knowingly—not unintentionally—violated the standard. Since much of the conduct that regulators seek to restrict cannot be described with the requisite degree of precision, criminal sanctions are often inappropriate. A variant is civil penalties, which are sanctions described by statute that call for the payment of fines, just as criminal sanctions often do.

Civil sanctions include the right of persons injured or the government, either on its own behalf or on behalf of injured citizens, to sue for compensation. The compensation for which suit may be brought can either redress losses alone or can include a punitive element. The Sherman Act, which covers monopolization and cartel arrangements, allows persons injured by a statutory violation to sue for threefold the damages actually sustained.

Equitable sanctions include those that prohibit action or require affirmative action on the part of violators. They parallel equitable remedies to some extent, but insofar as equitable sanctions are intended to penalize violators or deter others from engaging in similar activity, they constitute sanctions. For example, if the Federal Trade Commission orders a deceptive advertiser to engage in corrective advertising, it is attempting to correct the misleading impressions previously created (a policy goal); but insofar as the order compels the violator to announce that it engaged in deception in the same corrective advertisement, the FTC is imposing a sanction. Adverse publicity may be considered an informal sanction.

In summary, remedies and sanctions, in order to be effective, must be appropriate. They must not be too weak relative to the potential benefits involved in violating a regulatory statute, rule, or order. On the other hand, they must not be unrealistically stringent so as to adversely affect parties other than those charged with the offense. For example, the threat of closing down an automobile plant is not a credible or realistic sanction in no small part because of the adverse impact that would be imposed on large numbers of employees, shareholders, and suppliers who were innocent of the wrongdoing. To paraphrase Gilbert and Sullivan, the punishment must fit the crime.

As we observed, the regulatory agency also must be equipped with adequate resources to discover the information necessary to demonstrate violations. Regulatory statutes must provide the agency with procedures that permit it to move through the decisionmaking process effectively from developing information to the issuance of an order. We turn now to this critical element of a regulatory statute.

REGULATORY PROCEDURE

The Problem of Delay

While academic economists are apt to focus their criticism of regulation on the substantive provisions of statutes, rules, and orders, lawyers who practice before regulatory agencies are often far more concerned about the procedural elements, particularly the problem of delay. The results of a Senate Committee on Governmental Affairs questionnaire, distributed to approximately 1,000 lawyers who regularly practiced before regulatory agencies, indicated that 75 percent of the respondents considered procedural delay the major regulatory problem. And no wonder, for data compiled by the committee disclosed that agency licensing proceedings averaged more than 19 months, ratemaking proceedings averaged 21 months, and enforcement actions averaged more than 3 years.[13] Procedural delay not only has an adverse impact on private sector decisionmaking, often causing confusion and paralysis, but it also is a major factor in the excessive costs frequently incurred by firms seeking to comply with regulatory directives.

Delay also has a more subtle impact. As Bruce Owen and Ronald Braeutigam have persuasively argued, delay tends to favor the status quo against those interests who seek change and innovation.[14] But one should not infer that delay necessarily always serves vested interests, regulated firms, or big business. The enormous delays associated with Food and Drug Administration procedures for licensing new drugs offer a clear advantage to existing drug firms and pharmaceuticals already marketed. But, on the other hand, the delays occasioned by Nuclear Regulatory Commission procedures for licensing new atomic power plants work in favor of environmentalists and others opposed to this technology—and against the interests of plant construction firms, uranium suppliers, and electric utilities. The only ones that uniformly benefit from delay are lawyers who practice before regulatory agencies.

While legislators and many critics tend to blame regulators exclusively for delay, a closer look reveals that statutes and the Constitution are often "at fault" (if that is the appropriate characterization). Regulators are charged not only with their substantive mission but also with the responsibility of doing it in a fair and orderly manner, which inevitably occasions delay. One can be sure that if regulators could operate like authoritarian potentates, there would be no delay. But are we willing to surrender our claim to justice in judicial and administrative proceedings? Most of us are not. The U.S. system is based on the belief that any person who may be adversely affected by a decision must be afforded an opportunity to present his views, confront his accusers, and be given reasonable time to prepare a defense.

Balancing Delay and Fairness

The problem, then, is balancing regulatory delay with fairness. Most regulatory statutes, accordingly, contain basic statements that seek to assure a balance between delay and fairness with the additional statement that regulatory bodies may prepare rules and regulations in accordance with their basic statutory guidelines.

The original 1914 Federal Trade Commission Act provided a model for some regulatory procedures. It stated that: (1) the agency shall issue a complaint stating the charges, which must contain a notice of hearing at least 30 days after service; (2) the person charged shall have the right to appear and show cause why an order should not be entered; (3) other persons interested or affected by the proceeding may apply to the commission for the right to intervene; (4) testimony in the proceeding shall be taken down in writing and filed with the commission; and (5) the agency must make a written report containing findings of fact and an order that it must serve upon the other parties to the proceeding.

The FTC statute set forth elaborate rules concerning appeals to the courts, methods of serving documents, and other matters. Based on these provisions and amendments to the original law, the Federal Trade Commission periodically issues, amends, and revises a large body of internal procedural rules that amplify and clarify those in the authorizing statute.

Rulemaking and Adjudication

A major mechanism employed to reduce delay without sacrificing the values of orderliness and fairness is substantive rulemaking. Rather than conducting business on a case-by-case basis, agencies call in all parties who might be similarly situated, conduct hearings with all present, and then impose a general substantive rule applicable to all parties. For example, a large number of firms market gasoline at retail, giant as well as small firms. Seeking to impose octane-posting requirements equally applicable to all the firms, the Federal Trade Commission undertook that activity under its rulemaking authority rather than through the more tedious process of issuing complaints upon each of the affected parties and complying with all of the other requirements of the FTC statute.

However, rulemaking is hardly the panacea that some opponents of the case-by-case approach claim. First, rulemaking is not an appropriate procedure for ascertaining facts of particular cases. Rulemaking at the Interstate Commerce Commission is an inappropriate procedure when the issue is, for example, the "reasonable rate" for transporting cement from Peoria, Illinois, to Davenport, Iowa; a different set of facts, of course, will pertain to the reasonable rate for moving electric motors from Orlando, Florida, to Richmond, Virginia. Under such circumstances a rule can only provide the most general guidance, and adjudicatory proceedings are required for particular decisions.

Many matters that regulatory agencies must resolve are simply not conducive to generalized rulemaking because the situations are unique. For example, the Food and Drug Administration was once called upon to determine the minimum percentage of peanuts required before peanut butter could be so labeled. A general agency rule was developed, but it obviously had little application to the innumerable other products under FDA jurisdiction. This example also illustrates that rulemaking is no guarantor of speedy decisionmaking: the FDA took 12 years to adopt final standards on the minimum peanut content for peanut butter.

In summary, both rulemaking and adjudicatory processes have a place in regulation, and most regulatory statutes provide agencies with both procedures. Rulemaking is more applicable to general policy pronouncements than it is to the resolution of factual disputes and the specific principles that arise from such disputes. When adjudicative facts are an issue—"who did what, where, when, how, why, with what motive or intent"—our values dictate that interested parties should have the right to set forth their views in an orderly fashion.[15] This, in turn, requires the statutory provision of mechanisms for complaint, notice, answer, hearings, rational decisionmaking, and appeals. Obviously, these adjudicative procedures are subject to abuse, but unless we are willing to abandon our belief in fairness and vest unbridled discretion in the hands of administrators, we will have to accept delay.

As the foregoing review of the essential components of regulatory statutes indicates, regulation is often a cumbersome means by which to achieve policy results. Regulation is costly and time-consuming, and it directs resources that might otherwise be employed in productive activities into uses that do not directly contribute to economic growth. However, sometimes regulation may be the most efficacious policy choice of the several imperfect alternatives available to achieve certain public policy goals. In any event, regulation has certainly been a widely employed technique throughout United States history.

THE WAVES OF REGULATION

Regulation is as old as government, but it has been more common during some periods of history than in others. Great spurts of growth in the United States, usually occurring at all levels of government, have been followed by periods of relative dormancy in which few important regulatory statutes were enacted.

In general, the different paces and the substantive thrust of legislation during any particular period are reflections of an underlying public attitude toward the proper role of government. The New Deal (1933-1939) was an intense period of regulatory legislation, largely in response to economic and social problems resulting from the Great Depression that began in 1929. In contrast, the prevailing public philosophy during most of the 1920s—an era of theretofore unprecedented growth and prosperity—saw little need for regulation. But in every period until recent times, the institutional regulatory structure previously emplaced has continued to function. In this way, the aggregate regulatory structure in the United States has grown and expanded.

Early History

Historians agree that 1887 was a watershed year for regulation. It marked the birth of the Interstate Commerce Commission, the first independent regulatory commission at the national level. There were other federal regulatory bodies prior to the ICC, most notably the Treasury Department's Office of the Comptroller of the Currency, which has jurisdiction over national banks. Individual states had begun regulating infrastructural services such as banking, gas, and railroad and street car transportation shortly before 1887.

But the ICC ushered in an era of theretofore unprecedented regulatory growth that continued through approximately 1916. In both the earlier part of this period and the later years—the Progressive Era—states and municipalities greatly expanded regulatory jurisdiction over infrastructural activities. They also expanded the number of occupations and activities that required licenses. In 1902 New Jersey began licensing architects, and today they must be licensed in all states. At the national level, the period from 1887 to 1916 witnessed the creation of the Federal Trade Commission, with jurisdiction over unfair methods of competition, and the Federal Reserve Board, with jurisdiction over practices of member banks. The first national statutes dealing with monopoly (the Sherman Antitrust Act) and with pure food and drug products (the Food and Drug Act) were enacted in 1890 and 1906, respectively.

Considerable controversy exists among historians on what accounted for this spurt of intense regulatory activity. One thing is clear: the era witnessed a significant erosion of the principle that unrestricted markets constituted the best method to attain performance goals, with regulation as the chosen alternative. In the 1920s, however, the prevailing ideology changed to one that thought voluntary arrangements between economic units, without government intervention, could better attain performance goals in most cases. However, no significant statute or agency that came into existence during the 1887-1916 period was dismantled (in fact, railroad regulation became even more comprehensive). The only important regulatory additions at the national level were statutes regulating radio transmission, aviation safety, and commodities future trading.

The New Deal

An abrupt change in public philosophy took place during the New Deal, with a host of important new statutes—some creating new agencies—enacted between 1933 and 1939. Confidence in the power of the free market to achieve performance goals was very low in the face of the dismal record of the economic system during the Great Depression. One important statute, the National Industrial Recovery Act (subsequently declared unconstitutional) virtually abolished competition. According to many of the New Dealers, how to stabilize prices and other economic indicators was the principal problem. Regulatory agencies were given an important role in the New Deal plans.

The long list of regulatory agencies created in those relatively few years included:

— The Federal Communications Commission (FCC), with jurisdiction over radio and communications common carriers.

— The Securities and Exchange Commission (SEC), with jurisdiction over stock exchanges and new issues of stock.

— The Civil Aeronautics Board (CAB), with jurisdiction over the economic affairs of air carriers.

— A new banking agency—the Federal Deposit Insurance Corporation (FDIC)—as well as the Federal Home Loan Bank Board (FHLBB), with jurisdiction over federally chartered savings and loan associations.

— The National Labor Relations Board (NLRB), with jurisdiction over collective bargaining disputes and unfair labor practices.

In addition to these new agencies, numerous statutes granted additional regulatory jurisdiction to older agencies. Motor carriers, drugs, natural gas, and price discrimination were among the new areas of regulated activity.

Postwar Era

During the period following World War II through 1968, the regulatory apparatus in place at the end of the New Deal largely remained intact. In the postwar era, government policymakers primarily were concerned with economic growth, employment levels, and overall price levels; new regulatory policies played a secondary role. The only major regulatory agencies established during this period were the Atomic Energy Commission (AEC)—from which the Nuclear Regulatory Commission (NRC) was spunoff in 1973—and the Federal Aviation Administration (FAA), which regulates the national air traffic control system, licenses pilots, and certifies airplane airworthiness.

But by the late 1960s the era of consumerism had begun. Spurred by the 1966 publication of Ralph Nader's *Unsafe at Any Speed*, which decried the lack of automobile safety, and other critiques of business conduct, Congress enacted numerous new statutes regulating health, safety, and the environment. The new agencies created included:

— The Environmental Protection Agency (EPA), with regulatory jurisdiction over air and water quality, toxic substances, and noise levels.

— The Consumer Product Safety Commission (CPSC), whose mission was to reduce product-related injuries to consumers by regulating product design, labeling, and use instructions.

— The Occupational Safety and Health Administration (OSHA), responsible for safety and health conditions in work places.

— The National Highway Traffic Safety Administration (NHTSA), which regulates vehicles in an effort to reduce the number and severity of traffic accidents.

Additional consumer-oriented responsibilities were given to older agencies such as the FTC, and economic regulation expanded rapidly, most notably over the energy industries.

Deregulation

About 1977 a backlash occurred that clashed with the consumerist trend. The enormous regulatory apparatus was considered by some observers an impediment to U.S. economic growth and a significant source of inflation and declining competitiveness in world markets. Ronald Reagan's election to the presidency in November 1980 made it official. The impetus to reduce the extent of government regulation became an important part of the new public philosophy, characterized by cries of overregulation and calls for deregulation.

Public policies toward regulation, culminating in the recent pleas to reduce it, have come about in waves of changes in thinking about the proper place of regulation in U.S. public policy. And if history is a guide, we may be sure that the future will see new attitudes towards regulation. In every period of regulatory history, however, changes in public philosophy have always been related to the overriding end of attaining certain performance goals.

CONCLUSION

Regulation is a pervasive public policy technique that governs activities as diverse as devising traffic rules, labeling peanut butter, installing machinery in factories, and determining who may lawfully practice medicine. Regulatory decisionmaking embraces three levels: legislation, general rules, and specific decisions. Of these three, legislation is the most critical. Regulators' day-to-day activities must follow the guidelines in the language of the statutes governing their activities. Accordingly, regulatory officials must be continuously attentive to each of the elements of their authorizing statutes: form and subject matter, information, sanctions and remedies, and procedure.

There are certain costs associated with this sharp focus on the regulatory statute, however. One must be careful not to lose sight of the economic and social performance goals that the regulatory statute is expected to meet. Chapter 2 will discuss these goals and the question of performance.

NOTES

1. "How Public Regards Regulation," *New York Times,* November 30, 1978.
2. See "Regulators and the Polls," *Regulation* (November/December 1978):10-12, 54.

3. Donald G. McNeil, Jr., "Hooker Corp. Papers Indicate Management Sanctioned Polluting," *New York Times*, August 5, 1979, pp. 1, 34.

4. Theodore J. Lowi, "American Business, Public Policy, Case Studies and Political Theory," *World Politics* 16 (July 1964):677-715.

5. U.S., Congress, Joint Economic Committee, *The Economics of Federal Subsidy Programs, Hearings*, 92d Cong., 1st sess., 1971, p. 15.

6. Gabriel Kolko, *The Triumph of Conservatism: A Reinterpretation of American History, 1900-1916* (New York: Free Press, 1963), p. 59.

7. For example, see Walter Adams and Horace M. Gray, *Monopoly in America* (New York: Macmillan, 1955), pp. 52-54.

8. See Thomas Sowell, "Landmark or Curiosity," *Regulation* (September/October 1978):30-34.

9. Max Weber, *Economy and Society*, trans. E. Fischoff et al., 3 vols. (New York: Bedminster Press, 1968), 1:335.

10. A general discussion of these and other subpoena requirements is contained in *United States* v. *Powell*, 379 U.S. 48 (1964).

11. *Camara* v. *Municipal Court*, 387 U.S. 523 (1967) and *See* v. *City of Seattle*, 387 U.S. 541 (1967).

12. See Howard Margolis, "The Politics of Auto Emissions," *Public Interest* (Fall 1977):17.

13. U.S., Congress, Senate, Committee on Governmental Affairs, *Study on Federal Regulation, Vol. 4: Delay in the Regulatory Process*, 95th Cong., 1st sess., July 1977, p. ix.

14. Bruce Owen and Ronald Braeutigam, *The Regulation Game* (Cambridge, Mass.: Ballinger Publishing, 1978), pp. 23-25.

15. Kenneth Culp Davis, *Administrative Law Text*, 3d ed. (St. Paul, Minn.: West Publishing Co., 1972), p. 160.

2

Competition and Regulation

As we have noted, government structures and policies do not exist simply for their own sakes but are intended to achieve certain performance goals. Adam Smith in *The Wealth of Nations* did not advocate the free market as the best solution to most economic and social problems because he admired the business community (he did not) nor because he felt that it accorded with some metaphysical conception; in his judgment, the market best attained performance goals.

Smith's conceptions, which at once were novel and simple, have been enormously influential since their publication in 1776. Yet notwithstanding the enormous respect that political actors as well as academics in the Western world have granted to Smith's ideas, governments have intervened in private decisionmaking far more often than he would have approved. Regulation is one of the most important state interventionist techniques that uneasily coexists with the free market principle in the contemporary western political economy.

This brief description provides the structure of this chapter. First we will examine the economic and social performance goals that the free market, regulation, and other governmental techniques are expected to achieve. Then we will look at how the free market—the ideal of many economists—is expected to achieve these goals. In this discussion, I will attempt to state the free market idea as positively as possible, but this should not necessarily be construed as an endorsement of it. Finally, we will discuss some questions that should be asked to determine the appropriate type of public policy—or nonpolicy—that will best attain specific performance goals. These questions are based on the very broad assumption that relatively free competition is generally preferable to regulation. Citizens and policymakers can make different choices to solve different policy problems. The same solution will not necessarily fit every problem.

PERFORMANCE AND POLICY

There are a wide variety of governmental techniques, including regulation, to accomplish policy goals. Of course, there is also the possibility that such goals can be attained without significant government intervention, either through individual pursuit of economic gain or through voluntarily formed cooperative ventures. Under both of these alternatives, government's sole tasks are to provide for collective security and to enforce contracts on behalf of private parties or cooperative associations. But most of us also expect government to build parks and playgrounds and to assure that the canned food we eat does not contain poisonous ingredients.

In other words, we expect some government intervention but also considerable private discretion. Almost all of us accept that material well-being is one of the major components of human happiness and that economic and political arrangements should be designed to help us in this pursuit. More particularly, we expect a society to achieve certain performance goals, often unarticulated, and we favor public policies and economic arrangements that will best achieve them. In a word, our preferences for particular policy solutions or a market solution to specific problems is based upon unarticulated performance goals that we share. We will seek to clarify some of these goals that are relevant to this book, but first a few words about performance are necessary.

Performance can be looked at both in terms of a society as a whole and in terms of individual units. The performance of the economy at the macroeconomic level may be bad, but a particular sector or even a specific firm may be doing quite well. Of course, the opposite may be true. The level of analysis *may* make a difference in the particular criteria employed to evaluate performance. For example, we may decide that a high level of employment in the economy as a whole is evidence of good performance, but, ironically, a low level of labor input per unit of output may be considered good performance at the microeconomic level of individual sectors or firms.

Performance may also be viewed in static or dynamic terms with respect to the societal, sectoral, or individual levels. And performance may be compared with that at a different time period or with a different society. The U.S. economy during the 1970s might be viewed as having performed badly relative to that same economy in the 1960s, but it may have performed very well compared with the economies of most other countries.

Finally, one should note that in analyzing performance, as in most evaluations, we are concerned with a continuum of values ranging from very good to very bad. Just as with students' grades, certain arbitrary points are marked off in assigning qualitative characterizations—a 90 is an "A," an 80 is a "B," and so forth. Consequently, in setting forth basic performance criteria I will be forced to use such terms as "good," "bad," "adequate," etc., to describe these goals. Unfortunate? Yes, but unless one looks at specific cases there is no other choice.

ECONOMIC PERFORMANCE GOALS

Employment and Efficiency

The major economic aspects of performance that are pertinent to regulation have been well summarized by economist Joe S. Bain.[1] At the macroeconomic level these performance goals are, first, a high level of employment and, conversely, a low level of unemployment and under-employment. The second goal is that production be highly efficient; that is, the society's output should be high relative to inputs. In a dynamic sense, the society's efficiency gains should be high over time, which in turn breaks down into the relative efficiencies of the various factors of production. The efficiency criterion further implies that aggregate plant capacity should be such that there is neither chronic excess capacity nor substantial shortages relative to demand over time.

At the microeconomic level the efficiency criterion further implies that firms use employment and managerial policies that are not wasteful; featherbedding and inefficient duplication of tasks are to be avoided. Plants and firms should be in an efficient size range for that particular industry. The efficient size range of steel mills, for example, had been quite large, but more recently smaller mills have become highly efficient.

One could draw additional conclusions about performance from the efficiency criterion, but the critical point is to provide a sufficient articulation of performance goals in order to be able to assess critically the relative efficacies of the more-regulation or less-regulation schools of thought. For example, critics of contemporary U.S. regulation assert that both the aggregate costs of complying with government regulations as well as the alleged misallocation of resources—especially in installing devices to meet environmental and safety requirements instead of employing these resources in more efficient facilities—have been a major cause of America's recent productivity decline.[2] Assuming for the moment that there is truth to the claim that scarce resouces must be put to unproductive rather than productive uses because of government regulation (which will be taken up in a later chapter), the relevance of comparing competition with regulation with respect to the goal of efficiency is clear.

Prices, Costs, and Profits

The third major economic aspect of performance concerns the relationships between prices, costs, and profits. Assuming that costs reflect efficiency (our second criterion in evaluating performance), both profits and prices must be "reasonable." Under this conception, it is initially clear that when firms operate at a loss or when there is no profit, performance is bad. Under such circumstances a firm would be incapable of making a return on investment, expanding capacity, or investing to increase efficiency. At the other extreme, profits that are far above all-industry rates—except insofar as they reward: (1) persistently recurring innovation, (2) a very risky enterprise, (3) a rapidly depleting resource, or (4) an undertaking that involves increasingly greater marginal costs—do not indicate good performance. Rather, these excessive profits would tend to reflect monopoly conditions of contrived scarcity and heightened price that exclude large numbers of potential purchasers.

In the short run, excessive profits may be justified by any one or combination of other factors—superior product or major cost-cutting breakthroughs, for example—but in the long term, monopoly conditions or a cartel arrangement among competitors that simulates monopoly is usually the explanation (absent the four factors listed above). While numerous other factors contribute to the variety of profits experienced by different firms and industries, profits in the long run should tend toward the all-industry average. Under most conditions, excessively low or excessively high long-run profits and prices indicate either inefficiencies or monopolistic conditions and therefore are also signs of bad economic performance. We can do no better than state that profit rates within a zone of all-industry reasonableness are indicators of good performance.

The Quality of Products

The fourth relevant set of performance criteria concerns the quality of products and has both subjective and objective aspects. On the subjective side, it is desirable that prospective purchasers be able to judge products reasonably. Otherwise, the presumed benefit that commercial rivalry brings would not occur. Why expend money and energy producing superior products if consumers will not be able to discern the difference between your product and your competitors?

Insofar as this competitive dynamic has been operative over time, it has led to an interesting irony. More often than not, product improvement means increased product complexity. For example, compare the modern stereophonic system with the hand phonograph of the 1920s or modern "wonder drugs" with the simple medical remedies available at the turn of the 20th century. Consequently, as products improve, the ability of the ordinary (as well as the educated) consumer to judge product quality has declined commensurately.

This fact has led to another important issue in the debate between those who lean toward greater regulation and those who favor market forces. How are purchasers to obtain the information necessary to make a reasoned judgment about relatively complex products that they buy, such as automobiles? Does the answer lie in regulating product quality and requiring mandatory information disclosure by the producer? Or does the market system still provide the best mechanism for informing the consumer and assuring that firms compete in product quality as well as in price?

The objective component of product quality is twofold: the first aspect concerns general product quality and the second, product variety. In terms of quality, the critical trade-offs are the level of quality and price. Too low a *general* quality level is obviously undesirable since it might involve rapid depletion of resources, defective products, and wasteful servicing charges. The Soviet economy notoriously suffers from these problems. But too high an average quality level is also undesirable since numerous potential purchasers would be foreclosed from the market. It simply would not be practical to have the Rolls-Royce as the average quality automobile, for example. The revolution wrought by the Ford Model T that permitted many Americans to purchase automobiles attests to this point.

The formulation that economists have devised has been succinctly set forth by Bain:

> The general quality level of the products of an industry [should be] neither too high nor too low in view of the costs of increasing product quality and in view of buyers' desires relative to product quality. Products should not be excessively deteriorated in the sense that they reach such a level that buyers would prefer to pay the extra costs to be incurred in improving quality. Neither should they be excessively improved, enlarged, nor made elaborate in the sense that buyers would prefer a lower quality product with the resultant saving in cost.[3]

When government mandates design standards, does it interfere with this rule for product quality?

The same sort of argument is made with respect to product variety, the second objective component of product quality. We assume, based on the experience of consumer purchasing patterns over a long period of time, that consumers demand a wide range of quality, price, and design for most goods. Product variety is frequently lacking in societies such as the Soviet Union and is a major source of consumer dissatisfaction. In any industry or service there should be "a more or less maximum variety of designs, qualities and costs offered, so long as production volume of the industrial designs is maintained sufficiently that inefficiently small scale production does not offset the ... advantages of variety." [4]

Social Performance Goals and Economic Ends

Product quality most frequently is regulated not for its own sake but rather as a means to attain other goals. These are usually social performance goals related to public health, safety, and welfare. Of course, in some instances the motivation for high performance standards has little to do with attaining health and safety goals. For example, economist George Stigler reports that in the early 1930s the railroads, concerned about increasing long-haul competition from trucks, sought to enact state regulatory statutes limiting the size and weight of trucks to cripple that mode of transportation. [5] Notwithstanding this and similar cases, product quality regulation is usually directed toward the goals of safety and health, the two major social performance goals that we will now examine.

SOCIAL PERFORMANCE GOALS

The foregoing list of economic performance goals is by no means intended to be exhaustive, of course. An evaluation of these goals and other economic ones is necessary to determine whether an industry meets the standards of what economists term "workable competition." The concept, introduced by economist J. M. Clark, rejects the classical model of perfect competition as unachievable and instead sets up performance goals that are to be *approximated* through a mixture of market arrangements and public (principally regulatory) policies. The closer an industry achieves these economic performance goals, the more it is said to be workably competitive.

Can this same framework apply to the two other great subjects of regulation—morals and social performance goals? Social performance goals, like economic ones, are premised upon the common values of material and physical well-being. Economics is the science of maximizing these shared values. Morals, on the other hand, vary considerably from society to society and over time within the same society; they do not lend themselves to analysis within the law-and-economics approach. The diversity of human morals—best left to theories devised by sociologists, psychologists, and anthropologists—will not be further discussed in this book.

The Cost of Social Regulation

Social regulation can be integrated within the framework of workable competition. In recent years a distinction commonly has been made between the "old regulation" directed towards economic performance goals and the "new regulation" devoted to social performance goals (principally health and safety), as if these are sharply distinct categories. While there are clearly significant differences between post-1970s statutes such as the Clean Air Amendments, Occupational Safety and Health Act, and Consumer Product Safety Act, on the one hand, and the earlier Interstate Commerce Act, Civil Aeronautics Act, and Motor Carrier Act on the other, these differences must not be overstated. Social regulation devoted to health and safety and earlier economic regulation are more closely related than might be obvious at first glance.

Both economic regulation and the new social regulation are ostensibly designed to enhance the material enjoyment of life. Regulation of railroad rates and routes is directed towards cheapening transportation costs (and hence the delivered price of goods), guaranteeing steady supplies, and assuring the quality of transportation service, all of which are intended to serve the end of material enjoyment, just as explicit safety and health regulation is directed toward that goal.

But more importantly, the imposition of social regulations imposes economic costs, which leads to the central problem in formulating social performance criteria. How do we measure and evaluate competing costs and benefits? For example, requirements compelling automobile manufacturers to install safety and pollution control devices add direct pecuniary costs that are reflected in the purchase price of cars. It is also clear that resources expended in complying with such regulations may result in forgone opportunity costs, which are the costs attributable to doing one thing rather than another. Thus, funds expended on pollution abatement might have been more fruitfully spent on new equipment or on the development of new products. General Motors has estimated that half of its research dollars are expended to meet the costs of complying with regulation; other major firms have made similar, if not quite as specific, claims.[6] One study conducted by economist Murray Weidenbaum estimated that the aggregate cost to business of complying with federal regulation was about $102 billion in fiscal 1979, about $500 for each person in the United States.[7]

But balanced against these costs are those costs imposed by unsafe and unhealthful products and manufacturing processes. These costs are both pecuniary and nonpecuniary. A person whose health is impaired because of unwholesome working conditions sustains pecuniary losses that are measurable, such as medical bills or lost wages. Nevertheless, the intangible losses occasioned by the pain and suffering of serious illness are just as real, although not *immediately* measurable. Similarly, the losses resulting from intangibles such as excessive noise levels or filthy surroundings are just as real as directly measurable costs. The fact that we would pay more for a house located in quiet surroundings than for the same dwelling located in a filthy, congested area illustrates that these "nonpecuniary" costs indeed are pecuniary and that intangible costs are measurable.

Now let us consider two important factors that are critical in establishing performance goals in the area of social regulation. First, intangible and so-called nonpecuniary costs are measurable, but they are simply more difficult to measure than pecuniary costs. Nevertheless, persons selling real property and juries awarding damages for pain and suffering have found ways—albeit imperfect ones—for measuring such costs. Thus, a cost-benefit analysis may theoretically be conducted when tangible gains must be weighed against intangible losses.

Second, when we balance costs against benefits in a responsible manner, very few of us would be willing to take absolutist stands; we seek instead a reasonable balance. For example, it is likely that continued use of automobiles will always lead to some deaths that are caused by accidents. Not many of us would be willing to ban all motor vehicle use because it will result in some deaths, but most of us are willing to pay for the installation of some safety equipment in cars, whether on a voluntary or mandatory basis. To take a more realistic example, most of us are willing to permit the marketing of drugs that are apt to save many lives, even though some lives will be lost as a result of adverse side-effects.

How to Measure Social Performance

How then can we articulate performance standards in the safety and health areas without adopting absolutist positions? An assessment of costs and benefits is the obvious starting point—but what costs and what benefits? And how do we measure intangible costs and benefits?

One of the most probing and convincing analyses of these questions has been supplied by economist Larry E. Ruff, who has argued that the most important conceptual distinction that one must make is between *aggregate* cost-benefit analysis and *marginal* cost-benefit analysis.[8] Attempting to show the logical flaw in aggregate cost-benefit analysis, Ruff used the following example. If the national cost of air pollution is $11 billion a year and public expenditures are $50 million a year, it does not follow—as some zealots have asserted—that we should be spending an amount equal to the costs of pollution abatement, no more than it would follow that we would be spending too much on abatement if the cost and expenditure figures were reversed.

The fallacy in this sort of balance-sheet reasoning lies in the assumption that there is a linear relationship within the whole range of costs and benefits between public expenditure and pollution abatement. For example, this reasoning assumes that if, at the $3 to $4 billion range, $1 of expenditure will result in approximately $1 of abatement, the same approximate relationship will apply at the $5 to $6 billion range, the $9 to $10 billion range, and so forth. The assumption is unwarranted both logically and in actual experience. It is far more common in the real world of pollution abatement, as well as in other regulatory matters, for the additional benefits to decline relative to expenditures as one moves upward towards a 100 percent solution to a problem. Thus, the abatement costs in the $10 to $11 billion range are apt to exceed the measured benefits, which would most likely not be true in the $1 to $2 billion range.

For this reason, the appropriate conceptualization of safety and health regulation is in terms of marginal costs and marginal benefits, assuming for the moment that all costs and benefits are quantifiable. The critical question is how much extra benefit will be obtained with the application of additional cost at each point along the expenditure range. If, for example, $1 of expenditure will yeild $2 worth of benefit at the $2 billion expenditure point, the expenditure is warranted; but $1 of expenditure that yields only $.50 of benefits at the $9 billion point is clearly not justified. Thus, in health and safety performance, the goal must be to attain the optimum level where the marginal costs equal the marginal benefits. Reaching anything less than this point will indicate that we have achieved less than the desired performance, just as exceeding this point or range will mean exactly the same thing.

Of course, some may insist that this formulation might be reasonable in the abstract but that it cannot be made operational with respect to real world situations; therefore, the performance goal just set forth is of no practical use. The first answer to this objection is that, even if intangible costs and benefits cannot be precisely measured, the formulation can still serve as a general guideline—better a rough yardstick than none at all. Second, there are methods available to measure such intangibles, just as the fact that real estate located in a clean, quiet neighborhood commands a higher price than comparable property in a noisy, dirty neighborhood attests. Quantification and measurement are difficult, but they can be done. The critical problems are who will do the measuring and how they will do it.

These questions in turn imply a choice of technique. Should government attempt to attain these goals through regulation or subsidy policy, for example, or are they best achieved through free market operations? We will now discuss Adam Smith's arguments in favor of the free market to see how this system purports to achieve economic and social performance goals.

THE CLASSIC ARGUMENT FOR UNFETTERED COMPETITION

The year 1776 witnessed two momentous events, one rather violent and dramatic and the other quiet but no less dramatic. It is impossible to say whether the American War of Independence or the publication of Adam Smith's *Wealth of Nations* has had the greater effect on the modern world.[9] But it is clear that the impacts of both events have been extraordinary and in some ways interrelated.

Smith's great achievement was in providing a theoretical justification for relatively unfettered capitalism as the system most capable of realizing material happiness. This is not to suggest that he was an apologist or even an admirer of those engaged in business. To the contrary, Smith was often quite harsh in his judgment of them and their conduct, even to the point of suggesting that they would be the first to violate the rules of competition. At various places in the *Wealth of Nations,* Smith accused the business community of seeking to monopolize trade, inevitably conspire against the public, and direct the state into policies that serve their interests in conflict with the public good.

Smith did not completely reject state action. He noted many exceptions to the rules of competition where state intervention in the market was called for, although restricted to a relatively few tasks. Smith was not an idealogue seeking to show that state action is always harmful; rather he focused on the public benefits that would result if competition prevailed and was undirected by state regulation. The principal focus of Smith's enmity was monopoly, especially those monopolies and cartels that were created and protected by state action.

Smith, then, proposed a system of *relatively* unrestricted competition, the beauty of which was that it would work regardless of the wishes of its participants, similar to the way the laws of physics operate. According to Smith, if only the state would not meddle, the market system would achieve remarkable performance levels.

The power of Smith's ideas has been so great that many recent distinguished economists—including Nobel Prize winners—still adhere to the basic structure that he devised, notwithstanding the enormous changes that have taken place in the economy since 1776. Without extolling the business community, these modern adherents—notably the modern Austrian school (such as Friedrich Hayek and Ludwig Von Mises) and the Chicago school (including Milton Friedman and George Stigler) share a basic antipathy toward regulation and a belief that the best mechanism to attain both economic and social goals most often is the free market and the force of competition. Why?

The Case for Competition

The central concept fashioned by Smith in his elaborate free market argument was the "invisible hand." In a famous passage, Smith argued that each individual pursuing his own selfish interest would most effectively promote the interests of society:

> Every individual necessarily labours to render the annual revenue of the society as great as he can. He generally, indeed, neither intends to promote the public interest, nor knows how much he is promoting it . . . . By directing that industry in such a manner as its produce may be of the greatest value, he intends only his own gain, and he is in this, as in many other cases, led by an invisible hand to promote an end which was no part of his intention. Nor is it always the worse for the society that it was no part of it. By pursuing his own interest he frequently promotes that of the society more effectually than when he really intends to promote it.[10]

After extolling the market and competition, Smith went on to observe that the businessman pursuing his self-interest can

> judge much better than any statesman or lawgiver can do for him. The statesman who should attempt to direct private people in what manner they ought to employ their capitals, would not only load himself with a most unnecessary attention, but assume an authority which could safely be trusted, not only to no single person, but to no council or senate whatever, and which would nowhere be so dangerous as in the hands of a man who had folly and presumption enough to fancy himself fit to exercise it.[11]

Smith then advanced two interrelated propositions. As he saw it, the market is the best conceivable mechanism to attain most performance goals, although there are exceptions. Second, public intervention in the form of regulation impedes the attainment of these goals because: (1) regulation interferes with the natural workings of the market—the best possible system—and (2) public officials cannot know as much about the intricacies of any particular economic pursuit as do those engaged in it on a daily basis.

Smith remarked elsewhere that when the state regulates an activity, it usually does so not in the public interest but rather in the interests of particular business groups seeking some benefit or trying to thwart competitors or potential competitiors. He was not an anarchist envisioning no role whatsoever for government. Smith presumed against government intervention but allowed it some role, even including a small regulatory role. First, he conceded that government should protect society from the violence and invasion of other societies and therefore favored the support of a standing army.

Second, government has the obligation of "protecting, as far as possible, every member of the society from the injustice or oppression of every other member of it." [12] In other words, government must protect life, liberty, and property, through criminal laws that deter unwarranted force and fraud and through the civil actions brought by private parties in courts that enforce basic rules concerning contracts, private property, and tortious conduct. The function of these rules is to assure that the most basic economic and social arrangements are maintained. A commercial system, for example, could not function if one party could with impunity breach a contract into which both parties had freely entered. Nor could a system of private property be secure if a person could invade or injure it without punishment. The state, through the courts, therefore must protect such values when petitioned to do so by injured parties.

The third major task of government as envisioned by Smith also relates to the preservation of the social structure and the free market system. Government should establish and operate institutions necessary to these when for lack of profitability such activities will not be undertaken by private enterprises. A principal example is public works projects, such as canals and roads.

Adam Smith and Regulation

From the foregoing discussion of Adam Smith's principles we can now examine the role of regulation as envisioned by him and his followers. At the outset, it should be clear that we cannot define the issue between the Smithian perspective and contemporary proponents of regulation as a simple dichotomy between no regulation and regulation in the "public interest," as some have done. Smith and many of his contemporary followers do see a role for regulation, albeit a narrow one.

Smith set forth his view of regulation in a discussion of the banking industry and commended regulatory legislation directed at banking practices that severely impeded trade and commerce. Critical to Smith's perspective was that banking was considered a central infrastructural activity with a major impact on the aggregate level and growth of industrial and commercial activity.[13] Accordingly, certain banking practices that seriously retarded the development of trade and industry should be prohibited or otherwise regulated. Smith concluded:

> To restrain private people, it may be said, from receiving in payment the promissory notes of a banker, for any sum whether great or small, when they themselves are willing to receive them; or to restrain a banker from issuing such notes, when all his neighbors are willing to accept of them, is a manifest violation of that natural liberty which it is the proper business of law not to infringe, but to support. Such regulations may, no doubt, be considered as in some respect a violation

of natural liberty. But those exertions of the natural liberty of a few individuals *which might endanger the security of the whole society* ... *are and ought to be restrained.* ... The obligation of building party walls [a wall separating and common to two buildings or properties] in order to prevent the communication of fire, is a violation of natural liberty, exactly of the same kind with the regulations of the banking trade which are here proposed.[14] (Emphasis supplied)

It is important to specify the limited role Smith and his followers envisioned for regulation by contrasting it with what he is not saying. The party wall example at first might be considered an archaic analog to modern environmental regulation, since in both cases the failure to take precautions could have negative repercussions on innocent third parties; therefore the state should intervene with regulatory controls. But this justification for regulation, which we will look at in Chapter 4, was not what Smith had in mind. If he had, the state could justifiably regulate an enormous range of activities where one party's actions have an adverse impact on innocent third parties, which is clearly inconsistent with Smith's extremely limited conception of state action.

As the italicized portion of the above excerpt indicates, according to Smith regulation is to be limited to activities that *fundamentally* thwart the proper functioning of the social structure and the system of free competition. Thus, it is appropriate for government to regulate violent crime in order to protect society. Similarly, in view of the destruction of London by fire little more than 100 years prior to the publication of the *Wealth of Nations,* it was appropriate for the state to impose regulations requiring party walls that would retard the rapid spread of fire.

In other words, it is the degree of the harm to society that overcomes the strong presumption against regulation. In contrast, slight environmental damage to interests here and there, which falls short of undermining the social structure or market system, is not substantial enough to call forth the regulatory power of the state. While these problems involve matters of degree, the strong presumption in the Smithian system is always against public regulation since merely adversely affecting innocent third parties is insufficient to implement this governmental technique. In Smith's view, the proper procedure to remedy a situation where one party is injured as a result of another's harmful conduct is to petition the courts for damage compensation.

Similarly, Smith approved of the banking regulation discussed above because without it the very functioning of the commercial and industrial system would be severely impeded. By analogy we can hypothesize that Smith would favor that portion of modern antitrust regulation that prohibits collusive price arrangements, since collusion violates the fundamental principle of competition. Indeed, Smith probably would adopt the formulation advanced by economist Friedrich

Hayek that government regulation that is consistent with the preservation of free competition is permissible, while regulation that either restricts or shapes the direction of that competition is to be avoided.[15]

Two points follow from the structure of this formulation advanced by Smith and adopted by his followers. First, the issue dividing the Smithian view from the argument of those who advocate a far wider public regulatory role is not simply regulation versus no regulation. As we have seen, the Smithian perspective sharply limits, but does not preclude, regulation, while even the most forceful advocate of public regulation does not desire the abandonment of the unregulated market in every situation. The differences lie in establishing the principles that should determine when regulation should be used. We have seen the fundamental principle advocated by those identified with a very wide role for the free market: regulation is proper only when the social order or economic freedom could not otherwise effectively function.

But the second thing apparent from Smith's formulation is that it does not even come close to describing the realities of the contemporary U.S. regulatory structure, which is far broader than what Smith would have permitted and is today sharply criticized by his followers. Indeed, Smith no doubt would be horrified at the extent of the contemporary regulatory apparatus. We will examine the alleged defects in the free market and the justifications for the broad regulatory structure, but first we must look at the arguments made on behalf of the market system. Why do Smith and his followers claim that the free market yields the best economic and social performance?

COMPETITION AND ECONOMIC PERFORMANCE

Self-Interest and Public Benefit

We begin our examination of Smith's invisible hand concept with an observation found in most traditional introductory economics textbooks: Is it not remarkable that virtually every city, town, suburb, village, and hamlet in America contains stores that provide us with a wide range of goods to satisfy our demands? Is it not even more remarkable that the stocks of these goods are replenished on a continuous basis?

In contrast, there are societies that suffer from a chronic scarcity of goods; goods periodically appear, consumers queue up in long lines, the goods disappear, and replacements are not available again for a long time. These are typically societies that lack a market mechanism or in which there is a marked degree of government tampering with it. The reason for widespread availability in our society, of course, is that there are sellers in whose interest it is to provide this wide array of goods. And, to use Smith's framework, these sellers provide us with these goods not because they are motivated by a desire to serve the "public interest" but because they can profit thereby.

For the same reason, sellers are usually motivated to sell us their wares not just one time but on a continuing basis. Taken together, sellers—motivated solely by their desire for self-gain—constitute a system that provides us with our needs and wants. Through trial-and-error and marketing research techniques, sellers learn what consumers want and will buy. And when consumer tastes change—from large, powerful automobiles to small, fuel-efficient ones, for example—sellers adjust, although sometimes not as rapidly as tastes change. When smaller untapped markets or new consumer tastes are discovered that are not currently being fulfilled by extant sellers, new firms move in to fill the vacuum—as Volkswagen and later the Japanese automobile manufacturers demonstrated in the American car market.

At the same time, those producers that do not seek to compete in the mass market attempt to target their wares to narrower markets ignored by those firms aiming at the larger ones. For this reason Rolls-Royces and classical records are produced, even though they constitute very small fractions of the total markets for automobiles and recordings, respectively. Where there is a potential market or submarket not being tended by existing firms, a new entrant or one of the extant firms spotting the opportunity will avail itself of it. This is true despite the fact that the *general tendency* of firms is to seek out the largest part of a potential market, especially when regulatory controls limit the number of entrants.[16]

From the perspective of the consumer, relatively unrestrained competition means a high likelihood that individual particular tastes will be satisfied, even though a higher price may have to be paid to satisfy the more peculiar ones. And most important, the market system based on seller self-interest implies that consumers are free to choose pursuant to their individual and different tastes rather than have some authority impose standardized tastes upon them.

The Reality of Competition

The seller self-interest/consumer sovereignty dynamic depends on the presence of real competition—or at least potential competition—in the marketplace. A seller with an assured market and no competitors has little incentive to pay attention to what consumers want. On the other hand, competing sellers each seek to enlarge their market shares, and even a firm relatively content with its share must still compete out of fear that its rivals will erode its markets.

It is therefore important to examine how actual market operations compare with Smith's views on competition. One may object that in 1776 when Smith advanced his ideas market structures were quite different from those today, then consisting of large numbers of small firms owned by individual proprietors who had very imperfect information about each other's activities. In contrast, today many industries—certainly the leading ones—are oligopolies, comprised of a relatively few very large corporations dominated by managers with considerable and accurate information about each other's activities.

This objection continues by urging that, whereas in the market situation with which Smith was familiar firms had little choice but to compete, the modern oligopoly is a quite different situation. Why, for example, should U.S. Steel reduce its prices when its rival Bethlehem Steel will soon learn about it and imitate its move? Under such circumstances, there may be little reason for firms to compete in ways that their rivals can readily imitate, and a *modus vivendi* is reached where competition is restricted to relatively innocuous activities such as advertising and product packaging.

This objection to the views of Smith and his followers on the role of competition is obviously an important one. Indeed, the theoretical structure advanced by this school of thought would come tumbling down if it were true that such strong disincentives to competition exist. To rebut this argument, we should point out that price, quality, and service are hardly set arbitrarily. Each is affected by the existence of substitute products, level and elasticity of demand, condition of supply, bargaining power of buyers, level of imports, threat of new entry into the business, and other factors. And even if an industry is characterized by nonprice competition, a significant shift in market share may lead one of the losers to reintroduce price competition.[17]

Firms in such industries must search for ways to institute major advantages over their rivals in product quality, process, cost, or some other way, if for no other reason than the fear that rivals will take similar advantage of them. IBM, for example, was able to expand its market share rapidly in mainframe computers when it devised its 360 system. The continual changes wrought by firms in the so-called oligopolistic sectors attest to this dynamic. Moreover, virtually every major U.S. industry and retail trade has witnessed dramatic market share changes in recent times.

And price competition does exist in such industries, although in different forms. Instead of dramatic changes in list prices, sellers in oligopolistic industries are more or less apt to grant various surreptitious price concessions, rebates, and discounts in response to market conditions. Eventually the general price level does reflect the market impact of these individually made decisions. Accordingly, argue the

Smithians, it is not surprising that from 1947 to 1971 the prices of goods produced in oligopolistic industries displayed a generally slower rate of increase than prices in highly unconcentrated industries.[18]

While this brief summary does not purport to settle a rather intense controversy but only sets forth the contending views on this issue of competition, there is little doubt that sharp competition does exist in the modern industrial setting just as in Adam Smith's day. What is in question here is the extent of that competition. Prices, product quality, processes, costs of production, and every other aspect of competitive rivalry have changed in virtually every American industry during the past 25 years. New products have been developed and new substitutes invented; some industry leaders have lost their competitive advantage, with newer firms taking their place.

Competition is not moribund, and the equilibrium mechanisms that Smith conceptualized to explain the role and function of competition in satisfying consumer wants through producer self-interest are still at work in the marketplace. As he hypothesized, basic equilibrium mechanisms both assure availability of goods to consumers and guarantee performance goals in the best possible manner.

The Concept of Equilibrium

Equilibrium means there is a tendency for supply, demand, and price to come into natural adjustment. Suppose, for example, that at any particular time in the marketplace there is too much of some specific good relative to effective demand, as evidenced by high inventory and slow sales. Under such circumstances, production will slow down and prices will decline. Conversely, prices will rise and production will increase when too little of a good is produced relative to demand. In both cases there is a tendency for supply and demand to come into equilibrium at an equilibrium, or natural, price. The same simple principle applies to labor rates, rent, interest, and, perhaps most importantly, profits. Capital will tend to flow toward high-profit ventures and away from low-profit ones, which in turn will tend to increase production and reduce prices to natural levels.

Put another way, there is a long-run tendency for prices, supply, and demand to reach equilibrium, although at any particular time disequilibrium may exist. Because this long-run tendency leads to the correct adjustments of price, supply, and demand, the Smithian argues that any regulatory interference in the process creates market distortions. Thus, if regulation keeps prices below the natural price in a given market, producers will shy away from that activity and shortages will develop. Conversely, if prices are set too high because of state interference, the quantity of the product consumed is less than that which would prevail under free market conditions. The resulting decline in production below free market levels would occur because of lower effective demand. Similar and other market distortions will occur when there is regulatory interference with supply or demand.

To summarize the Smithian argument, price provides all the information necessary to optimize economic efficiency and allocate resources most effectively. The drive to maximize profits assures that producers and other sellers will minimize their costs, thus optimizing efficiency and preventing the waste of scarce resources. The same profit-maximizing motives also assure that funds will be available for investment purposes in the most profitable use, which (in a competitive situation) also means the most efficient use. And while any particular business decisionmaker's judgment may be fallible, the system taken as a whole assures the achievement of economic performance goals in a better manner than when government regulators—who do not operate with either the profit-maximizing motive or the detailed knowledge of those familiar with the marketplace on a daily basis—make economic decisions.

But even if we accept for the moment the Smithians' argument that the free market system is the best way to attain economic performance goals, are they also prepared to argue that the market performs equally well in achieving social performance goals?

COMPETITION AND SOCIAL PERFORMANCE

Those who advocate minimum state interference will confidently assert that the market system, supplemented by an effective judicial enforcement mechanism that will render justice to injured parties, provides the best guarantee of high levels of social performance. Of course, they concede that some sellers are unscrupulous and will make fraudulent representations to purchasers, but consumers can bring suit against such sellers and obtain damages to the extent that they were injured.

Certainly, proponents continue, *most* entrepreneurs have a strong incentive to sell safe and wholesome products to their customers. In most cases, a seller hopes for either repeat sales or sales to a large number of customers; since information about a product can readily be communicated, product defects will be discovered and buyers will no longer patronize that seller. Economically, it would be extremely irrational to sell unsafe and unhealthful products. Even in those instances in which safety defects or unhealthfulness are not easily discernible or in which health problems do not appear until long after the purchase, a seller will eventually develop a bad reputation that can cause irreparable damage to the firm's sales and profits.

Not only is it usually irrational for a firm to produce unsafe and unhealthful goods from its individual perspective, but the dynamics of competition also reinforce this tendency to sell wholesome products. Competition encourages cheaper production methods as well as the development of new products, improved products, and better service. And competitors are hardly bashful about informing prospective purchasers of the merits of their goods and services compared with rival products; so will they also not be reluctant to advise prospective purchasers about competitors' defects. Only in those rare instances where the generic product is hazardous—cigarettes, for example—will competitors refrain from such activities. Most goods are not *generically* unwholesome.

Information for Profit and Social Goals

But in any case, Smithians contend the market provides an additional protection for consumers, obviating the need for government intervention. In a free society, institutions and entrepreneurs are most happy to provide information—for a profit. For example, consider the many books available for sale that evaluate colleges and universities for prospective students and their parents.

A more dramatic example is the innumerable books and popular articles that supply information in the muckraking tradition about alleged business transgressions. Neither the muckrakers at the turn of the 20th century, nor Ralph Nader, who burst upon the scene in 1965 with an exposé of alleged defects in a popular automobile, nor any other critic with a plausible message has encountered much difficulty in getting media attention. From the quiet evaluation of Consumers Union to the most irresponsible rantings of antibusiness ideologues, consumers are veritably bombarded with allegations and information about health, safety, and other matters relating to social goals. Nor does the so-called "free rider" hypothesis, which argues that consumers will not pay for a benefit they can receive free of charge (in this case, information), negate this view. In fact, a sufficient number of people will pay for information, even though others may obtain it at no cost.

According to advocates of minimum state interference, the market supplies health and safety information more effectively than government. The market reflects the true cost of supplying information just as it reflects the true cost of supplying other goods and services. Government, which does not operate within the competitive market system, has no incentives to supply information efficiently. Consequently, it is not unusual for government to expend vast sums for the production of information about health and safety that is of minor benefit to consumers. But consumers do pay, in any event, as taxpayers—perhaps far more than when the market supplies information.

Private Law and Social Goals

The final protection that the market system provides to consumers is freedom of contract. One is not forced to buy any *particular* product that the market offers since choice is usually varied. A prospective purchaser of an automobile—a complex product involving *relatively* few choices and *relatively* few substitutes—may still choose between a new or used vehicle. If he decides to buy a new one, he may chose from among well over 100 models, and, although he will probably know very little about the reliability of any particular model, he may still protect himself by purchasing one that offers the best warranty.

If he buys a used car, the purchaser may negotiate with the seller in the contract of sale for warranties, which are enforceable in a court of law. Before entering into a contract the purchaser may seek the advice of a private source of information, such as an able mechanic or *Consumer Reports* magazine. Finally, if the prospective purchaser is still wary, nothing compels him to purchase a car at all. He still has the option of leasing an automobile or using public transportation, after weighing the costs and benefits of these alternatives. And what is true of a product that has been glibly described as a "necessity" is at least as true with respect to virtually every other service and product.

In brief, while the doctrine of *caveat emptor*—"let the buyer beware"—is often disparaged, it affords the consumer an important protective mechanism, for one may insist upon writing clauses into a contract in order to assure the safety and healthfulness of a product. Adequate private legal remedies exist to enforce such contracts.

The law also provides remedies to protect those who are not parties to a contract but whose health and safety may be endangered as a result of another's activities. These legal actions are called torts and include negligence, assault, and trespass. In such instances, self-interest will assure the assertion of rights, to which innumerable automobile collision court cases, based on negligence, attest. And while it is true that such actions may be brought only after the harm has been perpetrated or commenced, the threat of legal action will deter potential wrongdoers because the costs of remedying such a situation invariably exceed the costs of prevention. But in any event, the system of private tort enforcement, based on self-interest, is to the Smithian more efficient than a cumbersome regulatory apparatus, which usually operates without any regard to the balancing of costs and benefits.

The Free Market Concluded

The Smithian argument on social performance goals concludes that neither government nor the competititive market system envisioned by Smith can safeguard against all threats to health and safety, however.

Just as the pathological murderer will always exist, so too will the pathological businessman always be with us (although rarely, according to this argument). Social goals are protected as effectively as they can be primarily by the forces of competition, supplemented by consumer information, contract, and private legal remedies based on self-interest.

In contrast, government regulation—with its inherent inefficiencies, lack of proper incentives, and tendency to distort markets—is an inadequate substitute for the achievement of social goals. And ultimately the freedom of choice, built into the free market model, is preferable. It almost seems too perfect. But while the Smithian system based on a minimum of public regulation has numerous advocates, including many thoughtful and distinguished scholars, it also has its detractors, which also include many thoughtful and distinguished scholars.

More importantly, the public policies of the United States and every other western democratic nation have rejected the Smithian model for one favoring a much more extensive regulatory role. The reason is partly due to political pressures but part of it has to do with a reasoned basis for concluding that there are sufficient justifications for public regulation. Before proceeding to these justifications in the next three chapters, a preliminary problem arises. What questions do we need to ask when comparing the free market with governmental alternatives, especially regulation, in their achievement of economic and social performance goals?

QUESTIONS ABOUT MARKETS AND REGULATION

Asked whether the market or regulation is the better alternative, some observers are apt to look back wistfully at an earlier era where laissez-faire reigned supreme and the free operation of the market with its marvelous price mechanism solved virtually all problems. They argue that the economy performed better before the expansion of government intrusion into what theretofore were matters settled privately without public interference. From this perception they conclude that there is a presumption in most cases in favor of the free market, which achieved enormous economic progress in the United States and Britain before it.

But even aside from this questionable presumption, this wistful look at the past has doubtful historical validity. Price controls, transportation entry, wage and working condition controls, and a host of other regulations existed long before Adam Smith's idea of free competition.[19] Even during the so-called laissez-faire era in America, from the Revolution to the Civil War, regulation was employed at every level of government.[20] But should we then conclude that regulation is the "natural" state of affairs and that there is a rebuttable presumption against free market mechanisms? Clearly, there is no more logic in using history to support this presumption than there is for its converse, if for no other reason than that political-economic arrangements that guaranteed good performance levels in the past may be inappropriate under contemporary conditions.

Let us take another tack—the popular bias against government intervention, provided regulation can be avoided. If one could show that there is a sound basis for this attitude, we could establish that the presumption against regulation may be overcome—just as there is a presumption against the guilt of one charged with a crime that may be overturned by convincing proof to the contrary. This presumption against regulation is easily established if we assume, for the moment, that regulation and the free market unaided by government intervention are equally capable of achieving identical levels of economic and social performance. Under such circumstances, free competition is obviously the preferred choice, since regulation inevitably occasions what economists term "dead-weight loss"—economic costs that are not directed towards the production, distribution, and marketing of goods and services. At the least, salaries must be paid to those government employees who are not involved in these economic activities as well as to employees of regulated firms who must be employed for compliance or evasion. Starting from our temporary assumption of equal performance levels, the typical citizen would be better off not paying the taxes to support government regulators, and business units would be better off either reducing costs imposed by government or utilizing resources in productive activities.

Thus, all other things being equal, an unfettered enterprise—whether operated privately or publicly—is preferable to a regulated enterprise; there is a presumption against regulation. But, of course, all other things are not necessarily equal. Proponents of regulation are fond of pointing to alleged performance shortcomings that occur when enterprises are not regulated. According to them, we are allegedly served unwholesome food, breathe unwholesome air, and pay unreasonably high prices when there is no government intervention.

Nevertheless, we are now in a better position to evaluate the arguments about the benefits or harm of regulation. From the foregoing discussion, it is clear that the burden of proof lies with those who advocate regulation and that regulation should not be implemented without convincing evidence. This discussion permits us to structure the key questions that should be asked about regulation.

1. *Does the unregulated market achieve a high level of economic and social performance?* If the market does so in all particulars related to performance, our presumption against regulation dictates that our

inquiry is at an end. Little purpose is served by tampering with these arrangements in view of both the costs that might be involved and the unintended results that could occur; too often we are unhappily surprised when regulation is imposed on what was a satisfactory arrangement beforehand. If, however, economic or social performance in any respect falls significantly short of our realistic economic and social performance goals, we must ask a second question.

2. *Can regulation be justified?* Even the most ardent proponents of regulation as a public policy technique do not insist that it is appropriate in order to achieve every desirable public policy goal. For example, if a nation's industrial plant and equipment are woefully backward, even regulatory zealots will concede that firms cannot simply be ordered to modernize their facilities pursuant to certain regulatory standards. If that were all there was to it, every nation in the world could easily imitate Japan's economic successes.

Clearly, subsidy, planning, or some other governmental technique is more appropriate to achieve this particular goal than regulation. Indeed, regulation is a government instrument appropriate in only a few circumstances, which we will examine in later chapters.

3. *Will regulation lead to better performance than that which would prevail without government intervention?* Even if regulation is justified under certain circumstances, it still does not follow that economic or social performance under regulation will be superior to performance in an uninhibited market. An unregulated market may yield results that fall short (indeed, far short) of performance goals, but in an imperfect world the market still may yield better performance results than under regulatory conditions—an obvious point that is sometimes overlooked.

When the market fails to achieve desired results, legislators and the active public often automatically and unthinkingly search for a regulatory instrument that sometimes turns out to be worse than the unimpeded market conditions it replaced. Perhaps the most notorious instance in recent American history is the prohibition of alcoholic beverages during the 1920s and early 1930s.[21] Whatever social and moral harm might have been wreaked from the relatively unregulated liquor trade in the pre-Prohibition era was trivial to the harm occasioned by the ultimate form of regulation—prohibition.

4. *Do the costs of regulation outweigh the benefits?* This is a different question from the one just discussed. While the former compares regulation with an unhindered market, we are concerned here with an internal accounting of a particular regulatory scheme. It is important to address this question not only prior to instituting a regulatory scheme but also periodically afterward because the experi-

ence generated by regulation often supplies answers that at best could only be guessed beforehand.

For example, numerous critics of the 1962 amendments to the Food, Drug and Cosmetics Act and the regulations promulgated under it have charged that the law and its enforcement precipitated very drastic declines in the development and marketing of new drugs. They claim that more lives have been lost than saved through the more stringent safety and efficacy requirements imposed by the law.[22]

If the costs of regulation outweigh its benefits, one should be unwilling to institute or continue it, even though regulation might produce better performance goals than unrestrained competition in one particular area. In other words, regulatory costs that outweigh regulatory benefits frequently indicate performance declines in other areas. Thus, as the drug example illustrates, the 1962 drug law might have enhanced safety, but research and innovation suffered.

5. *Is there a public policy instrument that will achieve the particular performance goal better than regulation?* Even assuming we find that regulation will lead to better economic and social performance than unrestrained competition, it still does not follow that regulation should be instituted, for there may be superior policy instruments to effect the same or better results. Since the carrot is often more effective than the stick in getting desired results, subsidy policy might be a superior choice in some instances. For the same reason, tax concessions and loan guarantees are other instruments that have been employed instead of regulation, especially when the desired behavior requires a set of affirmative steps to be undertaken by private parties, such as delivering mail, searching for new petroleum deposits, or constructing merchant vessels that are readily convertible to military purposes.

Regulation, on the other hand, is often more appropriate to prohibitions and simpler affirmative tasks. Similarly, at other times, transfer payments or the provision of information to certain groups, such as farmers, are more suitable to certain tasks than regulatory policy. Finally, there are instances in which the government may prefer to undertake a task as a proprietor rather than regulate the private sector—the U.S. Postal Service and the Tennessee Valley Authority, for example. But no simple rule will provide us with an easy guide for choosing the policy instrument most appropriate to a particular task.

6. *What form of regulation should be employed?* This question is last, of course, because we momentarily assume that the answers to the prior questions inevitably lead us to conclude that regulation is the most efficacious means available to attain certain performance goals. But we are still faced with the problems of what forms regulation should take and how extensive it should be. The discussion of the components of

regulatory legislation in Chapter 1 emphasized the numerous permutations and combinations of regulatory statutes. An industry might be extensively regulated, as in the case of the maritime industry, or it might be regulated in only a few particulars; the sheer extent of regulation can make an important difference in performance levels. For example, some critics of regulation have complained that when there is little discretion left to management, initiative to improve products, services, and processes diminishes drastically.

Even after it has been determined that a particular situation warrants regulation, no simple answer is available about the appropriate form that regulation should take. So much depends on the particular tasks regulation is intended to accomplish that only one presumption can be made: unfettered market forces are to be preferred to regulation unless a convincing argument can be shown to the contrary, assuming that competition at least reasonably meets performance goals.

It therefore follows that less regulation is preferable to more regulation. Thus, if we decide it is desirable to regulate the practice of medicine, there is a presumption that regulating through a system of qualifying examinations, under which anyone who passes may practice, is better than licensing that restricts the number of practitioners. Of course, the presumption in favor of less regulation may be rebutted by showing that such a strategy is ineffective and that more stringent regulation is required.

CONCLUSION

We began this chapter by observing that political-economic arrangements should not exist in a vacuum. They exist to attain economic and social performance goals better than alternatives can. After specifying and discussing these goals, we looked at competition and the free market idea, powerfully developed by Adam Smith, and how they are supposed to attain performance goals. As we noted, few (if any) contemporary political economies rigorously adhere to Smith's prescriptions. Western economies are characterized by a mixed system embracing private markets and state intervention, including government regulation.

This indicates the pragmatic nature of modern western political economies, which recognize that no system is perfect. Policymakers accordingly choose what they conceive to be better policies on a case-by-case basis. But it is important to be precise in framing those questions necessary to evaluate whether the free market, regulation, or other arrangements are best capable of attaining economic and social performance goals.

NOTES

1. Joe S. Bain, *Industrial Organization* (New York: John Wiley & Sons, 1959), pp. 11-13.
2. See the argument in Alan Stone, "Planning, Public Policy and Capitalism" in *Nationalizing Government,* ed. Theodore J. Lowi and Alan Stone (Beverly Hills, Calif.: Sage Publications, 1978), pp. 434-439.
3. Bain, *Industrial Organization,* p. 16.
4. Ibid.
5. George Stigler, *The Citizen and the State* (Chicago: University of Chicago Press, 1975), pp. 120, 121.
6. Thomas A. O'Toole, "U.S. Industry Cutting Basic Research," *Washington Post,* November 28, 1977, p. 1.
7. Murray L. Weidenbaum, "Mr. Weidenbaum Answers His Critics," *New York Times,* November 4, 1979, p. F-18.
8. Larry E. Ruff, "The Economic Common Sense of Pollution," *Public Interest* (Spring 1970):69-85.
9. All references are to Adam Smith, *The Wealth of Nations* (1776, New York: Random House Modern Library, 1937). This is the most widely used of several editions.
10. Ibid., p. 423.
11. Ibid.
12. Ibid., p. 669.
13. Ibid., p. 304.
14. Ibid., p. 308.
15. Friedrich Hayek, *The Road to Serfdom* (Chicago: University of Chicago Press, 1944), pp. 88-100.
16. For an explanation of the "sameness" tendency, see Harold Hotelling, "Stability in Competition," *Economic Journal* 39 (March 1929):25-57.
17. See D. T. Armentano, *The Myths of Antitrust* (New Rochelle, N.Y.: Arlington House, 1972), pp. 132-137.
18. Arthur A. Thompson, "Absolute Firm Size, Administered Prices and Inflation," *Economic Inquiry* 12 (June 1974):240-254.
19. Martin T. Farris, "The Case Against Deregulation in Transportation, Power and Communications," *ICC Practitioners Journal* 45 (March/April 1978):307-312.
20. For example, see Louis Hartz, *Economic Policy and Democratic Thought* (Cambridge, Mass.: Harvard University Press, 1948).
21. Generally, see Charles Merz, *The Dry Decade* (Garden City, N.Y.: Doubleday, 1931).
22. William Wardell, "Rx More Regulation or Better Therapies," *Regulation* (September/October 1979):25-33.

PART II

Regulatory Justifications

In the last chapter we examined the benefits of the market system from the perspective of Adam Smith and his followers. Although we briefly touched upon some of the problems raised in the powerful theoretical structure Smith developed, we have not yet examined the questions raised about it by many political economists. This task will be undertaken in Chapters 3, 4, and 5. Many economists employ the term "market failure" to describe instances in which the free market fails to attain an optimum allocation of society's resources. That is, a situation where the excess of benefits over costs under the free market's use of resources is less than that under an alternative arrangement—such as regulation—is a market failure.

The notions of these costs and benefits must not be conceived too narrowly, however. Benefits include not only tangible goods and services but also the many amenities lumped together under "quality of life." Costs include more than expenditures for these goods and services; they also embrace impairments to the quality of life, such as dirty air or ugly physical surroundings. As we will see in the following chapters, however, we can put a price tag on amenities such as clean air and pleasant surroundings, just as we can for shoes or houses.

But that we can *theoretically* value these amenities quantitatively does not necessarily mean that we can do it *practically* or even easily. Nevertheless, that a house located 5 miles from a city has a greater market value than the same structure located 30 miles farther away (all other things being equal) is evidence that we often do assign quantitative market values to desirable qualities or features—in this case, proximity to what the city has to offer.

Market failures may be classified into various types. Since the topics of this book are regulation and its alternatives, I have chosen three categories of market failures, each with various subcategories, that best address those questions (discussed in Chapter 2) necessary to evaluate policy solutions to public problems. These categories—efficiency, externalities, and equity—are intended to compare the free market alternative with actual government interventionist alternatives, most importantly regulation.

In these discussions, it is important to remember that a *plausible* governmental substitute in response to *apparent* market failure will not necessarily always lead to better performance results than the free market. For this reason I call these categories of market failure regulatory *justifications*. They constitute defenses of regulation when there is apparent market failure, but that regulation is conclusively superior to the free market or another alternative does not necessarily follow. To determine the best or better alternative for a public problem, we must examine each situation on an individual basis in a responsible, ongoing analysis; the same solution will not fit every problem.

3

Efficiency

The first justification for regulation at which we will look is called *efficiency*. While in a broad sense every market failure involves inefficiency, I mean the term in a narrower sense, or more accurately, senses. After a brief review of how the free market is expected to operate efficiently, I will introduce the two efficiency concepts that will be employed in this chapter—technical efficiency and welfare efficiency—which both relate to the central notion that under certain circumstances the free market leads to less than optimum use of resources. That is, given a certain quantity of resources (land, labor, capital), output has less value than it might have under a different use of these same resources. We will look at four subcategories under the efficiency justification: (1) natural monopoly, (2) antitrust, (3) coordination, and (4) promotion. Examples of each of these subcategories will be discussed in detail, and regulation will be compared with alternative policy arrangements where applicable.

In this discussion, as in the ones in Chapters 4 and 5, we should remember that some historians have marshalled evidence that special interests have sometimes sought and obtained regulatory legislation not to advance the public interest pursuant to one of the three regulatory justifications that we will discuss but rather to advance their parochial economic interests. For example, it has been argued that airlines sought the enactment of the 1938 Civil Aeronautics Act in order to preclude the entry of new firms into that industry. This may have been the case, but it is equally true that a special interest seeking new regulatory legislation or the amendment of an earlier statute often must also show that the proposal serves a more general purpose in order to garner widespread legislative and public support. Otherwise, legislators are vulnerable to the charge of representing only special interests, which can adversely affect their re-election prospects.

For this reason (among others) the legislative discourse about regulatory proposals is almost always framed in terms of how the particular statute will serve the "public interest." As we will see in later chapters, this discourse is frequently reducible to one or more of the three justifications for regulation.

THE CONCEPT OF EFFICIENCY

Efficiency and Market Failure

As we saw in the last chapter, the Smithian argument for minimum government regulation rests on several assumptions. One of the most important of these assumptions is that the force of competition in an industry among rival firms, or potential entrants, will allocate resources most efficiently. In economist Arthur Okun's summary:

> A competitive market transmits signals to producers that reflect the values of consumers. If the manufacture and distribution of a new product is profitable, the benefits it provides to buyers necessarily exceed the costs of production. And these costs in turn measure the value of the other outputs that are sacrificed by using labor and capital to make the new product. Thus, profitability channels resources into more productive uses and pulls them away from less productive ones. The producer has the incentive to make what consumers want and to make it in the least costly way.[1]

Competition is the necessary ingredient that leads to efficiency. First, competition must be present *structurally* in the sense that there must be several units or potential entrants producing and/or selling the same product or close substitutes. Competition also is necessary in a *behavioral* sense; these firms must undertake sales, pricing, advertising, design, and other marketing strategies aimed at the same prospective customers. Competition in a behavioral sense does not necessarily mean competition in the structural sense, however, since firms may form a cartel arrangement, such as collusive price fixing, and thus agree not to compete in the behavioral sense.

Technical Efficiency and Welfare Efficiency

It follows that if it can be shown that the absence of competition in either the structural or behavioral sense leads to inefficiencies, a plausible case may be made for regulatory intervention. Our initial definition of efficiency is a simple one: *obtaining the maximum output from available inputs, including capital, labor, equipment, and raw materials.* The efficiency concept can be applied to any particular sector, industry, or firm as well as to the economy as a whole.

This observation leads to the first important point about efficiency—the difference between technical efficiency and welfare efficiency.[2] *Technical efficiency* simply measures output through different production techniques employing identical inputs. Thus, if production technique A yields 100 units from 50 input units, it is said to be more efficient than production technique B that only yields 75 output units from those same inputs.

Technical efficiency indicates little about society's aggregate welfare, however. For example, suppose that new production techniques were devised that increased efficiency in the manufacture of obsolete products such as piano rolls, horse-drawn carriages, and ladies corsets. These greater technical efficiencies tell us nothing about whether society would be better off if the resources used to produce these goods were employed in the production of other goods such as laser-read records, automobiles, and synthetic fibers. Because of this apparent limitation in the concept of technical efficiency, economists have devised the notion of *welfare efficiency,* which requires that each resource must be employed in its most productive *alternative* use.

These concepts suggest the most obvious kind of efficiency-related regulation—regulation directed against privately made collusive arrangements that restrict or prohibit efficiency gains, such as agreements not to introduce new products or processes of production. Similarly, the concept of welfare efficiency would permit regulation aimed at arrangements preventing the free flow of factors of production to where they can be employed most efficiently. These considerations lead to one subcategory of efficiency regulation—antitrust.

That resources should be employed most fully leads to another type of efficiency-related regulation—promotional regulation. Suppose an underdeveloped nation has considerable natural resources but lacks the transportation and communications networks to facilitate the marketing of products made from its resources; under these circumstances available resources would lie fallow. Or suppose that these transportation and communications networks were primitively or grossly underdeveloped, the result being that both technical and welfare efficiency were quite low. That resources should be employable and most efficiently employed is a principal justification for promotional regulation, such as the early regulation of commercial aviation, which, "by reducing the risk from entry or competition, allows investors in fledgling industries or in otherwise risky enterprises to reap rates of return high enough to justify the investment." [3]

That output should be high relative to inputs has been cited as a principal justification for coordination regulation, such as the Federal Communications Commission's licensing and regulating the use of radio and television stations. Without this kind of efficiency-related regulation, it is argued, users would interfere with each other's outputs leading in the aggregate to less than maximum output per input.

Another kind of efficiency regulation stems from the possibility that competition may not be feasible in some industries where monopoly is the natural market condition. In competitive situations, price is constrained by rivalry among sellers as well as by buyer demand and costs. In monopoly situations, the first of these factors is lacking, and the monopolist has a strong incentive to restrict output since the production of additional units above a certain point will force the reduction in price of all units produced in accordance with the demand curve. The monopolist therefore generally will tend to underemploy resources as compared with a competitive situation, and the monopoly price will be higher. Customers either would have to forgo other goods and services to the extent of the difference between the product's monopoly price and a competitive price or unduly restrict the use of the monopolized product.

In either event, in a monopoly resources have not been employed most efficiently in the welfare sense. These considerations have led to regulation in situations where monopoly is considered to be a natural outcome. Theoretically, regulation can be used to simulate the price, quality, and output that would prevail under competitive conditions.

NATURAL MONOPOLY REGULATION

One of the most important types of efficiency regulation is natural monopoly regulation of traditional public utilities. All 50 states, the District of Columbia, and Puerto Rico have regulatory agencies— usually called the public utility or public service commission—with jurisdiction over the rates, accounting practices, licensing, improvements, service standards, safety, financial practices, and service coverage of public utilities that operate in their respective jurisdictions. The businesses typically included within the jurisdiction of these commissions (usually comprised of three members) are electricity, gas, telephone, and water transmission. Unlike most other businesses, firms subject to the jurisdiction of these commissions must receive commission approval before proceeding with any alteration or change in certain activities—for example, any change in rate structure. These industries are far more intensively regulated than most others; the discretion that may be exercised by their managers is much narrower than that exercised by most other businesses—except in the extraordinary circumstances of price conrol.[4]

That these industries, characterized as natural monopolies, are somehow different from others was not always understood by government policymakers. After a period extending from colonial times until approximately the mid-19th century when government actively promoted the development of public utilities, these industries were characterized by a competitive phase that lasted until about the turn of the 20th century. During this competitive phase it was not uncommon for larger cities to be served by several electric utilities, each with a limited—but sometimes overlapping—market area.[5] Chicago, for example, granted 29 electricity transmission franchises from 1882 to 1905, while the towns it absorbed permitted 18. The relatively free granting of franchises occurred not only in electricity transmission but in the local supply of gas and telephone services as well, all as a means to force rates down to competitive levels.[6] However, in virtually every city, a single company after awhile would emerge as the sole franchisee in each of the transmission services. Moreover, the quality of service under the competitive framework was low with financial insolvencies not uncommon.

Thus, during this competitive phase, in city after city and town after town, public utility industries illustrated not only glaring inefficiency but also an inexorable tendency toward monopoly. This experience resulted in the concept that public utilities are natural monopolies and that, since competition and its benefits could not flourish in such industries, a public agency should regulate their activities. New York and Wisconsin led the way in regulating public utilities in 1907.

Characteristics of Natural Monopolies

Natural monopolies are, first, enterprises that supply, directly or indirectly, continuous or repeated services through more or less permanent physical connections between suppliers' plants and the premises of consumers. Second, under natural monopolies the bargaining power of most consumers relative to suppliers is low for several reasons: (a) the services tend to be necessities; (b) usually no close substitute products or services are available (nothing, for example, can substitute for telephone service); (c) the services are not storable (so that consumers cannot employ a stored surplus for bargaining purposes); and (d) the services are not transferable from one customer to another. The differences between electricity transmission and the choices involved in purchasing an automobile (discussed in Chapter 2) with respect to these four reasons are readily apparent.[7]

While a number of capsule statements have been advanced to summarize these characteristics of natural monopoly, perhaps economist Richard Schmalensee said it best: "An industry or activity is said to be a natural monopoly if production is most efficiently done by a single firm."[8] In many cases, this occurs when an industry's average costs inherently tend to decrease with increasing rates of output due to high fixed costs relative to total costs. Thus, the greater the number of output units over which these fixed costs may be amortized, the greater the tendency for average cost per output to decline. If, for example, an electric generator costs $1 million and constitutes a very large proportion of a firm's total costs, average costs will clearly be lower if fixed costs are amortized over sales of 1 million units than over sales of 100,000 units.

One may note that while some industries, such as food distribution, maintain constant average costs above a certain output, other industries, such as steel manufacture, are as capital intensive as public utilities, also manifesting high fixed costs and declining average costs over very high ranges of output. Indeed, some economists have argued that in most large-scale manufacturing industries, large firms almost always produce more efficiently and at lower average cost than their smaller competitors.[9] Does this mean that all of these industries should therefore be treated as natural monopolies and be subject to intensive regulation on efficiency grounds?

No—because of other cost characteristics, public utilities are different. First, they cannot gradually add to capacity as other capital-intensive industries may do:

> Water, gas, electricity and telephone companies have to dig up the streets and lay down pipes or build poles and string wires from the point of production to every point of potential consumption and install meters before a single drop, cubic foot or kilowatt hour can be sold or a single call placed.[10]

These high *initial* fixed costs tend to deter multiple entrants, which in other ventures may begin operation at relatively modest cost and which through product differentiation seek to carve out a portion of the market.

Even more significant, the physical nature of the more or less set connections between large supply points and many smaller consuming points has important cost characteristics. Average transmission construction costs also decline as capacity increases. This is best illustrated in the example of water pipe:

> Capacity is roughly proportional to its cross section area, while cost is roughly proportional to circumference. If the cross section of a pipe is doubled, the circumference less than doubles.[11]

In other words, capacity is a function of the formulation πr^2 where r is the pipe radius, while cost is a function of the formulation $2\pi r$. Thus, as the radius of the pipe becomes larger, average unit cost declines.

What is true of water transmission is equally true of other traditional public utilities, but this formulation understates the economies of scale in other areas. For example, friction in oil and gas transmission is reduced as capacity increases, while the amount of right-of-way that must be taken remains relatively constant regardless of pipe capacity. In the case of electricity transmission, the lowest cost between two points is obtained with a single high voltage transmission line.[12] In each of these industries, then, monopoly is the most efficient economic structure.

Of course, it does not necessarily follow that in these cases monopoly will *always* be the most efficient structure. An economic activity may be a temporary natural monopoly. First, a technological breakthrough may drastically alter the cost curves associated with an activity. For example, intercity telephone transmission during the 1940s was governed by natural monopoly cost considerations. But with the advent of microwave technology, average cost has flattened out at a level low enough to accommodate several competitors.[13] Second, a new form of competition may end the threat of monopoly, as illustrated by intercity truck transportation's impact on the former railroad monopoly. Third, as illustrated in Figure 3-1, it certainly is conceivable that, as demand for output increases over time, average cost also might increase due to rising coordination costs or more rapid deterioration of plant and equipment.

For the foregoing reasons, even if a natural monopoly can justify regulation on efficiency grounds, we are still bound to inquire whether it is a permanent or temporary natural monopoly. If it is temporary, periodic review of the activity is obviously required. But even if we do find changed conditions, we may still conclude that an industry is a natural monopoly because production may still be done most efficiently by a single firm.

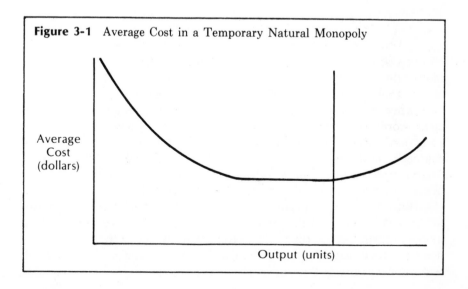

Figure 3-1   Average Cost in a Temporary Natural Monopoly

Average Cost (dollars)

Output (units)

For example, Alfred Kahn has shown that as the number of telephone subscribers increases, the possible connections among them increase at an even greater rate, leading to the initial impression that unit costs increase, not decrease. Yet, as he continued:

> This service is a natural monopoly: if there were two telephone systems in a community, each subscriber would have to have two instruments, two lines into his home, two bills if he wanted to be able to call everyone else. Despite the apparent presence of increasing costs ... monopoly is still natural because one company can serve any given number of subscribers ... at a lower cost than two.[14]

Moreover, as Kahn observed, this case is not really an exception to the rule of declining average cost since the quality of service increases as the number of interconnections rises, whereas the diminishing average cost standard only applies to cases of constant quality. Similarly, as economist James Bonbright has noted, an electric utility supplying most of its power needs from very cheap hydroelectric sources, but required to supply the remainder of an expanded market from more expensive steam plants, will manifest increasing average costs after a certain output. But

> the single company can secure the maximum advantages of economies of scale and of density, while on the other hand it is no more subject to the diseconomies of enhanced output resulting from scarcity of water power and of other natural resources than would be two or more companies if called upon to supply the region with the same total output.[15]

Why Regulate Natural Monopolies?

Given that natural monopoly exists, the next logical question is why it should be regulated. As we will see, some economists have argued that monopolistic price and output behavior does not *necessarily* follow from monopolistic structure any more than it follows that the sole successful bidder for a contract is charging a monopolistic price. Experience has shown that certain industries have been characterized by monopoly even when more than one firm was at one time operating in a market. In other words, experience has confirmed what theory predicts. We have seen that unregulated economic activity is posited on the premise of competition in both the structural and behavioral senses; without competition the arguments outlined in Chapter 2 in favor of largely unregulated business activity are without foundation.

But economic performance under monopoly conditions is unsatisfactory—although it still does not follow that the regulation of natural monopoly will necessarily yield better performance. Economic theory, however, posits that monopoly is associated with bad performance for reasons succinctly stated by Schmalensee:

> If a monopoly produces goods or services for which there are no close substitutes, its demand is likely to be relatively insensitive to the prices it charges. . . . It will likely charge prices that are well in excess of costs. Such prices can have sizable adverse effects on the efficiency with which scarce resources are employed. By reducing allocative or economic efficiency, prices well in excess of costs impose losses on the community or nation as a whole. There is a potential gain from controls that would force prices down to the level of costs.[16]

The critical notion here is "no close substitutes." If, for example, whole wheat bread constituted a natural monopoly, the foregoing reasoning would not apply since the price of whole wheat bread would be affected by the prices of competitive goods such as white bread, rye bread, rolls, etc.

Moreover, the product or service that is a candidate for natural monopoly or utility regulation must be one that cannot easily be forgone by consumers. For example, a natural monopoly in a product such as player pianos will not have the described impact because consumers can readily forgo the purchase in favor of acquiring a large number of other goods and services. In the economist's phrase, player pianos have high elasticity of demand. Regulation is appropriate for products or services with low elasticities of demand, such as electricity, gas, and certain transportation services that have no viable substitutes.

Some economists reject the view that candidates for natural monopoly should be regulated. Harold Demsetz, in an important article in 1968, argued that the degree of concentration in a particular market does not permit us to deduce whether price and output are competitive.[17] The reason is simply that when no legal barriers prevent bidding for the provision of a service and the costs of forming contracts with prospective customers are very low, the bidding process (absent collusion) among rival potential entrants will force the successful firm to charge a competitive price. Bidding for a utility contract will no more lead to monopoly prices and restricted output than will any other bidding process. Put another way, Demsetz contended that the theory of natural monopoly is deficient because it cannot logically show that scale economies lead to monopolistic conduct.

Despite Demsetz's convincing argument, there are still justifications for natural monopoly regulation. Utility commissions regulate more than just the level of rates; they also regulate service standards, safety, and coverage. And unlike the typical bidding situation where a large buyer transacts business with a large seller, the natural monopoly situation usually involves many small (as well as some large) recipients of a service. Thus, while litigation costs in the case of a single large buyer in a traditional bidding situation are usually commensurate with or lower than the amount that can be recovered in a lawsuit, that same relationship is much less likely in the natural monopoly situation. If, for example, the electricity voltage directed into my house is insufficient, the litigation costs required to redress the situation would very likely be disproportionately high relative to my recovery. Consequently, a regulatory agency representing service consumers is necessary to assure compliance with complex franchise contracts. Thus, regulation would appear to be a better way to deal with the problem of natural monopoly than the free market. In any event, the American experience of regulating private utility firms through law overall has been highly satisfactory compared with other nations.

The Law and Natural Monopoly

The common law of England and the United States developed an imperfect sense of the natural monopoly concept and the need to regulate certain businesses through the notion of businesses "affected with a public interest." But while in simpler times a certain theoretical fuzziness did not impede practical clarity in application, rapid industrialization in the United States after the Civil War and the development of a multitude of new manufactured goods and modes of distribution increasingly muddled the concept of a business "affected with a public interest."

The Supreme Court valiantly clung to the concept in the famous 1877 *Munn* v. *Illinois* decision, which declared that grain elevators were a business "affected with a public interest," thus allowing a regulatory commission to fix charges.[18] By the early 1930s, however, one way the Supreme Court was employing the concept of a business "affected with the public interest" was virtually synonomous with the idea of a natural monopoly or public utility; the Court struck down statutes regulating gasoline sales and the manufacture and distribution of ice on the grounds that these activities were not natural monopolies.[19] While this restricted notion of what could be regulated was later rejected by the Court for reasons extraneous to this discussion, the concept of economic natural monopoly was recognized for long enough a time to allow the institutionalization of regulatory agencies with jurisdiction over public utilities at both the state and local levels.

ANTITRUST

Monopoly may result not only from "natural causes," for which public utility regulation has been the traditional response, but also from the deliberate design of those engaged in business. Antitrust legislation has been the favored response of policymakers to these problems.

The Principles of the Sherman Act

The initial principles of the 1890 Sherman Antitrust Act were extremely clear and simple as understood by its sponsors and supporters: unregulated monopoly and collective arrangements among would-be competitors that ended competition among rivals were not to be tolerated. Their objection was precisely that unregulated monopoly and cartel arrangements among competitors violate the rules of the competitive framework that Adam Smith explicated. Since the basic rules of competition were violated, the benefits of unrestrained competition envisioned within the Smithian system would not be realized.

On this basis, various states and municipalities were proceeding to regulate natural monopolies during the very period that Congress enacted the Sherman Act, with states enforcing their own antimonopoly rules. Congress and the state legislatures had enacted a host of other regulatory statutes as well, based on the other regulatory justifications that will be discussed in later chapters. Nevertheless, the principal mechanism for assuring economic performance was the relatively unrestrained market, and the principal regulatory means for assuring that the market would work as theory anticipated was the Sherman Act.

The sponsors and supporters of the Sherman Act did not conceive that the new law announced any new principles; rather, they relied on a long-held common law and state law tradition that embraced free market principles. The novelty of the Sherman Act was simply that, in keeping with the dynamic growth of the business community, it applied these free market principles for the first time in a *national* law.[20] The law's supporters focused on the harm that unregulated monopoly and cartel arrangements would perpertrate on prices: they would raise prices above "competitive" levels to "artificially" high ones. Likewise, the same result would be effected by restricting supply or by collusively boycotting vigorous competitors.

In seeking to prevent these undesirable results, the first section of the Sherman Act outlawed combinations, conspiracies, and contracts in restraint of trade—the phrase intended to embrace cartel practices and their variations. The second section outlawed monopolizing, attempts to monopolize, and conspiracies to monopolize. It is important to note that monopolizing, and not monopoly itself, was outlawed. Even with Congress's then-imperfect sense of natural monopoly, it was believed that monopolies could result from the nature of competition in certain industries, although most industries would naturally have competitive structures. Only when a giant firm employed tactics utilizing its great size could a monopoly result, according to this view. Thus, a national firm engaged in selective selling below cost in a geographical market where it faced regional competition, while subsidizing its losses through excessive profits in areas where it was a monopoly, would constitute monopolizing.

Antimonopoly and Pro-Competition

Thus far, the antitrust policy and its application seem simple indeed. A company that achieves monopoly through any means not explicitly related to product superiority or economic efficiency is in probable violation of the law. These methods might include below-cost territorial price discrimination, cornering the supply of a strategic raw material, or acquiring its competitors. Similarly, if a group of firms normally engaged in competitive rivalry agree to charge uniform prices, fix terms of trade, allocate sales territories among themselves, restrict supply, or boycott certain customers, they would be acting collectively as if they were a monopoly. Thus, the original Sherman Act policy might be characterized as one intended to prevent monopoly and cartel arrangements—an antimonopoly policy.

Few would quarrel with such a policy, but the difficulty arises when the emphasis shifts ever so subtly from an antimonopoly policy to a pro-competition policy and then strays even farther to a fair competition policy. Unfortunately, the term "antitrust" has been applied ambiguously to all three of these policies, each one of which has different implications and involves different justifications.

Suppose that three firms in an industry, each with 33 percent of the market, merge. There is no question that this merger would constitute monopolizing within the meaning of the Sherman Act and would offend an antimonopoly policy. But suppose that, in an industry comprised of four equally sized competitors, two of those firms merged. Would this merger constitute a monopoly, which is, strictly speaking, defined as a single viable seller? Or suppose that two companies merged in an industry containing 20 equally sized firms. Such a merger clearly would not constitute a monopoly. Yet if we shift our policy emphasis from preventing monopoly to maximizing competition, this merger *might* be offensive.

The same problem arises when we shift our focus from competition in the structural sense to competition in the behavioral sense. If a giant firm, such as the Standard Oil Company during the last decade of the 19th century, engaged in a series of local price discriminations designed to destroy its small local competitors, this would likely be considered monopolizing conduct. (Incidentally, there is a body of evidence, much of it subject to dispute, that Standard Oil did not as a matter of common practice engage in such predatory conduct.[21]) But suppose a firm with 40 percent of a market engaged in price discrimination in order to take customers away from a firm with 30 percent of that market—does this constitute monopolistic conduct? Or what about price discrimination undertaken by a firm with 5 percent of the market against one with only 2 percent?

Students of these questions disagree violently about their answers. On the one side are those who would restrict antitrust to its original antimonopoly intentions, while those on the other have devised various theories, the underlying thrust of which seeks to justify an expansion of antitrust to maximize competition in the structural sense. These latter analysts take a very harsh view of a decline in the number of units in an industry through merger, conceiving a close relationship between the concentration in an industry and the degree to which an industry behaves like a monopoly.

One major study adopting this perspective utilized the concept of unreasonable market power:

> A firm possesses market power when it can behave persistently in a manner different from the behavior that a competitive market would enforce on a firm facing otherwise similar cost and demand conditions.[22]

The issue is joined by analysts on the other side who have adduced evidence—sometimes disputable—that highly concentrated industries do not behave much differently than relatively unconcentrated ones; they compete in price and in other ways that are customary in unconcentrated industries. Others adopting this position have mustered evidence that large firms—characteristic of highly concentrated industries—are generally more efficient than smaller firms. These efficiencies result from both plant size and firm size. Consequently, breaking up large firms (such as General Motors) or preventing mergers, short of those that meet monopoly standards in the traditional sense, will lead to increased inefficiency in a market, according to this view.[23]

In summary, then, a sharp disagreement exists between proponents of what have been termed the "hard competition" and "soft competition" schools, with each claiming that its viewpoint yields more competition and higher economic efficiency.[24] The main point here is not to evaluate the arguments but simply to point out that the notion of antitrust contains ambiguities and, if the hard competition school is correct, contradictions as well.

We can frame the issue another way: does government protection of competition in the structural sense—undertaking policies deliberately designed to preserve or enlarge the number of firms in an industry— conflict with a policy of preserving competition in the behavioral sense? Does the prevention of mergers of firms in the same industry inhibit economic efficiency by precluding the benefits of technological integration, the ability to install costly processes that firms could not afford singly, the expenditure of resources large enough to absorb the enormous marketing costs needed to introduce new products, or the increased ability to take risks that result from large size?

Various administrations have used the two major agencies charged with antitrust enforcement—the Federal Trade Commission and the Antitrust Division of the Justice Department—to further one or another of these philosophies on competition. The policy argument, which has its counterpart within the economics profession, ultimately depends on whether market practices—such as merging, exclusive dealing, or discriminating in price between large and small customers—aid or inhibit efficiency.

COORDINATION REGULATION

Interference or Coordination?

Efficiency justifications for natural monopoly and antitrust regulation are fairly widely accepted as proper regulatory activity. This is not true of the coordination and promotional justifications, which are more controversial. In part, because these regulatory justifications are weaker than those for natural monopoly and antitrust, advocates of the coordination and promotional justifications supplement efficiency arguments with others based on externalities (the imposition of costs upon persons external to a transaction). The coordination and promotional justifications for regulation are hybrids that can be discussed within the framework of either efficiency or externalities, but we will examine them with respect to efficiency since it is the dominant justification.

Regulation of airport safety through the Federal Aviation Administration (FAA) and regulation of radio and television spectra via the Federal Communications Commission (FCC) are the most prominent instances of coordination regulation. But a simpler example best illustrates the principles involved—automobile traffic control or regulation. Every major city and town in every country, regardless of social system, contains numerous traffic control indicators including electrically operated signals and road signs stating "stop," "yield," maximum speed limits, etc. Traffic control personnel—usually police—are expected to enforce these regulations. Densely populated areas use these indicators at virtually every traffic intersection, while less congested rural areas do not contain as many. But why regulate traffic at all, and why does the extent of regulation vary with traffic density?

Our first inclination is to frame a response in terms of interference. My automobile and yours cannot physically occupy the same space at the same time, at least not without a serious mishap. Traffic regulation provides rules that greatly reduce the risk of our automobiles interfering with each other. Without these rules, the likelihood of automobile damage and personal injury would greatly increase.

However, a closer look at the problem reveals that coordination, rather than interference, is the better descriptive term underlying traffic regulation. We will see that this distinction is not merely a question of terminology but also has important substantive implications for this justification of regulation. Suppose we lived in a place without property rules. Under these circumstances, my use of a piece of land for dwelling purposes would interfere with another person's proposed use of the same land as a slaughterhouse. Interference is as much a problem in the case of land use as it is in automobile traffic. Indeed, almost all resources are scarce, and one person's use necessarily interferes with another's. Property rules and a market system of allocation are sufficient under most circumstances to deal with the problem of interference. What differentiates traffic control from other interference examples? Why does traffic control mandate public regulation rather than a market system with property rules?

The answers lie in the high discoordination costs that a market mechanism imposes when the potential for interference is high. Suppose we wished to travel from Second Avenue and 14th Street in Manhattan to Tenth Avenue and 42nd Street. Suppose further that each street was privately owned, each owner collected a toll at every intersection, and every owner had a separate set of traffic regulations. Clearly the inputs would be high—in terms of time lost, gasoline used waiting to pay tolls, etc.—relative to output—traversing that distance—compared with the free use of public throughfares.

In short, a market system produces significant inefficiencies when coordination is necessary due to the high likelihood of interference. But the same principle would not apply to long-distance roads, where the justification for traffic regulation stems from the negative externalities that would affect an innocent motorist from the dangerous use of a car by another. Efficiency considerations would exist, of course, but they would be secondary to the more important ones related to externalities. Whereas in the city street situation coordination problems resulted from the high risk and costs of interference, the efficiency justification is at least as important as the externalities justification for regulation.[25]

The central issue in the coordination justification for regulation is how great the efficiency losses from discoordination would be compared with the efficiency gains that would result from the employment of a market system with property principles. In the city street example, the obvious answer is that a coordinating body is necessary to impose regulations. A similarly relatively uncontroversial case is Federal Aviation Administration regulation of airport safety. It would be inefficient—to understate the obvious—if airplanes crashed into each other with great frequency at take-offs and landings. The high interference risks require coordination not just for safety reasons but also to prevent problems of traffic delay and congestion—all of which weigh in efficiency considerations. It is also clear that, for a number of reasons including cost and noise, the sites where airports may be located are extremely limited.[26] Given this set of factors, the need for a central coordinating mechanism to institute certain regulations is obvious to most observers.

But why should not this central coordinating institution be a private person or corporation rather than government? First, due to the scarcity of airports, a single corporation or collective entity might tend to develop into a local monopoly and thus be subject to the same objections discussed earlier regarding monopolistic behavior. This private entity could further abuse its monopoly position by arbitrarily excluding some airlines from using its facilities. Only government can achieve fairness in that respect. Third, airline traffic density and the coordination problem have reached the point where airports must attain a high degree of coordination among themselves. Without government supervision there is always the possibility that one or more airports would fail to participate in an agreement; only the sanction of government regulation can assure this necessary coordination. These arguments do not necessarily call for government proprietorship of airports but rather for their regulation. Because of this need for coordination, Congress created a number of agencies—culminating in the FAA's birth in 1959—to regulate airport and airline safety, traffic, and congestion.[27]

Broadcasting Industry Regulation

A more controversial area where the coordination justification has been applied is the broadcasting industry. The controversy extends to two independent questions. First, can public regulation still be justified in view of the advent of new broadcasting technologies such as cable television, signal importation, and video cassettes? As noted earlier in our discussion of efficiency, the technological limitations that at one time may have led us to conclude that regulation is appropriate may be overcome, rendering further regulation superfluous. The second question is an even more fundamental one: Was regulation of broadcasting ever necessary in the first place? This question might strike readers as a little odd in view of the fact that virtually every nation in the world either operates its own broadcasting facilities or regulates them strenuously. Nevertheless, in a ground-breaking article in 1959, R. H. Coase vigorously argued that such regulation came about because of faulty analysis and specious analogies. Further, Coase concluded that a free market system could have developed in radio and television spectra, resulting in a more efficient industry than what exists today in a heavily regulated environment.[28]

The efficiency argument made on behalf of over-the-air broadcasting is straightforward. Without government regulation to assign conditions of broadcasting such as frequency, time, and area of transmission, the signals of one station would interfere with those of other stations. Chaos would result because there are a limited number of frequencies that can be employed in any particular broadcast band such as AM radio, FM radio, or television. Therefore, without assignments the output of most stations (as measured by the range within which broadcasts may be heard or seen with reasonable clarity) would be lower for any given power input. The critical efficiency consideration here is interference. Even if the same area could be reached with the same power output under conditions in which government did not allocate through licensing, the *quality* of the output would be lower. Consequently, the argument concludes, government-imposed coordination is necessary for efficiency reasons.[29]

Advocates point to the history of radio broadcasting in the United States to illustrate their argument. The number of AM broadcasting stations increased substantially during the early 1920s. Because a 1912 radio statute did not authorize government to allocate wavelengths among particular stations, a series of radio conferences in which government and the industry participated attempted to solve the problem on a voluntary basis. The conferences failed, however, and by late 1925 every channel in the broadcasting band was occupied by at least one station; many were occupied by several stations. The situation worsened:

> From July 1926 to February 23, 1927 when Congress enacted the Radio Act of 1927 almost 200 new radio stations went on the air. These new stations used any frequency they desired, regardless of the interference thereby caused to others. Existing stations changed to other frequencies and increased their power and hours of operation at will. The result was chaos and confusion. With everybody on the air, nobody could be heard.[30]

Congress enacted the Radio Act of 1927 as a result of these chaotic conditions. The statute was later amended by the Communications Act of 1934, which did not significantly alter the original act. Rather, its purpose was to embrace within one commission jurisdiction over all forms of interstate communication. Herbert Hoover, secretary of commerce during most of the 1920s, more than any other person was responsible for the intellectual framework of the Radio Act. Analogizing radio transmission to automobile travel, he stated:

> We can no longer deal on the basis that there is room for everybody on the radio highways. There are more vehicles on the roads than can get by, and if they continue to jam in all will be stopped.[31]

Because efficiency was a paramount consideration, Hoover saw no better alternative than federal licensing and regulation of the airwaves in the public interest. And because the decisions about who should be licensed and on what terms were technical and required a high degree of discretion, Congress created an administrative agency, the Federal Radio Commission (after 1934, the Federal Communications Commission), with jurisdiction to: (1) allocate space in the spectrum; (2) assign location and power; and (3) regulate stations in the public interest.

Since the enactment of the Radio Act, most Americans have become so used to the system of FCC regulation that they have not questioned whether the system was justified in the first instance. How great would the efficiency losses from discoordination be compared with the efficiency gains resulting from the employment of a market system with property principles? Since Coase's landmark article in 1959, a number of other studies as well as the development of new communications technologies have continued to cast doubt on the reasoning that led to the 1927 Radio Act. Coase argued that, prior to the act, the courts were in the process of creating a system of property rights for spectra in the same way they had created property rights for tangible property (such as land) and representational property (such as stock certificates and negotiable instruments). Had the government followed that route instead of licensing coupled with regulation, it would have auctioned off spectra in such a way that interference would have largely been avoided. A market would then have been created in spectra in the same way that land or stock certificates are subject to market operations.

Coase belittled the viewpoint that spectra are physically limited in a way that land is not. After all, he asserted, the number of original Rembrandt paintings is even more limited, yet the market satisfactorily deals with their sale and use without a need for government regulation. He similarly rejected the interference argument, since one person's use of land would interfere with another's proposed use of that same land if a property system did not exist. Indeed, one of the major functions of the private legal system is to devise rules regarding interference, and one of the most important conceptions it has devised is property rights protecting exclusive use. Precisely the same principle could have been employed in the novel case of spectra during the 1920s.

Coase and others who accept this argument have concluded that a system of auctioning off spectra would be far more efficient than a government regulatory apparatus. First, of course, there is the deadweight loss attributable to regulation and the apparatus designed to enforce it. Second, the danger of government censorship and/or arbitrariness is always present when an agency has broad discretionary authority. More important, a market system with property principles would lead to more efficient use of spectra, according to this view.

Another important study has pointed out that regulation has severely restricted the use of spectra; contrary to the interference view, there is not a market in the country in which anything close to the 95 UHF and VHF television channels are used. A market system would: (1) assure that use of any particular portion of the spectrum would be most efficient since one would have to purchase the quantity actually used and (2) simultaneously assure that aggregate use of spectra is most efficient. A system in which spectra are essentially free provides no such incentives.[32] In short, the situation would be similar to that which exists in the print media in which sufficient space exists for profitable (or subsidized) enterprises that have strong incentives to use their resources most efficiently.

While one might provide the rejoinder to this argument, there is little point.[33] The discussion illustrates the difficulty in determining whether a given activity should be subject to regulation pursuant to a given justification. More important, the advent of new technologies may render the disagreement moot; cable transmission of both audio and video programming as well as the development of video cassettes hold the promise of permitting a vast number of messages to be broadcast simultaneously without any threat of interference. These new technologies likely will not involve problems of coordination of the same magnitude as over-the-air transmission, and the market probably will be able to allocate resources effectively.

PROMOTIONAL REGULATION

Just as television and radio regulation may exemplify the need for temporary, rather than permanent, regulation so also may the final, and perhaps least persuasive, instance of efficiency regulation—promotional regulation.

This justification concerns the promotion of what for the moment we will term "key industries," which are industries upon which most other sectors greatly depend (such as transportation and communications). The argument at best justifies temporary regulation and, unlike the natural monopoly rationale, cannot justify permanent regulation; the argument maintains its force on efficiency grounds only to the point that the key industry has been developed or stabilized. After that point, further regulation must be justified on the ground of "positive" externalities, a concept examined further in Chapter 4.

For example, suppose (for the sake of illustration only) that it could be shown that regulation of telephone communication was the most effective way of promoting that industry's development in its infancy. Once the industry was developed and stable, any further regulation would have to be justified on the ground that continued regulation would render benefits to the commercial system, national defense, etc.—positive externalities—above the returns received by the owners of the facilities. To take another example, suppose timber companies were required by regulation to plant trees to prevent soil erosion to neighboring farms. In this case, other welfare gains would exceed the particular returns to the timber companies.

Two other points must be made before we set forth the argument that purports to justify promotional regulation. First, no other regulatory justification is as susceptible to the argument that better techniques are available to accomplish the same results. For example, if in the 1930s we had wished to promote the development of a commercial aviation industry, would it not have been better to have subsidized carriers than to have restricted the number of carriers through a regulatory franchise? Of course, both subsidy and regulatory techniques could have been employed simultaneously.

The second point is more subtle. The promotional justification argument has sometimes been confused and interwoven with another that seeks to justify regulation on the ground of preventing "destructive competition." As we will see in a later chapter, regulation allegedly has been imposed at times at the behest of firms seeking to escape the rigors of competition. Some observers have claimed that businessmen are often the worst enemies of competition and seek to use government-imposed rules to make competition illegal. For example, 15 states during the 1960s fixed the resale price of milk, while at the federal level a system existed that set the price at which dairy processors had to purchase raw milk from farmers.[34]

Politically motivated cartel arrangements premised on a need to prevent destructive competition have no relationship to the justification of temporary aid to an industry because the long-term gains stemming from developing or stabilizing that industry outweigh the losses from restrictions on competition. Nevertheless, the two conceptions of destructive competition and promotional regulation have sometimes been confused as one.

Risk and Regulation

What, then, is the promotional justification for regulation? The efficiency part of this argument is that certain activities that will result in long-run substantial gain to society will not be undertaken under a free competitive framework due to the extensive risks involved relative to the probable rates of return and size of investment. Therefore, the argument continues, government should promote these activities by restricting the number of franchises available and by regulating prices charged in such a way as to reduce risk of loss. In general, then, regulation's function is to reduce those investment risks significantly by promoting an activity in which investors otherwise would be disinclined to engage.

This rationale is similar to that which sought to justify high tariffs on goods imported to the United States during the 19th century to encourage the development of native industries. The granting of patents for new inventions is based on a similar rationale. As Alfred Kahn has observed:

> One way of inducing private investment in unusually risky fields—the East India trade at the end of the sixteenth century, the building of turnpikes or railroads into as yet insufficiently settled areas in the nineteenth century, or the development of commercial air transport in the twentieth century—is to offer the investors some protection against subsequent competition.[35]

Public Goods and Infrastructure

But what kinds of industries or activities should be so regulated? As noted earlier, the critical consideration is that benefits over the long run must exceed the losses engendered by the restrictions on competition in the short run. For example, many consider the benefits stemming from government promotion of a railroad system into the most remote areas of the country—extending the market, promoting economies of scale, etc.—to have outweighed by far the subsidies and other aids granted to railroads during the 19th century.

In some cases, the benefits that flow from a promoted activity are more difficult to measure than the promotional costs. Assessing some benefits may involve calculating social values into the balance sheet, which is not an easy task. In any case, those who propose promotional regulation bear a heavy burden of proof; at the least, the kinds of activities that appear to be plausible candidates for such regulation must provide public goods and be infrastructural.

Public goods are those that we consume collectively and therefore involve public expenditure; national defense, parks, and weather forecasting are obvious examples. The regulation of banks insofar as that industry's activities affect the money supply, and hence the aggregate economic activity of the nation, is a less evident example. Much promotional regulation is justified in part on this basis of public good or positive externality.

The efficiency aspect of promotional regulation is based on the notion of infrastructure, a concept widely used in development economics that refers to "the creation of services which would facilitate subsequent industrial investment and growth of industrial output."[36] These activities occur in sectors of an economy necessary for the economic development of other sectors; the most important involve the provision of transportation, power, and communication. For example, mining activities could not be carried out effectively unless the means of transport (roads or railways) were available to carry ores to markets economically and the means of communications existed to order supplies and parts rapidly. More formally stated, promotional regulation or subsidies may be justified on efficiency grounds if they

> jerk the industrial system out of its present poise at a position of relative maximum, and induce it to settle down again at the position of absolute maximum—the highest hilltop of all.[37]

The Civil Aeronautics Board

These justifications were precisely those made in support of the 1938 establishment of the Civil Aeronautics Board (CAB) and its regulatory jurisdiction over commercial aviation, which began in 1940. Lucille S. Keyes's scholarly study of that statute indicated beyond doubt that the natural monopoly justification played no role in the rationales advanced for creating the CAB. The legislative sponsors of the Civil Aeronautics Act emphasized the collective goods to which commercial aviation contributed—particularly national defense and mail carriage—but the most important consideration was securing the positions of the already-established carriers by preventing new entrants. The act did this by requiring that any new entrant in a route obtain certification from the CAB before being permitted to operate:

> It is actually the promotion of investment in particular [existing] carriers and the improvement of the financial status of these carriers that is advocated; the certification provision is to further these aims by entrenching the position of the established carriers and suppressing new competition.[38]

By protecting and advancing the interests of the commercial airlines, Congress felt it could further develop U.S. domestic and international commerce. Since the economic viability of the airlines was the critical factor in achieving this efficiency goal, the CAB was given additional powers, including the right to set exact fares, minimum and maximum limits, or both. Since airline profitability is dependent on the profitability of particular routes and the route mix, the new agency received extensive authority to regulate detailed aspects of this part of an airline's business, including scheduling. Finally, since there is a clear relationship between the quality of service, rates, and profitability, the CAB was authorized to regulate the quality aspect of the airline business as well. Thus, from an underlying efficiency judgment, Congress was led to establish a regulatory agency with authority over virtually every activity of the airline industry.

This leads directly to the question of whether regulation is the best method to promote the development of air travel, airmail, air freight, and other such activities. Are tax concessions, subsidies, or other techniques better? On one side of the ledger, regulation (unlike these other techniques) does not involve either a *direct* transfer of funds from the Treasury to private interests or the forgoing of taxes that otherwise would be paid to the government. But, on the other hand, regulation does involve substantial administrative and compliance costs incurred by the regulated interest. Regulation also has been criticized because it places government and industry in an adversary position rather than a collaborative one so that if a private interest does not wish to undertake some activity, it will either: (1) seek not to comply; (2) comply minimally; or (3) compensate for compliance by imposing unacceptable costs elsewhere.

In contrast, subsidy arrangements have the merit—in theory if not in actuality—of allowing government and private interests to work out all details in advance of the grant in much the same way that two parties to a private contract negotiate their agreement. Promotional regulation has the added problem of tending to continue to exist long after the temporary justification for it no longer applies, as in the airline industry.

Finally, as the airline case also illustrates, protective regulation puts a damper on free competition, innovation, and their benefits. Until the move toward airline deregulation in the late 1970s, no new trunk line carriers had been certified since 1938, and the costs of travel in regulated markets greatly exceeded the costs of travel in unregulated ones.[39]

CONCLUSION

In this chapter we saw that the market, free of government interference, may under certain circumstances lead to performance outcomes that are *apparently* less than optimal. This may result from a natural market tendency to monopoly (natural monopoly), collusive or monopolistic behavior by market participants (leading to the antitrust justification), or problems of coordination or industry promotion. We also examined the specific market characteristics that might qualify an activity for regulation under each of these subcategories of the efficiency justification.

But we also saw in the cases of natural monopoly, coordination, and promotion that an apparent market failure does not necessarily lead to the conclusion that regulation should be instituted, for it might be possible to reconstruct the free market with results superior to regulation, as the broadcasting example illustrated. Regulation might be a worse alternative than the free market, even though the market is less than ideal. Or, as some have argued in the case of airline regulation, another policy technique might be superior to regulation. Finally, as experience in antitrust as well as in the other subcategories of the efficiency justification shows, while government agencies sometimes begin their careers for justifiable reasons, gradual expansion *may* lead to unjustifiable activity. For this reason, regulation is an ongoing decisionmaking process that requires frequent re-evaluation.

NOTES

1. Arthur M. Okun, *Equality and Efficiency* (Washington, D.C.: Brookings Institution, 1975), p. 50.
2. The distinction is made by Donald Dewey in *Microeconomics* (New York: Oxford University Press, 1975), pp. 215, 216.
3. U.S., Congress, Senate, Committee on Governmental Affairs, *Study on Federal Regulation,* Vol. 6, 96th Cong., 1st sess., December 1978, p. xvii.
4. See U.S., Congress, Senate, Committee on Government Operations, *State Utility Commissions, Doc. No. 56,* 90th Cong., 1st sess., 1967.
5. Generally, see Martin G. Glaeser, *Public Utilities in American Capitalism* (New York: Macmillan, 1957), pp. 14-78.
6. Alfred E. Kahn, *The Economics of Regulation,* 2 vols. (New York: John Wiley & Sons, 1971), 2:117, 118; and Burton N. Behling, *Competition and Monopoly in Public Utility Industries* (Urbana: University of Illinois Press, 1938), pp. 20-23.
7. See James C. Bonbright, *Principles of Public Utility Rates* (New York: Columbia University Press, 1961), pp. 4, 8, 11-13.
8. Richard Schmalensee, *The Control of Natural Monopolies* (Lexington, Mass.: Lexington Books, 1979), p. 3.
9. For example, see Harold Demsetz, "Industry Structure, Market Rivalry and Public Policy" in *Industrial Concentration: The New Learning,* ed. Harvey J. Goldschmid (Boston: Little, Brown & Co., 1974), pp. 80, 81; and Harold Demsetz, "Two Systems of Belief About Monopoly" in ibid., p. 179.
10. Kahn, *The Economics of Regulation,* 2:120.
11. Schmalensee, *The Control of Natural Monopolies,* p. 4; and Richard Schmalensee, "A Note on Economies of Scale and Natural Monopoly in the Distribution of Public Utility Services," *Bell Journal of Economics* 9 (Spring 1978):270-276.
12. *Study on Federal Regulation,* p. 10.
13. Leonard Waverman, "The Regulation of Intercity Telecommunications," in *Promoting Competition in Regulated Markets,* ed. Almarin Phillips (Washington, D.C.: Brookings Institution, 1975), pp. 232, 233.
14. Kahn, *The Economics of Regulation,* 2:123.
15. Bonbright, *Principles of Public Utility Rates,* pp. 15, 16. For a somewhat different construction, see Kahn, *The Economics of Regulation,* 2:124-126.
16. Schmalensee, *The Control of Natural Monopolies,* pp. 5, 6.
17. Harold Demsetz, "Why Regulate Utilities?" *Journal of Law & Economics* 11 (April 1968):55-65.
18. *Munn* v. *Illinois,* 94 U.S. 113 (1877).
19. *Ribnik* v. *McBride,* 277 U.S. 350 (1928); and *New State Ice Co.* v. *Liebmann,* 285 U.S. 262 (1932).
20. See Alan Stone, *Economic Regulation and the Public Interest* (Ithaca, N.Y.: Cornell University Press, 1977), pp. 24, 25; and Robert H. Bork,

"Legislative Intent and the Policy of the Sherman Act," *Journal of Law & Economics* 9 (October 1966):39-48.

21. John S. McGee, "Predatory Price Cutting: The Standard Oil (N.J.) Case," *Journal of Law & Economics* 1 (October 1958):137-169.

22. Carl Kaysen and Donald F. Turner, *Antitrust Policy: An Economic and Legal Analysis* (Cambridge, Mass.: Harvard University Press, 1959), p. 75.

23. For example, see Yale Brozen, "Bain's Concentration and Rates of Return Revisited," *Journal of Law & Economics* 14 (October 1971):366; Stanley Ornstein, "Concentration and Profits," in *The Impact of Large Firms on the U.S. Economy,* J. Fred Weston and Stanley Ornstein (Lexington, Mass.: D. C. Heath & Co., 1973), p. 101; Demsetz, "Industry Structure, Market Rivalry and Public Policy," in *Industrial Concentration,* pp. 80, 81; Yale Brozen, "Concentration and Profits: Does Concentration Matter?" in *Industrial Concentration,* pp. 69, 70; and Betty Bock and Jack Farkas, *Concentration and Productivity* (New York: National Industrial Conference Board, 1969), pp. 4, 5.

24. See the interesting discussion in Robert H. Bork and Ward S. Bowman, "The Crisis in Antitrust," *Columbia Law Review* 65 (March 1965):366, 367.

25. See the argument in Milton Friedman, *Capitalism and Freedom* (Chicago: University of Chicago Press, 1962), pp. 30, 31. However, Friedman only considers externalities as a basis for regulation in these examples.

26. Generally, see Steven E. Rhoads, *Policy Analysis in the Federal Aviation Administration* (Lexington, Mass.: Lexington Books, 1974), chap. 3.

27. A brief history is contained in Robert Burkhardt, *The Federal Aviation Administration* (New York: Praeger Publishers, 1967), chaps. 1, 2.

28. R. H. Coase, "The Federal Communications Commission," *Journal of Law & Economics* 2 (October 1959):1-40.

29. See the opinion in *National Broadcasting Co.* v. *United States,* 319 U.S. 190, 213-217 (1943).

30. Federal Communications Commission, *Second Interim Report by the Office of Network Study: Television Network Program Procurement: Part 2* (Washington, D.C.: Government Printing Office, 1965), pp. 65, 66.

31. Ibid., p. 79.

32. See Roger Noll, Merton J. Peck, and John J. McGowan, *Economic Aspects of Television Regulation* (Washington, D.C.: Brookings Institution, 1973), pp. 53, 54; and Harvey J. Levin, *The Invisible Resource* (Baltimore, Md.: Johns Hopkins University Press, 1971), pp. 70, 71.

33. The interested reader should examine the latest round in the debate: Ronald H. Coase and Nicholas Johnson, "Should the Federal Communications Commission Be Abolished?" in *Regulation, Economics and the Law,* ed. Bernard H. Siegan (Lexington, Mass.: D. C. Heath & Co., 1979), pp. 41-56.

34. See U.S., Department of Agriculture, Economic Research Service, Agricultural Economic Report No. 152, *Government's Role in Pricing Fluid Milk in the United States* (Washington, D.C.: Government Printing Office, 1968); and Richard A. Ippolito and Robert T. Masson, "The Social Cost of Government Regulation of Milk," *Journal of Law & Economics* 21 (April 1978):33-66.

35. Kahn, *The Economics of Regulation,* 2:3, 4.

36. Alexander Gerschenkron, *Economic Backwardness in Historical Perspective* (1962, New York: Praeger Publishers, 1965), p. 107.

37. A. C. Pigou, *The Economics of Welfare,* 4th ed. (1960, London: Macmillan & Co., 1932), p. 141.

38. Lucile Sheppard Keyes, *Federal Control of Entry into Air Transportation* (Cambridge, Mass.: Harvard University Press, 1951), p. 85.

39. On these points, see Richard E. Caves, *Air Transport and its Regulators* (Cambridge, Mass.: Harvard University Press, 1962), pp. 438-443; and Michael E. Levine, "Is Regulation Necessary?: California Air Transportation and National Regulatory Policy," *Yale Law Journal* 74 (July 1965):1416-1447.

4

Externalities

One of the costs of living in an urban, industrial society is that activities in which we are not directly involved can significantly influence us. Whether it is the emissions of automobiles, factories, or a smoker in a restaurant, we are constantly confronted with the problem that economists call *externalities*. As we will see in this chapter, externalities present a complex problem to which no single solution is wholly satisfying.

This chapter begins by examining the concept of externalities, which may be defined as an activity that imposes costs or benefits upon persons who are not parties to a transaction or contract. Thus, the transacting parties in the case of automobile emissions—manufacturer, dealer, and purchaser—have imposed a cost (in the form of polluted air) upon parties who are not part of the transactions. Our next task is to show that economic analysis is the best way to look at the problems raised by externalities; to decry polluters is no substitute for the use of sense and judgment. This analytical framework will help to explain why externalities constitute a type of market failure.

Almost every act in a complex, crowded, industrial society involves externalities, but we would not expect government to institute rules for all of them. Consequently, an important task is to determine which externalities might be candidates for government intervention and which should clearly be ruled out.

We will then be in a position to evaluate the various policy arrangements that have been proposed to deal with externalities. These are: (1) the private legal system, which allows persons injured by externalities to bring suit; (2) taxing negative externalities and subsidizing positive ones; (3) constructing a property system in pollution rights;

and (4) regulation. As we will see, none of these solutions is wholly adequate because each involves significant costs. Thus, in this imperfect world, the problem of externalities is "solved" not by searching for a perfect solution but for the least unacceptable one.

In following this discussion, the reader should recall that the appropriate way to consider social performance goals is through marginal—not aggregate—analysis (see pp. 42-44). Always a key problem is how to locate the point at which marginal abatement costs just begin to exceed marginal benefits.

THE LOVE CANAL DUMP SITE

In 1942 the Hooker Chemical Corporation acquired a parcel of property on the Love Canal in Niagara Falls, New York, and used it to bury wastes resulting from the manufacture of chemicals. Eleven years later, the company sold the site for one dollar to the city's Board of Education. The deed transferring ownership asserted that the site had been used for dumping chemical wastes, some of which might be hazardous, and transferred all liability for damages resulting from the dumping to the board. The deed further required that any subsequent transfers of the property contain a similar notice and transfer liability to the new owners.

Residents of houses built along the canal since 1953 began smelling unpleasant odors in their basements in 1978. An investigation revealed that the dumped chemicals had spread to surrounding areas. Subsequent tests indicated the presence in the soil of dioxin, one of the most dangerous chemicals known to man that can lead to cancer, liver and heart diseases, and neurological disorders. In May 1980, a controversial study undertaken on behalf of the Environmental Protection Agency (EPA) suggested that a high proportion of the residents in the Love Canal area had suffered chromosome damage.

While the question of whether there was a relationship between the leakage and the adverse health effects suffered by some people who had resided in the Love Canal area is far from settled and the findings made are subject to dispute, the tragic incident illustrates both a practical problem and an intellectual one. The practical problem, of course, is what to do about the disposal of hazardous wastes—a subject subsumed under the broader heading of pollution, which in turn is subsumed under the broader heading of externalities. The intellectual problem is how to determine the best public policy approach toward externalities.

The problem of hazardous chemical wastes is a vast one, and the Love Canal incident is hardly unique. By mid-June 1980, the EPA had found that approximately 100 of more than 600 inspected waste sites posed health threats (and at the time the agency had many more sites yet to be examined).[1] When one adds to the problem of hazardous wastes other environmental concerns such as air pollution from mobile and stationary sources, discharges into water, atomic power plant operations and their waste disposal problems, and so-called noise pollution, it is clear that we are dealing with an issue of vast impact on public health, safety, and welfare that is crying out for resolution. And these environmental problems are not the only ones that must be considered within the context of externalities.

The scope of the problem illustrated by the Love Canal episode is not a matter of controversy; regardless of differing opinions on how to treat the problem, almost everyone acknowledges its importance. It is the intellectual problem that is the most difficult. When faced with a tragedy such as the Love Canal incident, the propensity of most people (including members of Congress) is to think in human—even moralistic—terms. They say punish the wrongdoer and compensate the victims, even though no amount of financial recovery can ever compensate the victims for their suffering. To think in the "heartless" terms of the economist is foreign to most people, who consider incidents such as Love Canal matters for anger and sympathy, not coldblooded calculation.

From this general perspective evolved the division of problems into categories of social and economic. There would appear to be vast differences between problems that involve human lives and those concerned with the prices that we pay for services. And since conduct leading to high social costs must be prevented, the appropriate approach is to regulate such conduct stringently so that it does not occur and to punish it when the rules are not scrupulously observed.

The Love Canal incident precisely illustrates this typical approach. The EPA busily prepared stringent rules promulgated under the Resource Conservation and Recovery Act of 1976, which covers chemical dump sites. At the same time, Congress sought to assure that the chemical industry—the alleged transgressor—footed most of the bill for the necessary cleanup. Finally, the EPA brought suit against the Hooker Chemical Corporation, seeking to compel the payment of $45 million in cleanup costs and civil fines.

DEFINING EXTERNALITY

Like so much else in contemporary economic thought, the concept of externality can be traced back to the writings of the great economist Alfred Marshall. But the development and implications of the concept were first worked out by the English economist A. C. Pigou in *The Economics of Welfare*, published in 1920. It is no exaggeration that Pigou set the agenda for all future discussion of the externality concept.

The principal distinction Pigou sought to make was between situations in which an enterprise fails to receive all of the returns from its operations and those in which its costs are not entirely internalized but are borne in part by others. For example, a firm might plant trees that prevent soil erosion for the entire surrounding community. Conversely, a railroad might damage and dirty the area near its path with sparks and soot. Pigou asserted that

> all such effects must be included—some of them will be positive, others negative elements—in reckoning up the social net product of the marginal increment of any volume of resources turned into any use or place.[2]

To take an extreme case, resources would clearly not be used in an optimum manner if the smoke output from an industrial plant reduced to nothing the value of other activities in the surrounding area—and the value of amenities such as recreation and clean air is to be taken into account in this reckoning of costs and benefits.

The concept of externalities evolved from this basic idea. *Positive externalities* are those that confer benefits on others with which the subject firm has no contractual relationship, as in the tree planting example. *Negative externalities* are those in which the costs of an activity are not entirely internalized and are imposed on parties not privy to contractual arrangements concerning the activity, as in the case of railroads polluting with smoke and soot. A firm that dumps sewage into a river, rather than disposing of it through internal processes, is said to externalize costs that could be internalized.

Economists refer to the distinction between *private costs*—those borne by the contracting parties, the consumer, and producer—and *social costs*—those borne by persons external to the contractual arrangement. Of course, social costs are borne not by society as a whole on an equal basis but by a few or many individual persons and firms. It also follows from these definitions that production techniques often can be chosen to make private those costs that were formerly social, as in the case of the installation of pollution control devices in automobiles, the costs of which are borne by the sellers and purchasers.

A definition devised subsequent to Pigou stresses other aspects of the externality concept. Economist Peter Nijkamp noted:

> [First,] *interdependency:* there is an interaction between the decisions of economic agents. Second, there is *no compensation,* so that the one who creates costs is not obliged to pay for it, nor is the one who creates benefits completely rewarded for it .... [Third] the environmental spill-over must be *unintended* or an incidental by-product of some otherwise legitimate activity.[3] (Emphasis in the original)

A somewhat different definition, couched in the language of modern welfare economics, focuses not on the creator of the externality or its contracting party but on the recipient of the externality or its victim:

> An externality exists when the utility function of an individual (or the cost or production function of a firm) depends not only on the variables under his control but also on some variable under the control of someone else where the dependence is not effected through market transaction.[4]

From this definition it follows, of course, that if one has contracted with another party (a market transaction), the externality concept is not appropriate to the relationship. Thus, if one purchases from a grocer a can of soup that causes botulism, the appropriate justification—if any— for regulation is (as we will see in the next chapter) equity, not externality. Conversely, if a factory's emissions cause cancer in people living near the plant, the regulatory justification—if any—would be externalities.

Economics and Externalities

Now that we have defined externalities, our next step is to develop an analytical framework in which to examine possible alternative approaches to remedy the externality problem. And since externalities involve costs and benefits, the appropriate framework is economics.

The gap between the American public and policymakers, on the one hand, and economists, on the other hand, in this area is certainly a wide one. But if we reflect on the problem, we will realize that the notion that economics is inappropriate for analyzing social problems simply does not hold. It does not necessarily follow that the now customary technique of imposing stringent regulations upon would-be transgressors is the most effective method of dealing with externalities.

More than a few complaints have been registered charging that the so-called social regulatory agencies are ineffective. For example, a January 1979 General Accounting Office (GAO) report concluded that the Environmental Protection Agency inadequately monitored and ineffectively enforced national air pollution laws. The GAO even charged that the EPA reports were inaccurate.[5] It is odd that this conclusion stemmed from an agency whose personnel is generally considered highly competent, dedicated, and honest. The GAO findings compel us to ask whether better techniques are available than the regulatory ones largely being employed to attain environmental goals— and this is an economic question.

Externalities must be examined in economic terms because different governmental techniques that accomplish the same goals usually involve different public costs. Although the two are related, this issue is not the same as the problem of the effectiveness of any particular technique. The problem here is which one of a set of alternative governmental techniques will most efficiently accomplish public goals from the government's perspective. Which means will consume the least public expenditure to attain a desired result?

But we are compelled to look at externalities problems from the economic perspective for another reason. This point is best made by an exaggerated example. Suppose that we unthinkingly adopted a performance goal that would require all industrial pollution to cease in five years. Barring a remarkable scientific breakthrough not likely to occur, this policy would entail the closing down of an enormous percentage—if not all—of our industrial facilities and the adoption of a way of life without the myriad of consumer goods available today. Not only would comforts and luxuries disappear (which the more ascetic among us might welcome) but the supply of necessities such as food would also shrink because the efficiency of commercial U.S. agriculture is greatly dependent on pesticides, fertilizers, and the use of machinery such as tractors, harvesters, etc.—all of which cause externalities problems. To carry this example further, the resultant malnutrition might render us susceptible to dangerous diseases.

Probably none of us would be so insistent on environmental purity as to be willing to give up all of the material benefits associated with a modern advanced society. The critical questions, then, involve the problems of balance and alternative uses of scarce resources. How much clean air are we willing to sacrifice for how much industrial production, and vice versa? This questions leads inexorably to the next: What criteria may we employ to determine the best alternative resource use to the end of maximizing our welfare? Clearly, as the extreme examples of wholly rejecting environmental concerns or wholly rejecting industrial concerns indicate as we follow their full consequences, a mixed strategy will probably yield more satisfaction than extreme ones.

Ruling out these extreme cases may not advance us very far in developing a framework that will establish criteria for judging alternative uses of scarce resources such as clean air, but at least we can identify the appropriate paradigm to use when scarce resources are involved—economics. Perhaps it is a "coldblooded" paradigm, but we use it for precisely the same reason that we prefer a coldblooded physician to an emotional and sympathetic quack. Using economic analysis to specify the key questions, make the important distinctions within the subject matter, and reasonably predict the best technique to employ in different circumstances may not be as emotionally satisfying as ranting against the transgressions of polluters and demanding that they should be brought to justice; but it does give us a clearer picture of the problems and possible solutions. From such an explication we may be able to determine more confidently when regulation is a justifiable technique to deal with externalities problems and when other techniques—or doing nothing—are more appropriate.[6]

To summarize, externalities represent an economic problem because they involve scarce resources. In a less industrialized society abundant supplies of clean air and pure water were free goods, but that is not the case today. Consequently, a market, regulation, or some other mechanism must allocate their use. From the perspective of producers, externalities that are not included in cost calculations inexorably lead to inefficiency for reasons succinctly set forth by economist Larry Ruff:

> The efficiency of competitive markets depends on the identity of private costs and social costs. As long as the ... producer must compensate somebody for every cost imposed by his production, his profit-maximizing decisions about how much to produce, and how, will also be socially efficient decisions.... If wastes do affect others, then the social costs of waste disposal are not zero. Private and social costs diverge, and private profit-maximizing decisions are not socially efficient.[7]

Externalities therefore constitute a market failure.

Where do we Draw the Line?

We are now able to note some of the important preliminary considerations and problems concerning externalities. Strictly speaking, virtually every activity involves an externality. Not only does the appearance of my house affect the market value of my neighbors' houses, but the demand I assert for goods also has a slight impact on the price that other prospective purchasers will pay for the same products. Since few of us would want government to intervene in the whole of our lives, this leads to an important problem. What externalities should we consider appropriate for government intervention on the basis of impact? Why do we feel that government intervention may be appropriate in the case of a steel mill emitting smoke but inappropriate to compel our neighbors to maintain attractive lawns?

It is clear that every externality situation does not require public action. If a person sitting next to me on a crowded bus smells of garlic to my displeasure, government intervention does not seem appropriate. In this section, we will look at some concepts that will aid in determining when public intervention may be appropriate and when it clearly is not.

Public and Private Goods. The first critical distinction is between *public* and *private goods*. If a messy yard diminishes the value of a small, definable group of neighboring properties, the owners may bring lawsuits against the offender or contract with him to clean up his yard. Public intervention—other than using the public courts for private litigation—is not required under these circumstances. On the other hand, public goods are involved when a homeowner or a factory dumps dangerous chemicals within its own property. The risk of poisons spreading to other persons in this case is very high. In formal terms, externalities in which the state might have an interest involve common, usually nondivisible resources such as clean air, water, and subsoil. These are public goods.

Public goods, then, *may* justify governmental intervention in cases of externalities; the fire wall requirement discussed in Chapter 2 that Adam Smith used to justify regulation was intended not to protect adjacent property owners but to prevent the conflagration that might spread through a whole city. An externality whose probable impact is restricted to one or a small group does not warrant public action.

Marginal and Inframarginal Externalities. A second distinction further limits the scope of public intervention. Economists James M. Buchanan and W. C. Stubblebine distinguished between marginal and inframarginal externalities.[8] *Marginal externalities* are those in which the decisions of one actor *at the margin* (the addition of one more unit) affects the welfare of others, while *inframarginal externalities* occur when one party's action makes marginal changes that do not affect the welfare position of other parties. These categories help to determine activities that may justify public intervention and also compel us to consider the ranges of any particular activity that justify or do not justify intervention.

A common example involves the effect of a 10 percent traffic increase on the area surrounding a busy airport. The additional increase in traffic constitutes an inframarginal externality because the additional traffic does not render the surrounding area less suitable than it already is. Graphically, this can be illustrated by Figure 4-1, where Δw is the marginal change in the social welfare of the population affected by the externality and Δx is the marginal change in the externality.

Obviously, such figures will vary from case to case. In the traffic example, marginal welfare decreases when the airport has little traffic, shows no change when there is moderate traffic, and declines again when traffic increases. The area B through C is an inframarginal range, while A through B and C through D are marginal ranges.

The marginal-inframarginal distinction compels us to think with more precision about when public intervention might be appropriate in externalities rather than make blanket condemnations or approvals. From a regulatory perspective (assuming that this is the desired policy technique), this distinction leads to the notion of standards and would exclude activity levels that are inframarginal from public intervention since marginal public costs necessarily would exceed marginal welfare.

Relevant and Irrelevant Externalities. Buchanan and Stubblebine introduced still another important distinction that allows

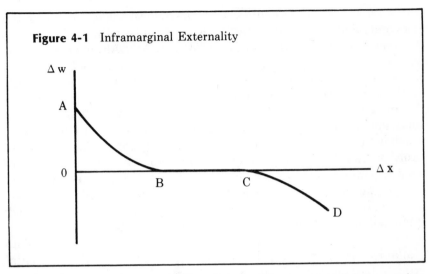

Figure 4-1 Inframarginal Externality

us to exclude other activities from potential government intervention. We have observed that virtually every activity in a complex, highly interdependent society involves externalities. According to Buchanan and Stubblebine, *potentially relevant externalities* are those that generate a desire by the damaged party to modify the behavior of the party causing the externality through bargaining, persuasion, or other means. An externality that generates no such desire is termed *irrelevant*.

While these definitions cover extreme cases, they may be operationalized for policy analysis purposes by asking damaged parties how much they would pay for the other party to give up or reduce its objectionable behavior. Obviously, different people prefer different things, but framing the question this way lets us place quantitative exchange values on activity modifications so that we can rule out certain options. For example, most people probably would be willing to pay $50 more per automobile in order to reduce certain emissions by 10 percent. However, few might be willing to expend $2,500 more per automobile to reduce those same emissions by 15 percent.[9]

While the accumulation and dispensation of relevant information is costly and the tallying of honest preferences difficult (if not impossible), framing the problem in terms of potentially relevant and irrelevant externalities considerably sharpens the question of when government might intervene and the range through which it might intervene. In some cases, public consensus might be substantial enough to exclude activity or include it within the range of possible government action.

Actual and Potential Externalities. The difficulty of obtaining information is even greater when we consider another distinction within the genus of externalities, which introduces the factor of risk. If a steel mill emits noxious fumes, the externality with which we are concerned actually exists—an *actual externality*. Although the information cost of ascertaining damage to health and aesthetic values in such a case is sometimes very high, data nevertheless are usually available to assess a situation based on fact.

In contrast, *potential externalities*—those involving possible adverse impacts on noncontracting parties—are typical in situations in which data concerning both probable risk and probable damage are not easily knowable. Regulation of the construction and operation of nuclear power plants is a good example. The potential externality is, of course, the enormous damage that could ensue if a plant seriously malfunctioned to the extent that a substantial radiation leak resulted. While potential risk and damage assessment procedures clearly do exist in such a case, they are qualitatively inferior to the existing data available for many actual externalities. Consequently, potential externalities must be viewed in the "worst possible case" scenario in considering whether an externality is marginal or inframarginal, irrelevant or potentially relevant.

It is clear that externalities are commonplace and that merely describing some activity as "pollution" does not *necessarily* justify regulation or any other governmental technique. The foregoing externalities categories are designed to help us identify those externalities that *might* be appropriate candidates for governmental intervention. These categories also help us to make the preliminary judgments on how to evaluate particular cases. Thus, if externalities damage public goods, including scarce resources such as clean air, then a stronger case can be made for public intervention than if private goods have been damaged.

Similarly, public intervention can more easily be justified if externalities are marginal rather than inframarginal. This distinction also helps to determine the tolerable and intolerable ranges of any particular externality. Finally, the potentially relevant-irrelevant distinction compels us to ask the cost-benefit question over the entire range of an externality. The distinction between a potential and an actual externality must be superimposed upon all these other categories, however, because when actual risk and damage are less likely to be known it is best to plan for a worse (rather than a better) scenario than might be anticipated. Consequently, a potential externality is more likely to be a candidate for public intervention than an actual one.

Several public policy techniques are available to deal with externalities. Indeed, the technique that we will discuss first—private law—is centuries old. But since litigation cannot handle every externalities problem, other techniques have been advocated. The first, known as tax-subsidy, taxes negative externalities and subsidizes positive ones. The second technique involves the construction of a property rights system for externalities so that the market mechanism, with its efficiency benefits, may be employed. The third technique at which we will look is regulation.

PRIVATE LAW

The Action of Nuisance

The Anglo-American legal system began dealing with the problem of externalities as early as the 12th and 13th centuries through an action now known as "nuisance." Its origins were in the land law, and its fundamental objective still is to protect rights in land. A nuisance consists of some unreasonable interference by a defendant with a plaintiff's use and enjoyment of his property interest in land. Thus, a party that dumps trash into water, thereby interfering with a plaintiff's use of his property downstream, might be liable for nuisance.

Since it is the interest in land that is protected, the plaintiff's personal inconvenience is not the subject of the action of nuisance. For example, a plaintiff could not use the action of nuisance to compel a defendant to prevent his dog from barking incessantly during the night. Thus, the first principal difficulty with private litigation is that it covers only a small portion of externalities. One reason that the issue of externalities—the pollution problem—is so high on the public agenda stems from its impact upon persons, not land.

Nevertheless, the development of the common law action is instructive when considering other policy techniques, for the courts have examined a large number of factual situations in developing the notion of "unreasonable interference." Clearly, if every use of a defendant's land that interfered with a plaintiff's enjoyment and use of his property was considered a nuisance, an industrial society could not have developed and could not function today.

The courts therefore, while conceding the near impossibility of articulating a simply stated rule applicable to all circumstances, have attempted to weigh numerous factors in rendering decisions. In general, they have viewed as most important the societal benefit of a defendant's acts (adopting the values of an industrial society) and the *objective* extent of harm to the plaintiff and others similarly situated. Thus, mere inconvenience to the plaintiff is insufficient to sustain such a cause of action if the defendant's activity is economically productive.

Other factors that the courts take into account include: (1) the extent and duration of the interference, (2) whether there is a practical possibility of preventing or avoiding the harm, and (3) the relative land uses by both parties given the locality's nature. On the last factor, courts will look more favorably on the plaintiff's claim if the harm to his residence is in a predominantly residential neighborhood than if his residence is located in a predominantly industrial area.[10]

Problems of Private Litigation

Notwithstanding that the courts apply principles of balance in deciding cases, private litigation does not lend itself to producing a balanced result—which constitutes a major defect of the process. An important 19th century court decision illustrates this point. The plaintiff sued a coal company for discharging mine water into a stream, which destroyed fish, rendered the water unfit for consumption, corroded the plaintiff's water supply, and caused him to abandon his residence. Nevertheless, the Pennsylvania Supreme Court held for the defendant coal company, stating that the plaintiff's interest

> must yield to the necessities of a great public industry. . . . To encourage the development of the great natural resources of a country, trifling inconveniences to particular persons must give way to the necessities of a great community.[11]

The most important defect of private law with respect to externalities is that there are inevitably winners and losers. In contrast, other techniques can balance interests more effectively by applying economic principles that seek to find those points for activities that pollute where marginal costs just begin to exceed marginal benefits.

Private law as a mechanism for dealing with externalities suffers from other defects as well. First, there is the danger that a socially useful lawsuit will not be brought to court. Although lawsuits are occasionally brought on behalf of a class of people similarly affected, it is far more common for individuals or firms to bring suit on their own behalfs against other individuals or firms. There is the strong possibility in many instances that, from the perspective of one person contemplating bringing suit, costs will exceed personal benefits, and consequently the suit will not be brought. The "free rider" problem also exists where a person has a strong incentive not to participate in cost-incurring litigation if others might do so and bring the same beneficial results. In many important modern situations involving externalities—automobile emissions or industrial air pollution, for example—the aggregate damage consists of a small amount of harm done to a large number of persons.

A second important consideration concerns economies of scale. A single entity, such as the government, instituting action on behalf of everyone affected by an externality can obviously achieve substantial savings compared with a large number of individuals bringing suit, since in the latter situation each attorney must duplicate the investigative and legal activities of the others. For these reasons, too, public intervention in general is a better instrument than private litigation to reach the points at which marginal costs just begin to exceed marginal benefits.

The final flaws in private litigation as a method to control externalities arise from the nature of legal causation. Simply stated, if A is to recover damages from B or enjoin B's activities, A must show that B's activities were *the cause* of B's harm. Situations involving relatively short time frames and no intervening factors allow the private legal system to operate most effectively. For example, if A shoots B, who thereupon dies, there is a strong causal inference that A's action was the cause of B's demise. If A shoots B—who lingers in the hospital, contracts pneumonia because of his weakened condition, and then dies one week after the shooting—the causal connection can still be made.

But private law is simply not equipped to deal with the complex causal questions that many modern externalities problems involve, since many harmful effects take place long after the occurrence of an event that might have contributed to the harm. Investigative costs can be enormous, and much of the pertinent evidence may no longer exist. For example, it was not until 1974 that the adverse health effects became known to persons who had been breathing significant quantities of vinyl chloride gas since the 1950s.[12]

Moreover, there are apt to be a large number of contributors to a harmful effect. For example, a person who suffers from a respiratory ailment attributable to automobile emissions must look to literally hundreds of thousands of defendants, each of whom partly contributed to his illness. Clearly, the system of private litigation cannot handle this difficulty. In many modern pollution problems, so many factors enter into the harm that tracing the chain backward to a triggering event in a simple causal relationship becomes a near impossibility.

For example, in the vinyl chloride gas situation, the fact is that most people who breathed the fumes did not suffer known health damage, although the rate of appearance of some illnesses was very high for this group relative to the general population. Therefore, the gas did not cause illness in any direct, easily perceivable causal sense that would constitute good evidence in a court. Rather, it is likely that in some very complex fashion the gas in combination with a range of other factors ultimately led to the harm.

Private litigation therefore is not an appropriate way to deal with many externality problems, especially those currently considered most pressing. Rather, its utility is limited to traditional situations involving simple causation, harm done to one or a few persons or firms, instances in which litigation and investigations costs are low, and situations where there is a virtual congruence between the legal result in which one side loses while the other side wins and a sound economic result.

For these reasons, there is almost complete consensus that some form of public intervention is necessary to deal with externalities: (1) taxes and subsidies, (2) property rights, or (3) regulation. Of course, each solution may be used in combination with the others or may apply only to certain categories of externalities.

TAXES AND SUBSIDIES

The Pigouvian Approach

The use of taxes and subsidies as a method of dealing with externalities originated, as we previously noted, in the work of the distinguished English economist A. C. Pigou. His basic idea was simplicity itself:

> It is plain that divergences between private and social net product . . . cannot . . . be mitigated by a modification of the contractual relation between any two contracting parties, because the divergence arises out of a service or disservice rendered to persons other than the contracting parties. It is, however, possible for the State . . . to remove the divergence. . . . The most obvious forms which these encouragements and restraints may assume are, of course, those of bounties and taxes.[13]

Thus, the railroad that damages and dirties with sparks and soot the area that it traverses should be taxed, while the firm that plants trees that prevent soil erosion at neighboring farms should be subsidized.

The tax-subsidy scheme for negative and positive externalities should be restricted, however, to those situations in which "payment cannot be extracted from the benefited parties or compensation enforced on behalf of the injured parties." [14] In other words, situations in which there are only a few clearly identifiable benefited or injured parties should be handled through the private legal system. In all other externalities cases, Pigou prescribed

> a system of taxes and subsidies which will modify the cost function of an externality-creating firm in such a fashion that the firm must produce at the socially optimal level if it wishes to maximize profits.[15]

Before looking at the problems presented by a tax-subsidy scheme, we must examine its virtues and some of the instances in which it might be appropriate. As a practical matter, neither the Environmental Protection Agency (EPA) nor any other regulatory agency with jurisdiction over externalities has employed a tax-subsidy policy, except on an experimental basis—and even then only in conjunction with regulatory policy, the predominant technique.[16] Indeed, the EPA has resisted adopting a tax policy on negative externalities—known as effluent fees—notwithstanding strong support from economists, business groups, and environmental groups.[17] Yet the important voices raised in support of a tax-subsidy approach refuse to be silenced.

The advocates of tax-subsidy policy readily concede that ascertaining precise taxes, covering the numerous polluters over an economy as vast as ours, would be no easy task. Nevertheless, even a reasonable estimate of what such fees should be is a better solution, they argue, than present alternatives, including regulation. Proponents argue that the administrative costs of a tax-subsidy system are apt to be lower than those required for policing, enforcing, and interpreting a vast regulatory apparatus.[18]

The starting point to understand why this is so is that society is—or at least should be—concerned not with the output of *each* polluting source but rather with a maximum allowable amount of each pollutant in a given geographical region. Thus, if q_2 is the maximum amount of sulfur dioxide that should be permitted consistent with the rule that *we will pay up to the point that marginal abatement costs just begin to exceed marginal benefit,* it does not matter if the reduction results from the efforts of one source or of all the sources.

Indeed, the most efficient approach to pollution control would be to concentrate reduction among firms and sources whose marginal reduction costs were lowest. Assume that firm A's costs of reducing pollution from q_3 to q_2 were, say, $1,000, and firm B's costs for a comparable reduction were $20,000. Under these circumstances, society would benefit most from a strategy that concentrated reduction on firm A rather than on firm B or both. It is important to remember that these reduction costs are not free; consumers would have to pay for the higher costs, while producers would have forgone other uses of their resources.

Given the *desired* result (q_2), advocates of the tax-subsidy solution argue that regulation is a far less effective technique to deal with externalities. Although regulation theoretically can lead to efficiency, it does not as a practical matter. In order to achieve the optimum result, the EPA in the above example would have to undertake a cost-engineering study of every industrial facility and other polluting source in the United States, covering every kind of pollution in order to assign the maximum amount of pollution allowed for each source. Given the enormous number of facilities and the substantial cost of each study, no demonstration is required to conclude that the total cost would be prohibitive.

In contrast, a tax or effluent fee would work in the following way, using sulfur dioxide emissions as the example:

First ... EPA sets a tax on which the firms then base their reductions in SO_2 emissions. The EPA then observes the resulting total reduction. If a further reduction is desirable, the tax is increased; or if the reduction is in excess of that required, the tax may be lowered. Such a process can result in a final position where the effluent charges correspond to the politically determined marginal willingness to pay.[19]

In much the same way that an electric utility measures monthly charges, this scheme would require the metering and policing of virtually every pollution source for collection purposes as well as the metering of the total emission level for each pollutant. But unlike a regulatory scheme, it has the advantage of permitting each firm to incorporate the tax into its optimum production decision and thus would not involve government administrators in decisions about which they have sparse knowledge. Presumably the same principles could be employed when a firm undertakes an activity that provides positive externalities—the planting of trees that prevents erosion to the surrounding neighborhood, for example—with a similar process of adjustment.

The Baumol Approach

Economist William J. Baumol has devised a variation on the tax-subsidy scheme that requires the gathering of even less information and consequently less cost. Rather than trying to ascertain the public's marginal willingness to pay for marginal decreases in externalities, Baumol has proposed a simpler, although more arbitrary, system. He recognized that polling the public (even the informed public) about the point at which they would no longer pay for additional resource purity is an extraordinarily difficult task. One would find considerable variation among respondents about the desired level of purity, so that large numbers of people likely would be dissatisfied regardless of which level was ultimately selected.

Consequently, Baumol argued, the most practical way to solve the problem is to analogize the tax-subsidy principle to economic stabilization policy. In stabilization policy, it is decided—somewhat arbitrarily—that an unemployment rate or inflation rate exceeding designated levels is unacceptable, with fiscal and monetary policies designed accordingly. In the case of negative externalities, a judgment on unacceptable levels of each pollutant could be made, a tax designed to achieve the acceptable level instituted, and adjustments made as in the previously described tax-subsidy scheme.

The alleged advantages of this method are that, compared with regulation, it would greatly reduce administrative costs, reduce the need for compulsion and difficult lawsuits, and correspond with the goals of economic efficiency.[20] The information required is as easily obtained through metering as is the information of electricity use obtained by public utilities—which involves a very small portion of a utility's total costs. Finally, as with other taxes, the scheme provides entrepreneurs with a strong incentive to devise new technologies and businesses to install updated equipment that will reduce or eliminate the effluent charge.[21]

Difficulties of the Tax-Subsidy Solution

At best, the tax-subsidy scheme would apply to actual externalities and not to potential ones. How, for example, could one impose a tax on a nuclear power plant for radiation that has not yet leaked? Clearly, funds would be better employed by installing additional safety devices than by providing the government with taxes for damage that has not yet been sustained. In a word, regulation would clearly be the better alternative in that case.

At a more mundane level, regulation that separates parties who might be damaged from others who create externalities before any damage has occurred is often a better method than a tax-subsidy plan. Zoning and other land use regulations at local levels are intended to accomplish this by geographically segregating commercial, industrial, and residential areas so that potential damage will either not occur or will be minimized. It is obvious that separating factories from residential dwellings by long distances, so that homeowners will not have to breathe noxious odors, is a more effective scheme for both minimizing damage and reducing costs than is the information gathering, metering, and policing required by a tax-subsidy scheme. The tax-subsidy scheme would appear to be inappropriate in cases of potential externalities and where separation can be attained at low cost.

Some economists suggest, moreover, that a tax-subsidy scheme will not guide affected firms toward making the efficient decisions that tax-subsidy advocates argue is one of the system's outstanding advantages. The distinction is complex, but we can convey the essence of the argument.[22] *Separable externalities* are those that the damaged party can treat independently of the decisions of others. This does not mean that the actions of others are not taken into account; they are accounted for, but, once known, the damaged firm may incorporate these actions into its decisionmaking.

For example, an office building near which a blasting facility has just located will have to install thicker windows and perhaps take other precautions. But these costs can readily be ascertained and incorporated in the potentially damaged firm's price-cost calculations. Under the circumstances of separable externalities, then, a tax-subsidy scheme could promote efficiency since both the damaging and damaged firms can readily incorporate the tax in their otherwise known costs and make profit-maximizing decisions accordingly.

But instances of nonseparable externalities are common and, both theoretically and practically, make the efficient allocation of resources far more difficult. A *nonseparable externality* occurs when one firm's cost decisions are affected by the production decisions of others. For example, if a water company purifies water that is polluted by other firms utilizing the same stream, its costs are dependent upon the production decisions—including the amount of discharges—of the other firms. Consequently, unless all the firms agree on specific pollution outputs—or are assigned these outputs by a regulatory agency—the water company cannot determine its cost curve. Therefore, the firm so affected cannot plan what its most efficient private production solution should be to the pollution problem. As a practical matter, then, the tax-subsidy scheme would not necessarily achieve efficiency where firms' costs are particularly sensitive to the rates of pollution outputs emanating from others—which probably includes many businesses, especially those that must maintain high sanitary standards.

The tax-subsidy solution has been criticized in more general ways as well. Foremost among the problems are

> the costs of collecting the necessary information and the costs of supervision, costs which would be particularly heavy for industries in which demand and supply conditions are apt to vary frequently.[23]

Among the difficulties in ascertaining cost is the problem of how to assess the psychic costs that are such a major part of pollution. How would the Pigouvian tax collector determine the proper point at which the marginal willingness to pay just exceeds the marginal damage over a population, given the diversity of taste and different perceived impacts of externalities? If public opinion rather than an arbitrary government decision is to play the major role in this assessment, how can we even be sure that the public will think about these issues intelligently within the desired framework or respond honestly—especially since many people will not appreciate that ultimately they pay the cost but rather will assume it is borne entirely by the polluter?

Even assuming that the problems of diversity of tastes, honesty of response, and correct thinking can be overcome, consider the factors that must be taken into account to determine just how much one would pay to reduce externalities. Among others, these factors would include: (1) the marginal damage reduction cost curves of numerous firms; (2) probable private expenditures such as medical bills, at various levels of pollution; (3) costs because of the pollution, such as decline in property values; (4) costs imposed on goods that one purchases from firms that must respond to externalities imposed upon them; (5) the marginal value of noise abatement; (6) damage to amenities such as parks, trees, recreational areas, and environmental appearance; and (7) the value of psychological well-being. It is difficult not to agree with the delicately phrased conclusion of a leading economist, who is sympathetic to the tax-subsidy approach, that such a system "is still far from operational."[24]

The Baumol approach to externalities does not suffer from these difficulties since the tax would be adjusted not on the basis of the enormous amount of information that would have to be weighed under the Pigouvian approach but rather on the basis of setting arbitrary maximum limits for each pollutant. In defense of his system, Baumol has argued that

> it promises to be operational because it requires far less information for its implementation. Moreover, it utilizes global measures and avoids direct controls with all of their heavy administrative costs and their distortions of consumer choice and inefficiencies.... Its effects are long lasting, not depending on the vigor of an enforcement agency, which all too often proves to be highly transitory.[25]

Thus, Baumol concluded, this approach may not be perfect, but it is probably a better system than any other for achieving the optimum level of externalities.

However, critics argue that this system almost entirely dispenses with efficiency considerations and economic judgments. It is based entirely on subjectively derived optimum amounts of pollution and value judgments about "reasonable" standards. It is possible that purely political infighting will determine permissible externality levels without any scientific standard or theory employed to make the appropriate judgments.[26]

In summary, then, while it is certainly conceivable that tax-subsidy policy *could* be used in such a way as to achieve the optimum position— the level at which the costs of pollution abatement just begin to exceed the benefits—the means are not available. Consequently, proponents of the tax-subsidy approach must fall back to a position that essentially abandons the search for an objective optimum in favor of a subjective standard that would be politically derived. Proponents of this position argue that it is still superior to regulation for reasons previously set forth—especially considerably lower administrative costs—as well as because of alleged inherent defects in regulatory techniques.

Clearly, a tax-subsidy policy is most promising in situations where there is near unanimity on the optimum points of the externality, short of entirely banning the activity (in which case regulation is clearly the solution). The tax-subsidy technique is least promising when considerable difference of opinion about the optimum is likely, which is the more typical situation.

A MARKET FOR POLLUTION?

Because of the problems of the tax-subsidy solution and the difficulties that many see in regulation, many analysts are enthusiastic about a market approach to externalities in which divisible blocs of rights to pollute are sold and traded as private property.

The Concept of Property Rights

The connection between the notion of property rights and externalities, other than that private property is a major source of pollution, is not immediately apparent. Indeed, not until the publication of an important paper by economist R. H. Coase in 1960 was the tax-subsidy approach seriously challenged.[27] But since that time, due to Coase's brilliant analysis, the converts to his position have increased and begun to influence policymakers. Although government administrators have not adopted a full-scale property rights system of the sort that its advocates desire, a modified version has been instituted—on an experimental basis—in conjunction with standard regulatory techniques.

For example, the Environmental Protection Agency announced a new policy in late 1979 that would permit companies, under some circumstances, to "bank" the differential between permissible emissions and the lower amount actually produced. "Banked" pollution rights could be used later. Similarly, the EPA has considered adopting a policy in which the total amount of fluorocarbon used for refrigeration, air conditioning, and many other purposes would be established. This set amount then would be divided into many units, each one to be auctioned off to the highest bidder, who in turn could then resell or trade the units. Production rights to fluorocarbon would go to their most efficient use via this kind of market system.[28]

Coase's views may be divided into two parts, the first attacking the underlying Pigouvian notions and the second advancing a positive theory. But first we must examine the meaning of property rights in detail. Lawyers treat property as a collection of rights, avoiding any metaphysical attempt to define the essence of property. For example, if I lease an apartment, I have the *right* to occupy it to the exclusion of others for a given term. Similarly, if I own a piece of property, I have the right to use it for certain purposes forever or until I trade it.

These examples illustrate some of the essential characteristics of a property system. First, property *may* differ from the physical possession of a thing. Thus, if someone steals my automobile, he has possession of it, but the car is not his property; conversely, I do not have possession of the automobile, yet it is my property. The concept of property, then, involves legal rules that determine who has rights in a thing, who does not have such rights, and what those rights are.

Property rules also describe the kinds of things over which rights may be exercised and those to which the rules do not apply. For example, before the abolition of slavery, property rights could be exercised over human beings; after its abolition these property rights were withdrawn. Just as property rights and rules apply to objects with inherent utility (such as food), they also may be extended to things without any apparent utility as objects whose value is symbolic or representational—such as paper money or stock certificates. As society's commercial needs have developed, the property concept has been extended to new things to meet these needs. In the last chapter, we examined Coase's argument that property rights should be extended to radio and television spectra and that such a system might have been superior to current Federal Communications Commission regulation.[29]

If a property rights system can be utilized in connection with communications spectra, why not also use it in connection with the right to pollute? The first question that must be asked is whether any general principle exists that embraces the large number of things that are subjects of property rights. Yes—they are all scarce resources for which the system of property rights provides a method of allocation. Neither clean air nor clean water were subjects of property rules when they were so abundant that they could be treated as free goods. But as the demand for clean air and water increased rapidly, they became relatively scarce, crossing what has been termed the "scarcity threshold." [30]

Under these circumstances, property rules that allocate rights to the scarce resource can be developed. The system of property rights, then, is concerned with the same central problem as the study of economics—the allocation of scarce resources. It follows that insofar as we value the central goal of economics—the attainment of efficiency—property rules and economic science should (and can) be synchronized.

Environmental Goods and Property Rights

Environmental goods therefore fit at least one major characteristic of a property system: they are scarce. But what are the principal facets of a property rights system that proponents claim are its great economic merit? There are four characteristics of property rights that environmental goods may also embrace: (1) alienability, (2) use, (3) exclusion, and (4) possession. Alienability means that one has the right to buy, sell, or lease things. Environmental goods—or rights to pollute—can be the subjects of trade and negotiation; and once rights are initially auctioned off, they may readily be traded.[31]

For example, suppose the government created for each geographic region 100,000 pollution units, auctioned in unit blocs. The aggregate unit is based on a judgment by public authorities of a "reasonable" amount of pollution that is consistent with economic well-being. Company A, a large firm, bids for 100 units, while B decides to acquire only 5 units. Company C decides it can more cheaply treat its emissions so that they do not discharge into the air. From this point, firms purchase and sell pollution rights, each making its own decision about whether it is more efficient to pollute or treat its emissions.

Thus, the ability to alienate these pollution rights internalizes what once were external costs and promotes efficiency by compelling firms to take into account: (1) the market price for pollution rights and (2) the costs of pollution control equipment. Finally, advocates of property rights argue that, as economic growth increases while the number of rights remains constant, their market price will increase, providing a strong incentive for firms to install efficient pollution control equipment for two reasons. They can make a profit by reselling these rights, and they can avoid having to purchase increasingly more expensive rights.

From this description one can readily see how pollution rights possess all the principal characteristics of other things that are subjects of the property rights system. First, pollution rights may be alienated— in the same way that other property may be traded, bought, and sold. Second, pollution rights may be used just as other property may be used. Thus, an owner of pollution rights may use the rights in any way it sees fit within a region; a steel company may use all of its rights in plant A or plant B or perhaps divide them according to the proportion it has decided. Third, the owner of pollution rights uses them exclusively as the sole lawful possessor. And fourth, the owner of a pollution right possesses a piece of paper that supports the claim in the same way that the owner of a stock certificate supports certain claims to the profits of a corporation.

The claim has been made that a system of property rights enjoys five distinct advantages over regulation, succinctly summarized by political scientist Alfred Marcus. These are:

> minimization of coercion and emotional appeals to obtain compliance, reduction in the need to obtain hard-to-get information from companies, flexibility of company response to changing economic circumstances, increased production efficiency, and the ability to direct innovation into socially desirable directions.[32]

Using property rights to deal with externalities has been sharply criticized, however, on several grounds. The first concerns the problem of symmetry, which arises from another pairing of externalities into symmetrical and asymmetrical categories. *Asymmetrical externalities* include cases in which (assuming a two-party case for the sake of illustration) one party imposes costs on the other party, but the latter imposes no costs on the first. For example, a polluting plant imposes costs on the people surrounding it, but the neighborhood residents impose no costs on the plant. Similarly, smokers in an airplane impose costs on nonsmokers, but the nonsmokers do not impose costs on the smokers.

In *symmetrical externalities,* however, each party imposes costs upon the other. Thus, the emissions of two adjacent plants, one a steel mill and the other an aluminum smelter, might corrode each other's equipment; a traffic jam involves symmetrical externalities since each car imposes costs on the others. Symmetrical externalities would appear to be likely candidates for solution through a property rights system, since both parties have as strong incentives to increase their respective welfares as, say, two parties involved in the exchange of tomatoes for money. Both parties presumably will enter into a mutually beneficial contract.

The application of property rights in cases of asymmetrical externalities, however, has been criticized on the ground that it is wrong for the victim to have to pay the aggressor to abate his behavior. Should the surrounding community really have to pay a plant emitting noxious odors to stop an activity that endangers health? Should the nonsmoker have to pay the smoker to refrain during the airplane trip? Furthermore, the case of assymetrical externalities opens up the possibility of extortion by the aggressor to curtail his or her behavior.

Joint Costs

Defenders of a property rights system maintain that the foregoing argument misunderstands the nature of the costs involved. First, real contracts involve the forgoing of something that may otherwise *lawfully* be done; extortion is unlawful. Second, our examples of so-called asymmetrical externalities actually involve joint costs and not costs imposed by one party upon another. Coase has written:

> The question is commonly thought of as one in which A inflicts harm on B and what has to be decided is: how should we restrain A? But this is wrong. We are dealing with a problem of a reciprocal nature. To avoid the harm to B would inflict harm on A. The real question that has to be decided is: should A be allowed to harm B or should B be allowed to harm A? The problem is to avoid the more serious harm.[33]

Citing an example that will be clear from the context, Coase argued:

> In the case of the cattle and the crops, it is true that there would be no crop damage without the cattle. It is equally true that there would be no crop damage without the crops. . . . If we are to discuss the problem in terms of causation, both parties cause the damage. If we are to attain an optimum allocation of resources, it is therefore desirable that both parties should take the harmful . . . effect into account in deciding on their course of action.[34]

While the notion of joint costs is not the traditional way in which we think about externalities, it substitutes personal preference and economic neutrality for the imposition of one group's values. Thus, the smoker on the airplane would suffer damage—irritation, anxiety, etc.— if he was forbidden to smoke; the presence of the complaining non-smoker is as much a cause of the damage as the smoking of the other passenger. Consider also the extreme case of a massive steel mill whose smoke damages the house of a single resident while supplying its products to tens of thousands of customers. Few would suggest that the steel mill, rather than the homeowner, should relocate.

The principle of joint costs, then, has the additional benefit of not imposing the fruitless burden upon us of making ethical judgments about each of the innumerable activities that involve externalities. Instead, we are asked to make the far more modest effort to assess and balance harm, both in the aggregate and at the margin, and to devise systems that minimize harm. The probable optimum solution in the airplane example was separate smoking and nonsmoking sections in the aircraft.

Transaction Costs

The greatest difficulty of the property rights system as a general method of dealing with externalities is hidden in the costs of conducting a transaction. Some would argue that for most real-world externalities problems transaction costs are so high that the trading and bargaining—one of the presumed benefits of a property rights system—rarely would take place.

Consider the case of a large number of automobiles, each one of which has pollution rights. Assume that a property rights system exists and a pedestrian wishes to enter into negotiations to pay motorists who will reduce their noxious emissions. This example will, of course, strike the reader as absurd, since the property rights system is impractical, at best, in this situation. A far better solution would be through regulation at the ultimate source of emission—the automobile manufacturers. Not only would such a regulatory system be more effective than a property rights system, but the costs of administration (even granting a high degree of government inefficiency) would be much lower than those resulting from a large number of pedestrians negotiating and contracting with a large number of motorists.

Because of the high transaction costs that almost necessarily ensue in what would have to be complex multiparty transactions, some economists have argued that a property rights-market solution could not work for most real-world environmental problems.[35] The market system is better suited to the two-party case, but it is simply not useful for common environmental problems, such as air and water pollution from various sources that admix and affect whole communities or even the dumping of wastes from easily traceable sources that adversely affects a relatively large number of neighbors.

What are these transaction costs that preclude the formation of agreements in many practical externality problems? While the term is not without ambiguity, economist Carl Dahlman has concretely spelled out its various components.[36] First, the costs involved in searching out the other possible parties to a bargain must be considered. At the outset, we can see that these search costs rise substantially as the number of parties required to make an effective contract increases. For this reason alone, the automobile pollution example effectively precludes the consummation of contracts.

Second, there are costs incurred in the development and exchange of information. Third, each of the parties sustains private costs in the decisionmaking process. Fourth, each party incurs costs in the actual bargaining process, and, obviously, the larger the number of parties, the greater will be these costs. Each party also must sustain policing costs to assure that the other parties with adverse positions will uphold any agreement that is reached.

It is clear that the number of factors that might inhibit contract formation include not only large numbers of actors but also high policing costs, complex and difficult negotiations, and very high information costs. In short, given this imposing list of transaction cost components, it appears likely that the high transaction costs associated with most actual externalities problems would effectively preclude contracts from forming and, indeed, negotiations from taking place. Without this vital component of a market system, the benefits of a property rights solution to the externalities problem do not follow.

Coase and other careful proponents of the property rights system have been well aware of this impediment. They have suggested government should reduce transaction costs but have not proposed ways to do so. Coase has recommended a valuable way that policymakers can examine alternative approaches to the externalities problem in order to settle upon the least unacceptable alternative:

> It would seem desirable to use an [opportunity cost] approach when dealing with questions of economic policy and to compare the total product yielded by alternative social arrangements.[37]

Such an assessment should embrace not only economic values but aesthetic and moral ones as well.

REGULATION: THE LEAST WORSE ALTERNATIVE?

For the foregoing reasons, regulation is the last technique to be examined. Although regulation is often subject to considerable criticism, its justification for the control of externalities might be based less on its clear benefits than on the view that regulation is a technique superior to private litigation, tax-subsidy, or property rights (notwithstanding some glaring deficiencies). Or we might conclude that the least undesirable solution consists of blending regulation in some fashion with the other techniques so as to utilize the best of each approach. As we noted earlier, this is the course the Environmental Protection Agency has tentatively and awkwardly been taking.

Regulation and Flexibility

Critics of regulation frequently point to its rigidity and all-or-nothing character as its worst trait. They argue that the tax-subsidy solution and the property rights approach, in contrast, allow considerable flexibility. For example, a firm may adjust its externality output under a tax-subsidy approach throughout a wide range so as to incorporate the tax or subsidy into its other business decisions. The choice is essentially each firm's to decide whether to pay a high tax, no tax, or anything in between when it pollutes the air.

Similarly, the market-property rights solution is relatively flexible. A firm, for example, might decide to use some of its pollution rights, sell others, or lease still others for a term of years. It can also decide to use its rights in plant A rather than in B or in production process X rather than Y. Critics of regulation argue that choice and flexibility disappear when government regulates, with everyone compelled to accept the same quality and quantity established by the regulator. The result is that some people are unhappy and freedom of choice—a most important value inherent in the market system—is denied.[38]

The defender of regulation as the least worse technique will answer that the foregoing argument is misplaced for several reasons. First, regulation can permit some degree of choice, depending on how the legislation is drafted. For example, the New York City ordinance that bans smoking on all subway cars is inflexible and obviously makes some consumers of this service unhappy. But the London rule that allows smoking in some subway cars and forbids it in others gives sufficient flexibility so that all riders are happy (except perhaps authoritarians who wish to rule the lives of others).

Similarly, regulation can be used in conjunction with other techniques to promote flexibility and a reasonable degree of choice. For example, the Environmental Protection Agency in late 1978 announced the "bubble" concept under which the agency places a "bubble"—or maximum amount of emissions—for an *entire* industrial facility. The firm can then vary the amount of emissions from each source at the facility, as long as it does not exceed the overall maximum. A manufacturer might choose not to control emissions from one source in the plant that involves very high control costs and instead might emphasize controls at sources in the plant where these costs are considerably lower. In any event, the decision on how to meet the maximum lies with the plant's managers in contrast to the former regulatory system where the EPA set emission standards from each source within each plant.

In brief, regulation does not necessarily require the sacrifice of individual choice. Rather, in an imperfect world, regulation may be designed in a way to allow considerable private discretion in meeting standards—although, as we have observed, it also may not.[39]

Prohibition

Defenders of regulation also point out that the technique itself is highly flexible and subsumes a variety of ways to obtain desirable results. The appropriate type of regulation is dictated by the nature of the problem. The first category of regulation is *prohibition*, which is appropriate when the danger and risk of an activity are so high that the marginal damage is considered to exceed the marginal benefit at all levels of output. Opponents of the generation of electricity through nuclear power plants wish to outlaw it based on this kind of assessment; of course, advocates of that technology make a very different marginal damage-marginal benefit calculation.

To take another case, there is nearer unanimity about the prohibition of the sale and use of certain pesticides for which there are reasonably satisfactory substitutes. In all cases for which prohibition is advocated—nuclear power is the prime example—the facts and risk assessment techniques should determine its appropriateness. Nevertheless, as nuclear power again shows, there may still be a considerable gray area where differences of judgment reasonably may exist.

Separation

Another category of regulation that may be appropriate to deal with certain externalities is *separation*. Land use planning and zoning are the best examples, the theory of which is that if activities that may interfere with each other are geographically separated, subsequent externalities problems are less likely to develop. For example, if industrial facilities are kept at some distance from residential areas, the difficult "balancing-of-competing-uses" problem is avoided at the outset. Similarly, the separation of trains into smoking and nonsmoking cars—or where this is not possible, as in the case of commercial airliners, into separate sections—provides the least unsatisfactory solution to the most people. Of course, separation is not always practicable; for example, in a building containing few elevators, complete prohibition of smoking in the elevators would appear to be the better regulatory solution.

Separation, especially zoning, has been subject to considerable criticism, even when it appears appropriate. The most important criticism has been that the market more cheaply accomplishes what regulated separation purports to do.[40] Houston, Texas, for example—a nonzoned city—does not have discernibly different land use patterns than zoned cities. The reason is that industrial firms making a location decision will always seek cheaper land than expensive residential areas, while commercial enterprises seek to locate on busy thoroughfares; and residential buyers prefer quieter streets with little or no traffic. In addition, the private legal system through the device of restrictive covenants can protect the land use patterns of neighborhoods.

It is also argued that most actual zoning patterns are devised for the principal benefit of business interests and upper-class residents.[41] Others charge that zoning decisions are not consistently applied and in their inconsistency tend to favor businesses, realtors, and those with political connections.[42] Finally, critics of separation techniques argue that market arrangements effectively can handle a demand for separated facilities, as illustrated by the way motion picture theatres were traditionally separated into smoking and nonsmoking sections.

Standards

Clearly the prevalent approach to deal with externalities, the third category of regulation is *standards*, where specific activities are required to attain certain pre-established standards. Failure to attain these standards subjects the regulated party to sanctions. Probably the best known recent example is the emission standards imposed on automobile manufacturers.

Standards may be divided into various subcategories. For example, regulation may impose minimum standards, or it may impose exact standards from which the regulated subject may not vary. Automobile manufacturers must reach the minimum emission standards, but they may, without fear of punishment, attain even higher standards. On the other hand, the Nuclear Regulatory Commission has moved toward imposing very explicit operating standards from which no deviation is permitted on electricity companies employing nuclear power.

Standards also may be strict, as in the foregoing case, or flexible. For example, a statute may impose higher standards on larger firms than on smaller ones. Similarly, a statute may provide for an administrative board that may grant exemptions and variations from standards in particular cases, as in zoning. Standards may be employed in conjunction with either a qualification system or restrictive licensing system; that is, *any* person who attains the minimum standards may be permitted to undertake a particular activity or only a designated number who achieve the standard may be permitted to undertake the activity. In the latter case, the regulatory agency is far more concerned about the total quantity of emissions than the emissions from any particular source and, consequently, rations the total permissible amount among a limited number of emitters.

The Environmental Protection Agency's "offset" policy provides an example of a modified restrictive standard system. Under this system, employed since 1977, the agency has allowed the construction of a new plant in a region only on condition that: (1) the firm offset the new pollution by commensurately reducing its pollution at its other plants in the area or (2) other firms in the area have reduced their emissions in the same amount. Third-party firms have been induced to decrease their emissions through the coaxing of local governments or chambers of commerce, anxious to have the new firm locate in their areas.

In summary, contrary to the views of its critics, the technique of regulation does provide a considerable degree of flexibility to meet particular problems. Prohibition, separation, and the many varieties of standards may be combined not only with each other in numerous ways but also with modifications of the tax-subsidy and market-property rights systems. Sophisticated advocates of regulation concede that there are numerous applications that are wrongheaded and that there are inherent defects in regulation as a technique to deal with policies toward externalities—but they conclude regulation is the least worse alternative.

Clearly, in the case of prohibition there is no substitute for regulation nor is there in the case of potential externalities. Neither a tax-subsidy scheme nor a market-property rights system can substitute for regulation of nuclear power generation, for example. And even if one concedes that in such cases firms have a strong incentive to prevent the manifestation of the externality—a nuclear power meltdown, for example—the risks and dangers are apt to be so high that regulation is well worth the added cost. Add to these observations the defects in the other systems intended to meet the externalities problem, and the regulation advocates conclude that theirs is the best possible way to deal with the problem.

The Problems of Regulation

Nevertheless, considerable doubt exists among economists and others that regulation is the least undesirable policy alternative for externalities, because of the efficiency problem *inherent* in it. They point not only to the innumerable difficulties that agencies have had as symptomatic of regulation's inherent defects but to theoretical principles as well.

Critics of regulation first note that this technique promotes the inefficient use of resources, especially in the case of across-the-board standards. For example, assume all firms were required to achieve a hypothetical discharge limit of 10 units so that total emissions would be 20 units (given a two-plant economy). If both firms A and B started with emissions of 15 units and the reduction cost for A was $5,000 per unit, while the reduction cost for B was $100,000 per unit (assuming for the sake of simplification that each firm's average reduction costs and marginal reduction costs are equal and the same throughout their respective reduction schedules), it would have saved far more of society's resources to have achieved the same result of 20 total units entirely through A's efforts.

While this example is purposely simple, the principle is precisely the same when other complexities are added. Moreover, the principle applies if, instead of requiring an across-the-board emission reduction, each firm was required simply to reduce its emissions by a constant percentage or even if there were variations based on size of firms or some other factor. For this reason, critics conclude that regulation of externalities through standards is *inherently* inefficient and wasteful of society's resources.

The EPA and other regulatory agencies, of course, have been aware of these arguments and for these reasons have moved away from the imposition of rigid standards. But as the agencies have moved toward greater flexibility and specificity in individual cases, they have laid themselves open to other criticism. In order to appreciate the scope of the problem, one must consider the complexity of the task that externality regulators face in an economy as complex as ours.

First, an agency that is charged with controlling pollution must take into account the wide variations in costs and emissions among different industries as well as the large number of industries for which flexible standards must be set. Second, even within the same industry considerable variation may exist from firm to firm in product mix, pollution control technologies available, and costs of each product. Third, even with the same product, plants can vary considerably with respect to the technology used in the production processes. Fourth, the age of the plant and the equipment used within it can have a major effect on emissions; generally speaking, the older the plant, the greater the polluting emissions. Taking all these factors into account in a vast economy, it is clear that for an agency to do a thorough job of point-by-point regulation the costs of investigation, administration, and policing would be enormous and impractical.[43]

Furthermore, regulation is open to the charge that the polluter is provided with no incentive to reduce emissions below the permissible maximum. For example, if a polluter can reduce its emissions below the maximum, say, of 10 units, there is a strong disincentive to do so since additional costs will be incurred but no rewards reaped. It also follows that there is no strong incentive under a regulatory scheme for producers of pollution control equipment to manufacture goods that will reduce pollution below the allowable maximum. Buyers will not purchase such equipment if it is more costly than equipment that just meets the maximum since nothing is gained by incurring the additional expenditure. And, in general, those who must install such equipment seek to retard the development of new pollution control technology since they might be forced to replace older technology at high cost once the new device is proven.[44]

Critics of externalities regulation also charge that government has no incentive to operate efficiently since it is not disciplined by the market and that once innumerable regulations with highly discretionary language are promulgated, particular interpretations are often the result of political pressures and uneven enforcement. The public, too, develops a distorted view of the costs and benefits of policies, mistakenly believing that environmental goods are free. The public therefore demands large quantities of environmental protection, not realizing that other potential goods are forgone.

In summary, then, the critics of regulation point to all these political and administrative factors, add them together, and recognize that they inevitably play a major role in the process of regulation. Consequently, they conclude that externalities regulation is a much costlier and less consistent way to attain environmental goals than its alternatives. Only in the extremely unusual cases of a potential externality with exceptionally high risk of great danger or one in which prohibition is clearly called for should regulation be imposed. But even here, critics argue, taxes may be raised to prohibitive levels or property rights not granted for certain activities.

AN UNHAPPY ENDING

We have looked at numerous alternative techniques to control externalities and found that each has strengths and serious weaknesses. There is no satisfactory solution to the problem of externalities; at best, there are second best solutions or, perhaps more accurately, least worse solutions. Nevertheless, regulation is a justified technique to deal with externalities because no *clearly* superior alternative is available.

The categories of externalities discussed in this chapter provide at least some guidelines as to what techniques might be rejected or useful in solving specific public problems. Thus, when transaction costs are very high, a property rights system is least useful; when negotiation between a few parties to control externalities is likely, regulation is least justified. In short, as Coase essentially concluded, each case must be considered on its own merits to determine the appropriate technique. And each technique for each case must be evaluated with an opportunity-cost approach, comparing the costs and benefits that likely will ensue under each alternative.

NOTES

1. Anthony J. Parisi, "Who Pays? Cleaning Up the Love Canal," *New York Times,* June 8, 1980, pp. F-1, 4, 5.
2. A. C. Pigou, *The Economics of Welfare,* 4th ed. (London: Macmillan & Co., 1932), p. 134.
3. Peter Nijkamp, *Theory and Application of Environmental Economics* (Amsterdam: North Holland, 1977), p. 45.
4. Yew-Kwang Ng, *Welfare Economics* (London: Macmillan & Co., 1979), p. 167.
5. See Philip Shabecoff, "Environmental Agency Called Lax on Enforcing Air Pollution Curbs," *New York Times,* January 10, 1979, p. A-12.
6. For a discussion of the power of economic analysis to treat problems that traditionally have been treated as noneconomic, see Reuven Brenner, "Economics—An Imperialist Science," *Journal of Legal Studies* 9 (January 1980):179-188.
7. Larry Ruff, "The Economic Common Sense of Pollution," *Public Interest* (Spring 1970):72.
8. James M. Buchanan and W. C. Stubblebine, "Externality," *Economica* 29 (November 1962):371-384.
9. An example of the increasing marginal costs of purity at high levels is Thomas D. Crocker, "Externalities, Property Rights and Transaction Costs: An Empirical Study," *Journal of Law and Economics* 14 (October 1971):458.
10. See William L. Prosser, *Handbook of the Law of Torts,* 4th ed. (St. Paul, Minn.: West Publishing Co., 1971), pp. 591-612.
11. *Pennsylvania Coal Co.* v. *Sanderson,* 113 Pa. 126, 6 A. 452, 459 (1886).
12. The case history of this substance is recounted in David D. Doniger, *The Law and Policy of Toxic Substances Control: A Case Study of Vinyl Chloride* (Baltimore, Md.: Resources for the Future, 1978).
13. Pigou, *The Economics of Welfare,* p. 192.
14. Ibid., p. 183.
15. Stanislaw Wellisz, "On External Diseconomies and the Government-Assisted Invisible Hand," *Economica* 31 (November 1964):354.
16. Indeed, most regulatory agency experimentation with nonregulatory techniques has been of a modified market approach, not a tax-subsidy one. For a review, see "New Approaches to Regulatory Reform—Letting the Market Do the Job," *National Journal,* August 11, 1979, pp. 1316-1322.
17. For example, see Edwin S. Mills, *The Economics of Environmental Quality* (New York: W. W. Norton & Co., 1978), p. 218.
18. The literature advocating the use of effluent charges is vast. Among the most forceful and persuasive presentations are Allen V. Kneese and Charles L. Schultze, *Pollution, Prices and Public Policy* (Washington, D.C.: Brookings Institution, 1975), chap. 7; and Krister Hjalte, Karl Lindgren,

and Ingemar Stahl, *Environmental Policy and Welfare Economics* (Cambridge: Cambridge University Press, 1977), chap. 3.

19. Hjalte et al., *Environmental Policy and Welfare Economics*, p. 64.
20. William J. Baumol, "On Taxation and the Control of Externalities," *American Economic Review* 62 (June 1972):318, 319.
21. See A. Myrick Freeman III, "Air and Water Pollution Policy," in *Current Issues in U.S. Environmental Policy*, ed. Paul Portney (Baltimore, Md.: Resources for the Future, 1978), pp. 55-59.
22. For a full discussion, see O. A. Davis and A. Whinston, "Externalities, Welfare and the Theory of Games," *Journal of Political Economy* 70 (June 1962):241-262.
23. Ezra J. Mishan, "The Postwar Literature on Externalities: An Interpretative Essay," *Journal of Economic Literature* 9 (March 1971):15.
24. Nijkamp, *Theory and Application of Environmental Economics*, p. 124.
25. Baumol, "On Taxation and the Control of Externalities," p. 319.
26. Carl J. Dahlman, "The Problem of Externality," *Journal of Law & Economics* 22 (April 1979):157.
27. R. H. Coase, "The Problem of Social Cost," *Journal of Law & Economics* 3 (October 1960):1-44.
28. "New Approaches to Regulatory Reform," p. 1320.
29. Coase, "The Problem of Social Costs," p. 1, footnote 1.
30. James C. Hite et al., *The Economics of Environmental Quality* (Washington, D.C.: American Enterprise Institute, 1972), pp. 14, 15.
31. See the discussion in J. H. Dales, *Pollution, Property and Prices* (Toronto, Canada: University of Toronto Press, 1968), pp. 93-97. See also Bruce Yandle, "The Emerging Market in Air Pollution Rights," *Regulation* (July/August 1978):21-29.
32. Alfred A. Marcus, "Converting Thought to Action: The Use of Economic Incentives to Reduce Pollution" (Paper delivered at the annual meeting of the American Political Science Association, September 2, 1979), p. 6.
33. Coase, "The Problem of Social Costs," p. 2.
34. Ibid., p. 13.
35. Alan Randall, "Can We Trust the Market to Solve Externality Problems?" in *Economics and Decision Making for Environmental Quality*, ed. J. Richard Conner and Edna Loehman (Gainesville: The University Presses of Florida, 1974), pp. 47-64.
36. Dahlman, "The Problem of Externality," pp. 147, 148.
37. Coase, "The Problem of Social Cost," p. 43.
38. See Hite et al., *The Economics of Environmental Quality*, pp. 35, 36.
39. "New Approaches to Regulatory Reform," pp. 1317, 1318.
40. For example, see Bernard H. Siegan, "Non-Zoning in Houston," *Journal of Law & Economics* 13 (April 1970):71-148; and Bernard H. Siegan, ed., *The Interaction of Economics and the Law* (Lexington, Mass.: D. C. Heath & Co., 1977), pp. 159-171.
41. See S. J. Makielski, Jr., *The Politics of Zoning* (New York: Columbia University Press, 1966), pp. 7-41; and Edward M. Bassett, *Zoning* (New York: Russell Sage Foundation, 1940), p. 9.
42. Makielski, *The Politics of Zoning*, pp. 43, 44; and Curtis J. Berger, *Land Ownership and Use*, 2d ed. (Boston: Little, Brown & Co., 1975), pp. 820-825.
43. Dales, *Pollution, Property and Prices*, p. 86. See also Mills, *The Economics of Environmental Quality*, pp. 205, 206.
44. Mills, *The Economics of Environmental Quality*, pp. 207, 208.

5

Equity

One of the principal questions raised in the law-and-economics tradition is how legal conceptions facilitate or retard attaining economic and social performance goals. As we saw in the last chapter, property is one of the most important conceptions. Contract is an equally important conception and is the focus of this chapter. We will look at the notion of free contract and how it is critically related to the free market in achieving market goals. But just as there are instances in which the free market falls short of its ideal, so must free contract sometimes be supplemented with regulation.

After our look at the contract and its underlying assumptions, we will next examine four subcategories under equity regulation, which stem from problems of contract. In each case, considerable controversy exists as to whether regulation or the free market provides the best solution to the problem of market failure. And even if we assume that regulation is appropriate, in some instances much disagreement exists about the best possible type of regulation to implement.

DEFINING EQUITY

Although externalities and efficiency are concepts that are not unambiguous, they are nevertheless subject to being measured; to that extent they are value-free. But how very different is the third major justification for regulation—equity—which appears to be within the realm of values (often highly controversial ones at that).

One person's notion of equity is apt to be another's sense of inequity. For example, if the Interstate Commerce Commission should impose upon a railroad a below-operating cost rate between small communities and allow that railroad to subsidize the resulting loss by charging a high rate between large communities, both the favored and disfavored communities can point to reasons why the rate structure is equitable or inequitable—depending on whether the argument is made from the winner's or loser's perspective. The smaller communities will point to the need to help commerce and economic growth, lest large urban communities become even more congested than they are already and small communities virtually disappear. The larger communities will point to the discriminatory rate structure and the fact that large areas in effect are subsidizing smaller ones. How are we to determine which argument is correct? Is there some scientific basis to sharpen the debate once certain common values are agreed upon, as in the cases of efficiency and externalities?

Consider another case from an entirely different policy realm, which illustrates both the difficulty of establishing a reasonable framework for equity and the pervasiveness of the problem. In July 1980, Secretary of Labor Ray Marshall told the Firestone Tire and Rubber Company that it could no longer contract with the U.S. government, an important source of its business. The secretary's decision was based on an executive order that prohibited government contractors from engaging in racial and sexual discrimination.

But had Firestone actually engaged in such discrimination? All the company had done was to hire a lower proportion of minorities and women than the quota established by the Labor Department's Office of Federal Contract Compliance Programs (OFCCP). No discrimination charges against Firestone were made or proved. Rather, the OFCCP simply found that Firestone failed to meet a rigid quota for the 650 employees in its Orange, Texas, plant.[1] On the one hand, Firestone claimed it was being treated inequitably by the Labor Department's arbitrary judgment that failing to meet quotas is equivalent to discrimination. But on the other hand, the Labor Department reasoned that inequitable racial and sexual discrimination is rarely obvious and that failure to meet quotas without some justification is convincing proof of this inequitable practice.

So large a part of the U.S. regulatory apparatus is designed to deal with inequities that some basis for reasoned analysis of the problem must be found. Consider the following brief list of areas where regulation has been imposed on equity grounds:

— Physicians and other occupations are licensed and practitioners' conduct is regulated by agencies in every state because it is inequitable for lay people to be asked to judge highly technical qualifications without the state's expert guidance.

— The Food and Drug Administration will not permit drug products to be marketed without its approval for much the same reason.

— The Federal Trade Commission scrutinizes advertising because of the wide information gap between the sellers and buyers of many products. Allowing consumers to judge highly technical products without the discipline exercised by the threat of FTC sanction is considered inequitable.

— The inequitable gap in bargaining power between large corporations and employees is used to justify government regulation over occupational safety and health through the Occupational Safety and Health Administration (OSHA) as well as to justify minimum wage, maximum hour, and collective bargaining regulation.

— Rate and price discrimination between large and small customers is used to justify another large body of regulatory laws, while innumerable regulations are intended to prevent inequitable discrimination based on race, sex, religion, etc.

The dictionary defines equity in terms of fairness or justice. Such definitions certainly do not help us to determine why minimum wage regulation *might* be justifiable for some low-paid occupations, while at the same time it is considered inappropriate for physicians, architects, and oil company executives. Definitions in terms of other value-laden words are not very useful in exploring the topic of equity.

However, there is one thread common to all these examples of equity regulation that might generate a set of embracing principles by which we can evaluate particular regulations: they are all concerned with contractual relations, such as the sale of goods or labor contracts. Federal Trade Commission regulation of advertising content is premised on the fact that consumers will rely on that information to make purchasing decisions. Similarly, Food and Drug Administration regulations are intended to intervene in the buying decisions of drugs. The rules developed by the Occupational Safety and Health Administration, as well as minimum wage and other labor regulation, involve government intervention in labor contracts; discriminatory rate and price regulations involve government intervention in the terms of commercial contracts.

THE NATURE OF CONTRACT

To understand the justification for equity regulation, we must look closely at the nature of contract, the alleged benefits of contracts, and the assumptions behind the contract system. As we will see, the market system and the contract system are interrelated in both the historical and conceptual senses. It is no exaggeration that markets could not operate without a system of contracts and that contracts have little meaning outside a system of markets.

Of course, any of the regulatory categories that we will discuss in this chapter also may be justified on moral grounds, and, indeed, many are so justified when they are the subjects of active political debate. But the great difficulty with premising regulation solely on moral beliefs is that, in the final analysis, they provide no scientific basis for reaching policy conclusions. If one person believes that certain literature should be banned because it is pornographic, another maintains that the same literature is not obscene, and a third believes that printed matter should not be banned, no basis exists for reasoning from common principles to a better or best policy solution.

In contrast, when we proceed from economic principles—admittedly an underlying value but nevertheless a widely shared one—there is a basis for reasoning toward a better or best policy solution. As we look at the contract ideal and see how some situations vary from it, we will understand how these variations can lead to market failure and how some regulatory forms are expected to bridge that gap.

The Functions of Contract

In a society as complex as ours, on any given day millions of exchanges take place, including business, consumer, and labor transactions. Individuals and corporations entering into these transactions are considered autonomous in arranging the terms of these bargains. A supermarket firm, for example, autonomously decides to charge $1 for a dozen apples while each consumer autonomously decides whether or not to complete a transaction by purchasing at the offered price. A prospective purchaser may decide he will be better off on that particular occasion by purchasing bananas rather than apples or by purchasing apples at another store where the price is lower or the quality higher.

As noted earlier, the market system and the contract system are inextricably related. The processes of negotiation and bargaining and of resisting or rushing to buy have great impact on prices and markets. At the same time, they embody the very essence of the activity of contracting. Free contract thus leads to efficiency because it allows both producers and consumers to weigh alternative uses of their resources and select those that are most efficient.

Free contract is considered beneficial by its zealous defenders in still other ways. First, the contract system tends to increase welfare in what economists term a "Paretian optimal" way. The concept of Pareto optimality asserts that a change is desirable if it makes someone better off without making others worse off.[2] Thus, the contract system establishes a social gain whenever a consumer's satisfaction is increased without decreasing the satisfactions of anyone else. Contracts achieve this social gain since an exchange, whether of a good for a good or of money for a good, involves mutual satisfactions (assuming the absence of externalities). If I part with 50 cents for an ice cream cone, both the store owner and I increase our satisfactions; otherwise, neither of us would have voluntarily undertaken the exchange. In each case, the thing obtained in exchange was worth more to each party than the thing given up.

The private contract system contrasts sharply with the normal functioning of government. Government generally responds to demands for use of expenditures in such a way that there are winners and losers. Thus, given a set budget, government will choose to expend given portions for dams or military weaponry, with further choices made within these categories. By their very natures, government expenditures and taxes invariably fail to satisfy the Pareto optimality condition, whereas satisfactions obtained through the contract system do.

The second important benefit obtained from the contract system is embodied in the phrase "consumer sovereignty." Under the contract system, consumers *individually* are free to choose the goods that they want; nothing compels a consumer to purchase any particular thing except in the rare instances of natural monopoly or a government-imposed monopoly, such as the only passenger airline allowed to operate between two points. Except for such cases, consumers may choose to spend their money, for example, on baked beans or string beans, frankfurters or new clothing, a Ford or a Toyota, etc.

In contrast, government-made decisions inevitably are all-embracing with no room for individual choice. When the government purchases B-1 bombers rather than some other good, when it bans the sale of certain drugs, or when it imposes a specific regulatory standard, the government is making an all-or-nothing decision—which invariably makes some people unhappy. The contract system ideally

> guarantees to individuals a sphere of influence in which they will be able to operate, without having to justify themselves to the state or to third parties.[3]

Thus stated, the contract system appears to have so many virtues that government intervention is unwarranted except through the court system as umpire in cases of fraud, duress, breach of contract, or questions of interpretation. Certainly, according to this view, regulation of contractual terms or the events surrounding negotiations is not justified. In George Stigler's words:

> The system of direct regulation cannot allow flexibility in the application to individual cases because favoritism cannot be distinguished from flexibility and diversity of conditions cannot be distinguished from caprice.[4]

Equity, in this view, is better served through the contract system than through regulatory intervention in the contract process. Yet, as we will see, another school of thought argues that equity justifies such regulation, based on the nature of contract and its assumptions.

The Essentials of Contract

Although one might expect that as fundamental a notion as contract must have existed since the first bartering arrangements of primitive times, the modern concept of contract and the public policies embodied in the law pertaining to it are of fairly recent origin. In England—whose system of common law the United States adopted— the concept of contract came into being with the rise of capitalism.[5]

The first two essentials of a contract, as the concept developed, are: (1) an offer and (2) an acceptance in the *exact* terms of the offer; any deviation from the terms of an offer is not an acceptance but a counteroffer. If I offer to sell you a dozen red apples for $1 and you "agree" to purchase a dozen green apples for that price or a dozen red apples for 90 cents, you have not made an acceptance but rather a counteroffer.

The process of offering, counteroffering, and discussing precise terms constitutes the negotiations of a contract. The first assumption underlying this aspect of the contract system is that either party or both are capable of understanding the nature of what they are doing; for this reason, infants and mentally defective persons cannot legitimately make contracts. This is not to suggest that both parties are necessarily equally shrewd with respect to a prospective bargain or that most onlookers will not think that one side or the other benefitted more from a transaction. To the contrary, just as the New York Yankees proved when they obtained Babe Ruth from the Boston Red Sox, many transactions in retrospect are clearly one-sided; but if the parties have reasonable intellectual capacity, the law will look no further. Both the Yankee and Red Sox managements—who not only possessed sufficient mental capacity but also considerable expertise—rationally sought to increase their own welfares.

The second underlying assumption of the nature of contract is that the negotiating parties are *free* to enter into the bargain, reject it, or modify it. Such decisions, of course, are made by each party on the basis of contemplated gain. Thus, no bargain will be struck if a prospective seller wishes to sell apples at $1 per dozen and I am willing to pay no more than 90 cents, but it is possible that the parties will reach a compromise sum.

Regardless of what actually happens in the negotiating process, each party is free to do what it pleases. For this reason, contracts that are made under duress are not considered binding contracts. Force, fear, and undue pressure impede the party subject to such duress from exercising free will and judgment. Thus, a contract entered into as a result of holding a gun to the other party's head or threatening to expose him to great disgrace is considered not binding.

These assumptions of capacity and free choice lead to the third major element of a contract—consideration. At first glance, the concept appears to be a simple one: an enforceable contract must have a price tag attached to it. In other words, each side must give up or promise to give up something of value. I give you $1 and you give me a dozen apples, or I promise to pay you $1 in 30 days if you give me the dozen apples. A gift therefore cannot be a contract nor can a contract be formed when an obligation is *already* owing. If I give you apples free of charge, there is no contract; if a police officer promises to enforce the law upon certain payments to him, there is similarly no contract because he was under a pre-existing duty to enforce the law.

The notion of consideration obviously is designed for the needs of a commercial society; something of value must be sacrificed by both sides. Furthermore, in keeping with the views of a commercial society, the consideration and the terms of the bargain should be determined by mutual agreement, not by imposition of public authority. This element of free choice marked a radical departure from medieval commercial practice where numerous guild restrictions and the notion of "just price" governed bargaining relationships. The doctrine of consideration was thus an expression of the market system; in Adam Smith's words, the bargaining parties can, with respect to consideration, "judge much better than any statesmen or lawgiver." [6]

Consumer Choice and Instrumental Rationality

Several assumptions that are consistent with consumer choice underlie the doctrine of consideration. A consumer may choose any end that he wants, but the means he chooses to attain that goal should be rational. For example, one may fancy owning a pet rock—an end that I might find silly—but once having selected the end, it is assumed that the means chosen to obtain that goal are more or less rational.

This point is an abstract one, but it is crucial in understanding the equity basis of much regulation. The initial assumption is that the ends or things for which consumers contract are subjective. Consistent with freedom of choice, the law makes no judgment about taste or the rational basis for it; consequently, a consumer may contract for anything not clearly illegal. In contrast, a seller or commercial buyer is assumed to be pursuing goals of profit or wealth maximization and to have selected the means to attain these ends based on rational calculations. These principles are embodied in the contract system and the capitalist economic system, which the system of contract was designed to serve.

Thus, for the contract system to work smoothly the law must assume that each side undertakes its negotiations and reaches its bargaining positions in an "instrumentally rational" manner. Instrumental rationality entails

> consideration of alternative means to the end, of the relations of the end to the secondary consequences, and finally of the relative importance of different posible ends.[7]

One chooses to maximize gain through the cheapest possible means, which entails, first of all, arranging subjective wants in a scale of relative urgency. For example, one may desire both a house and a yacht, but the house, as a necessity, will rank above the yacht in a scale of urgency. Second, one examines the means at one's disposal to maximize gain. Continuing this example, one determines the amount available for a house down payment and the amount that can reasonably be employed for home-related expenses, which in turn determines the price range of housing from which one may choose.

The next step involves a search for the most desirable house at the lowest possible cost. Once again, both personal preference and instrumentally rational thinking play a role in this decision. One person may want a home surrounded by large trees, another buyer may prefer many bedrooms, etc., but regardless of the subjective preference, each prospective buyer seeks to minimize his costs relative to his chosen ends.

When a person lacks the capacity to engage in rational thinking, however, the state will intervene. Equally important, the state will also intervene in cases of fraud. Fraud consists of the *intentional* concealment or misrepresentation of facts pertinent to a transaction. In our example of choosing and buying a house, a seller *knowing* that his home is termite-ridden engages in fraudulent conduct if he states that the building is termite-free or undertakes steps to prevent prospective buyers from discovering termite damage. Such fraud can void a contract because it interferes with the rational calculations undertaken by the other party.

In summary, private law seeks to assure the operation of instrumental rationality in the process of contract formation. This does not mean that private law guarantees correct judgment; to the contrary, one always takes risks in contract formation. A petroleum company, for example, may employ expert geologists and on the basis of their expert judgments purchase a parcel of land—but still fail to find oil. It is the process of instrumental rationality that is protected by the private legal system—not that the desired result will necessarily follow.

But what of the wide disparity of information that often occurs between buyers and sellers? Is not the purchaser of an extremely complex device, such as an automobile, at the mercy of the seller? How is an ordinary consumer supposed to judge an automobile? And does not the wide information gap make a mockery of the rationality hypothesis in contract formation? Does not this gap justify government regulation of information so as to aid the relatively ignorant consumer?

Not at all, claim proponents of the contract system. First, the purchaser can contract with the seller for express warranties. House buyers, for example, are not experts on termite control, but they can contract with sellers to assure that the building is free of termites. Similarly, automobiles and most other complex equipment about which an ordinary consumer knows little are sold with warranties. Second, the law implies certain warranties of fitness for a product's intended use, upon which a seller may bring suit. Third, in some cases (usually involving expensive purchases) a prospective buyer may purchase expert information before entering into the contract. For example, home buyers frequently hire an expert inspector and await his report before signing the contract, while prospective used-automobile purchasers frequently rely on mechanics that they hire to judge a car's reliability. Even in much less expensive purchases, information about quality is frequently available from published sources or through word-of-mouth from persons whose judgment we trust.

Finally, we rely on merchandisers with reputations for selecting good products, such as major food chains and department stores. They do so not because of their solicitude for our welfares but because their profit positions depend on their reputations for selecting reliable, quality merchandise and making adjustments for their errors. Selling poisoned mushrooms, only one time, could drive even the largest food chain—or canner, for that matter—out of business.[8]

In summary, advocates of the system of contract consider the instrument sufficiently flexible to solve almost any problem. We will now examine the case for equity regulation, which argues that contract is often a flawed method of protection. Although the system of contract may have been adequate in an earlier age where goods were simpler and one knew personally and usually dealt face-to-face with producers, this is not true in a complex modern society. Contract and its remedies may not be adequate or suitable for many situations.

REGULATION AND THE DEFECTS OF CONTRACT

In the rest of this chapter, we will look at four subcategories under the equity justification for regulation: (1) government agreements, (2) discriminatory contracts, (3) bargaining power disparity, and (4) information disparity. In each of these cases, the justification for regulation stems from either the observation that one of the assumptions underlying the contract system cannot properly be made or that government must participate in the contracting process and should accordingly protect the public through regulation. In both instances, advocates of regulation maintain that regulatory intervention in the contract process leads to more efficient results than would occur if the free market operated without such intervention. We will briefly define these subcategories here and then examine them more closely in succeeding sections, beginning with government agreements.

On many occasions, the government must enter into contracts with private firms and individuals. In addition, private firms sometimes must seek governmental assistance to do something that advances their businesses. For example, railroads require government to condemn land before they can construct facilities or extend railway lines. In the course of this process, government uses its bargaining power in the same way that private parties do: to maximize benefits and minimize costs for itself institutionally as well as for the public. Accordingly, government has created regulatory agencies to assure long-term compliance with its goals in its contracts with private firms.

The principle of regulating discriminatory contracts is that under *some* circumstances the system of contract discriminates between different groups in ways that are either contrary to the instrumentally rational assumption underlying the contract system or that thwart the intended efficiency benefits of the free market system. The third subcategory of equity regulation—bargaining power disparity—pertains to contracts in which the element of duress is very close to being present. The cardinal principle of contract—that it is a *freely* entered arrangement—is subject to challenge under this justification.

The information disparity subcategory of equity regulation is largely based on the problem of capacity to form a contract. If idiots and infants cannot form binding contracts because they lack the ability to evaluate terms rationally and what they may be bargaining for, are ordinary people in any better position when they confront extremely complex products, services, and agreements? Although those who propose regulation in these instances respond "no," this subcategory, like much equity regulation, is rife with controversy.

GOVERNMENT AGREEMENTS

Government regulation of certain industries, conveniently categorized as public utilities, may come about for a variety of reasons. Sometimes, as we have seen, public intervention is necessary because an industry is a natural monopoly, as in the case of electric utilities. At other times, such regulation is based on promotional reasons, as in the case of the airlines during the 1930s. Often regulation may come about because government grants a valuable privilege to a private entrepreneur, demanding something valuable or protective in return.

Since well before the advent of capitalism, governments have granted valuable monopolistic privileges to individuals and firms in exchange for promises to undertake activities that benefit the public. Guilds in England, for example, were organized for such diverse occupations as tailors, goldsmiths, vintners, and fishmongers in the 14th and 15th centuries, in exchange for which their strict training regimen was supposed to assure high standards of workmanship.[9]

The watershed was 1553 when the Russia Company was formed in England and was granted a monopoly of trade with Russia in exchange for which the company agreed to grant a portion of its profits to the Crown. Soon the mutual benefits of the arrangement and the expanding English economy led to similar monopoly grants to trading and mining companies as well as to other ventures.[10] Through their new activities and expansion of trade, such ventures were presumed to benefit English society as a whole. While abuses in the sales of securities led to some retrenchment in the granting of such charters, the principle was nevertheless established for Britain and the United States that the government may grant monopolistic or other privileges to a business corporation in exchange for which the firm must undertake some activity that in turn benefits the government or the public.

The specifically American contribution to these developments began during the tenure of Chief Justice John Marshall. In 1819, the Supreme Court held, first, that Congress had the power to charter a corporation and, second, that a state's grant of a corporate charter constituted a contract that could not be altered without violating the Constitution's prohibition against impairing the obligations of a contract.[11] Since a corporate charter is a contract, government may impose requirements in such charters that regulate the business entity. In 1837 the Court paved the way for further regulation by divorcing corporate privileges from their association with monopoly.[12] Legislatures, it was then clear, could regulate corporations without the need to grant them monopoly privileges. Such privileges could be granted, but the state could extract what it wanted from a company without the need to grant such an extensive monopoly privilege.

The fact that regulation of chartered business entities no longer depended on the granting of monopoly privileges led to two important developments. While one direction resulted in the widespread adoption of the corporate business form, the other led to expansion of state regulation and restrictiveness over other corporate enterprises, especially in areas where company activities might otherwise be detrimental to the public.

The Certificate of Public Convenience and Necessity

From this background an important regulatory device called the certificate of public convenience and necessity (CPCN) developed.[13] The CPCN was first instituted in 1872 by the state of Massachusetts. Railroads in that densely populated state faced a problem that was of minor consequence in the West—the need to pass through occupied lands. In order to do this, they required the assistance of the state to condemn land along the path desired by the railway companies.

The state's response was to enter a contract with a railroad for which it was willing to condemn land. In turn, the railway company agreed to charge certain rates and abide by certain other regulations. In addition, an administrative board was created to pass upon requests to construct railroads in Massachusetts and to grant a CPCN. The theory under which the board operated was to limit the granting of applications so as to maximize the number of transportation possibilities but minimize the inconvenience to citizens caused by eminent domain and subsequent construction. Thus, if only one line was required to carry traffic between two points, only one CPCN would be granted. However, if probable traffic warranted it, more CPCNs might be granted.

The grant of monopolistic privileges, especially in densely populated areas, was most common, however. Sometimes such a monopoly would coincide with a natural monopoly, but in many cases it would not. The "man-made" monopoly was granted not for economic reasons but, as its name clearly implies, to minimize public inconvenience. In any event, since competition could not act as a discipline upon such a firm's behavior, a regulatory agency would have to do it.

The CPCN idea as a method of regulating railroads at the state level spread from Massachusetts to other states, particularly the more densely populated ones. The concept was applied not only to requests for new railroads but also to extension lines for precisely the same reasons and to new technologies that might cause similar disruption to the public. As Alfred Kahn succinctly remarked:

> Distributors of gas, water and steam have to have the right to dig up city streets; telephone and electric companies to put up poles and wires along the sidewalks, highways and across the country.... Why let several companies tear up the streets to lay competing gas or water mains or build their own telephone or electricity poles when one would suffice?[14]

The CPCN granted to a single recipient, even when not justified by natural monopoly considerations, has additional advantages stemming from its entry limitations. First, the fewer the number of firms, the easier it is for government to enforce whatever rules are set. Second, since entry is limited, the CPCN is a valuable privilege and thereby provides a strong incentive to the certificate holder not to violate its terms, conditions, and regulations for fear of being compelled to surrender the certificate. Finally, because of the certificate's value, the regulating body can require the holder to undertake burdensome services that it would not do under free market conditions, such as serving distant, sparsely settled, or unprofitable areas.

What things are regulated in exchange for granting a certificate of public convenience and necessity? There are obviously variations, depending not only on the kind of facility for which the CPCN has been granted but also depending on in which state or municipality. One of the more comprehensive studies of CPCN regulation, illustrating the scope of this kind of public regulation, was made on interurban railways, which flourished in the United States from about the turn of the 20th century until the late 1920s.[15]

First, governments imposed construction requirements on interurbans, both at the initial phase and during the certificate holder's operating phase when repairs were required. Interurbans thus were subject to very detailed paving requirements. Second, the quantity and composition of interurban service were regulated. Interurbans were limited to a given proportion of freight traffic relative to passenger traffic and were required in most communities to provide a designated minimum of service.

Third, the CPCN regulated interurban rates as well as the procedures and substantive rules by which rates could be increased, reduced, or otherwise adjusted. Rules set forth how costs would be computed and how they were to be considered in determining rates. Fourth, rules were provided concerning extension or abandonment of any part of the company's service. Requirements regarding conditions of service also were imposed; for example, interurbans were required to maintain clean washrooms in their cars and terminals. Fifth, the financial arrangements of interurban companies, including methods of raising capital for future service and facilities, were closely regulated. In brief, as the interurban example shows, accepting a CPCN is an invitation to extremely close and comprehensive public regulation.

The Costs of CPCN Regulation

In addition to the benefits of close governmental attention to company operation, presumably on behalf of the public, as well as the gain from avoiding the duplication of facilities and construction that would have disturbed the public, there are clear costs and difficulties attendant upon CPCN regulation. First, there is a strong incentive on the part of public officials to expand their realm of control, and a protective relationship with the regulated firms develops not because of bribery or some other crass reason (although possible) but for very practical business reasons. The firm holding the CPCN has invested a considerable sum of money in developing the property and has gained substantial experience in operating it. Consequently, compelling the sale of the property might be extremely difficult with very high transaction costs and could result in relatively inexperienced operators taking over the service with possible serious disruption during their learning period. Numerous third parties potentially could be injured, including shareholders, bond holders, and other creditors of the CPCN holder. For these reasons, it is extremely rare for regulators to compel certificate holders to give up their certificates.

Several costs flow from these observations. First, the certificate holder, aware of this dynamic, is not compelled by the force of competition to institute new technologies. It may do so for other reasons, such as adding to its rate base, but there is a strong incentive not to institute new technologies when they will reduce the rate base. Similarly, a firm that might produce better results than the certificate holder is essentially precluded from entering the market. Suppose that the food retailer who invented the supermarket, the automobile manufacturer who developed assembly line production, or the steel company that developed continuous casting never had an opportunity to utilize their innovations? Suppose that the first mainframe computer firm had a monopoly and IBM never had a chance to show its great improvement over early models?

This exact problem exists in cases where a CPCN holder is granted exclusive or near-exclusive rights. When the certificate holder's term expires and it applies for renewal, regulatory bodies almost always favor the existing certificate holder, even against a more promising applicant. This generally has been true in most cases at the federal, state, and local levels. The rationalization for strongly favoring existing applicants was succinctly stated by the FCC in an important policy statement:

> It would disserve the public interest to reward good public service . . . by terminating the authority to continue that service. If the license is given subject to withdrawal despite a record of such good service, it will simply not be possible to induce [good] people to enter the field. . . . It would be an inducement to the opportunist who might seek a license and then provide the barest minimum of service which would permit short run maximization of profit, on the theory that the license might be terminated whether he rendered a good service or not.[16]

The certificate of public convenience and necessity, then, like so many policies under the aegis of regulation, manifests both costs and benefits that are difficult to calculate and weigh. But one must be careful not to lose sight of the most obvious point in evaluating these costs and benefits: there must be a justification for the regulation in the first place. That is why the historical discussion concerning the origin of the CPCN and its relationship to public inconvenience is so important.

Once a device such as the CPCN is developed, it can be used thought-lessly for no other reason than that an activity somewhat resembles one for which a certificate has been employed. For example, should motor carriers that neither tear up the streets nor emplace poles be required to obtain certificates simply because, like railroads, they carry freight for hire? Should local cable television companies be required to obtain municipal licenses if they are simply using poles that have already been emplaced for telephone services? In both cases there might be other reasons for regulation, but the traditional one used to justify regulation pursuant to a CPCN is clearly absent.

Thus, we must vigilantly pursue answers to the questions asked in Chapter 2. Is regulation better than the market in each particular case? These questions also should be posed in each instance of the second subcategory of equity regulation: discriminatory contracts.

DISCRIMINATORY CONTRACTS

Discrimination—whether on the basis of race, religion, sex, etc.—involves contracts. For example, one common charge is that both black males and all women are paid less under employment contracts than white males. Banks have been accused in their lending contracts of charging higher interest rates and demanding higher down payments of blacks than whites for comparable housing. The same principle can apply to higher prices charged to small than to large customers, covered by the Robinson-Patman Act, or to rate differences between short-haul and long-haul shippers, which the Interstate Commerce Act is intended to address.

The Concept of Common Calling

The discrimination principle has its roots in the English concept of common calling, which says businesses holding themselves open to the public must not contract in an arbitrary way and shall not charge excessive rates to some customers. The concept of common calling originally embraced a large number of occupations in precapitalist times. Then, under the pressure of the idea of free contract, it shrank to a few occupations—most importantly innkeepers and common carriers such as railroads.

The principal characteristics of these businesses were: (1) by their very natures they held themselves out to serve the public; (2) they rendered important services to wide sections of the public for which there were no close substitutes; and (3) they exercised a considerable degree of bargaining or market power relative to many of their custom-ers.[17] To take a more concrete example, consider a situation in which there were few public lodgings and a person arrived exhausted at the only inn within a community. Equitable considerations should preclude the innkeeper from refusing lodging for capricious reasons or being able to extract a monopoly rent from a tired traveler.

During the 19th century, the concept of common calling became the idea of a business "affected with a public interest." As new occupations developed, courts were called upon to determine whether or not they were "affected with a public interest." If the finding was negative, free contract principles generally prevailed; but if the business was found to be "affected with a public interest," the state could regulate the activity and the proprietor was required to serve all customers willing to purchase the service and abide by reasonable conditions of use. In other words, discrimination could not occur for arbitrary or capricious reasons.

While the consequences of the concept of "affected with a public interest" were clear, the application to new industries was not. After the Supreme Court in 1877 enunciated the principle in the important *Munn v. Illinois* case—applying it to grain elevators and thus allowing a regulatory commission to fix charges—the essentially very flexible notion of a business "affected with a public interest" became more and more hazy.[18] The Supreme Court in 1934 abdicated the difficult task of applying the "affected with a public interest" principle, deferring to legislative judgment if any reasonable ground could be found to support regulation.[19]

The common calling principle did not, as some believe, die with the 1934 *Nebbia* milk pricing decision. Rather, it was modified and moved from narrowly defined economic areas to what are popularly conceived as social issues—especially regarding discrimination on the bases of race, religion, sex, etc. Antidiscrimination laws apply to enterprises such as banks, supermarkets, and department stores that hold themselves out to the general public, not just to a select few individuals or firms. And the discrimination outlawed is based not on rational grounds—such as credit-worthiness in the case of sales or skill in the case of employment contracts—but on capricious or arbitrary grounds such as race alone. Finally, legislative, executive, and judicial findings have concluded that the same pattern exists wherever the discriminated group turns.

Under these circumstances, economic efficiency—the principal justification for free contract—is impaired. For example, if a firm purchases labor not on the meritocratic principle directed at selecting those persons who will most efficiently aid the firm but rather by arbitrarily excluding certain groups, the firm is not utilizing the contract system in an optimal market manner. Advocates of regulation insist that the state should intervene in the contractual process in such cases.

Civil Rights

The word "discrimination" has undergone a subtle transformation in popular usage during the last 50 years. Discrimination was originally used in a highly positive sense to indicate the act of making "penetrating distinctions." Thus, one who discriminated was a person with the taste and judgment to make penetrating distinctions that less perceptive people could not. Today the word is commonly used in a pejorative sense to mean making unfair and biased judgments that do not take into account the "appropriate" criteria for evaluation.

The remarkable change in the underlying connotation that "discrimination" implies underscores the dilemma inherent in the concept. Virtually every human action involves discrimination in the literal sense; we choose one thing over another. We choose one person for a task or employment rather than another one, with attendant injured feelings. Indeed, every time we select one opportunity rather than another we are engaging in discrimination. Many public policies also work a discrimination; government policy designed to end one type of discrimination inevitably works another. Thus, when federal law overrode state "Jim Crow" laws that discriminated against blacks, it also discriminated against those whites who previously enjoyed a position of superiority.

The underlying question, then, is not whether discrimination must terminate but what types of discriminatory contracts are permissible and what types are not. The issue, of course, is a vast one where ethics, economics, sociology, and politics intersect, involving debate at the most profound level of values. No one could reasonably suggest that discrimination is close to solution; nevertheless, it is possible to strip away certain layers of discourse when we remember that our purpose is to examine not underlying philosophical principles but justifications for U.S. regulatory policy.

Thus, some philosophers may make cogent arguments for equality of condition in which each person's income is determined by need or in which per capita incomes are identical, but these arrangements do not agree with the underlying principles of most of the American public. Rather, our consensual ideology appears to support absolute equality only in legal standing and not in other situations. Most Americans accept inequality of condition but reject "inequitable" treatment. They accept the market and contract system but also accept state intervention when contracts are "unjustly" discriminatory. But where are we to draw the line?

Possibly the best example to explore these questions is organized baseball. Jackie Robinson became the first black ballplayer in organized baseball when he agreed to play for the Brooklyn Dodger organization in

1946 and the first black major leaguer when he began playing for the Dodgers in 1947. Interestingly, there were no explicit rules among the major league teams that forbade them from hiring blacks. Rather, an unwritten folkway prevailed among the team owners until the course was changed in 1946. What is more odd is that the overriding objective of a baseball team is to win more games than its opponents, yet the white-only policy conflicted with this goal. Not only the experience of previous years but also the fact that the pool of available baseball players would have been substantially enlarged should have dictated a colorblind policy for each club—especially those with losing records. Yet the baseball teams did not choose the instrumentally rational means to the ultimate goal of maximizing games won.

Today this kind of rank discrimination is contrary to federal, state, and local laws. But the example illustrates our point: the contract system is usually permissible when employed in a manner consistent with the goals of the business system—maximizing profit, which in this case usually translates into maximizing the number of baseball victories. However, in cases where the system is used in a manner inconsistent with such goals—working a discrimination against groups, individuals, or regions that does not appear to be instrumentally rationally related to the organization's legitimate goals—the state will often intervene and impose regulations designed to redress the inequity. This boils down to the principle that merit should determine hiring and advancement in employment decisions—the equality-of-opportunity position.

Baseball teams are expected to evaluate players in terms of their hitting, pitching, fielding, effectiveness, etc., and a black player will have no cause for complaint if his qualifications as a ballplayer are insufficient. Similarly, the people of Brooklyn could not cry "unjust discrimination" when the Dodgers—a business organization—concluded that Los Angeles afforded greater profit opportunities and moved the team there.

There are some people, of course, who do not recognize the meritocratic system that the foregoing structure implies. Some of these opponents want to remove all state regulation of discrimination, while others—bitter enemies of the former—seek to institute near exact quotas in place of merit as the governing criterion. Most Americans, as we noted earlier, accept the meritocratic structure as the governing criterion.

At this point we should recall the principles underlying contract and their application to the economic system. Since consumers, under the doctrine of consumer sovereignty, are free to indulge their tastes, they may refuse to patronize a baseball team because it has black players or refuse to purchase weapons at a particular gunshop because the clerk is a woman. No legal penalties attach to such consumer conduct, but sellers and business purchasers are expected to adhere to the standards that generally lead to economic efficiency. Thus, civil rights regulations apply to producers and sellers but not to consumers. And while moral standards clearly play a part in all civil rights regulations, this important distinction based on underlying economic behavioral principles indicates why such regulations apply to business but not consumer conduct.

One may object that a business may discriminate on racial or other grounds precisely because such conduct will maximize wealth or profit. For example, the gunshop owner may refuse to hire a female sales clerk because his clientele would have little confidence in a woman's knowledge or ability to guide the purchase of a weapon. Similarly, it can be argued that baseball club owners resisted employing black players because they feared this practice would drive away their white patrons. But this is precisely the point: these discriminations are ill-founded. Women can learn a great deal about guns, and the employment of black ballplayers did not drive away white patrons. Long-range profitability or wealth position would not be harmed in either case; indeed, by extending labor markets, they are furthered.

And all the state has done through its civil rights regulations is make the judgment that such distinctions based on race, sex, etc., have no reasonable basis per se. Businesses are required to develop additional information that will distinguish between the qualities of individuals. And the additional information aids—not detracts from—the goals of wealth and income maximization. An employer is not required to hire an incompetent employee; he is expected to hire only those who are competent, resulting in an expanded labor pool.

But this recognition does not solve the underlying problem of discrimination. The first difficulty—and controversy—lies in applying it to particular situations. The second issue is what is the appropriate public policy to best assure the standard described above. Discrimination, as economist Walter E. Williams has argued, may come about for one of three reasons: "... the indulgence of preference (tastes) ... or the attempt to minimize information costs ... or the recognition of real differences." [20] And it is particularly the inability to distinguish between these three motivations in many situations that renders policymaking such a difficult task.

A concrete example in the realm of the employment contract will illustrate the problem. An employer, determining who to hire for a position requiring high mathematical competence, may be faced with choosing between a black and an Asian job candidate. He may select one or the other entirely on the basis of in-house testing and considerable investigation of the qualifications of both candidates. But, as Williams noted: "Information is not a free good; it is acquired by the expenditure of time, effort, money, and income foregone." [21] If there are more than just two job candidates, these information costs rise substantially.

Since the firm may decide not to incur voluntarily such substantial costs—much of which would be passed on to consumers—employers will commonly resort to one of two other methods to reduce these costs. First, they may indulge their tastes without regard to merit. In the two-person example, the employer may simply prefer blacks to Asians. Or the employer may, on the basis of general experience or on his awareness that Asians *generally* score higher on mathematical tests, select from that group. This shortcut, unlike basing decisions on taste, is founded on a rational probabilistic calculation that it will result in the selection of a better employee—although, of course, the employer may be wrong with respect to any *particular* prospective employee.

The great difficulty and the source of much controversy is that both the employer engaging in a full examination and the one who uses short-cut information may feel that they are not racially biased, while the employer indulging his tastes will recognize his biases. Yet the outcome in many instances, from the perspective of the rejected employee, is likely to be the same in all three cases. Furthermore, in cases such as our example where shortcut information is used in hiring decisions, the inference is that the black candidate must show significantly better credentials than his competitor or provide some other incentive, such as a willingness to work for a lower wage.

Since determining the mental states of employers to find out why *apparently* discriminatory results occur is an extremely difficult—if not impossible—task, governments have devised new policies to rectify the situation. Whether these alternative methods in effect lead to a quota system that conflicts with the meritocratic principle is a source of intense controversy. The two principal federal agencies involved in racial discrimination are the Equal Employment Opportunity Commission (EEOC) and the Labor Department's Office of Federal Contract Compliance Programs (OFCCP), which were established in 1964 and 1962 respectively.

These agencies, frustrated since their inceptions by the nearly impossible task of determining "intentions" to discriminate, now employ a concept known as "affirmative action" in which those subject to civil rights laws and regulations must take affirmative steps to eradicate the effects of past discrimination. The easiest measure to determine whether past discrimination is being eliminated is the percentage employed of a group allegedly being discriminated against relative to: (1) past percentages in the same company, (2) percentage of the group represented in similar firms and occupations, and (3) the group's proportion of the population. Regulators have sometimes mechanically employed such comparisons to judge whether unfair discrimination has taken place. Consequently, opponents of affirmative action have argued that such actions amount to a quota system in conflict with the merit principle; after all, different abilities are found disproportionately in different groups and not necessarily in proportion to their population percentage.[22]

Railroads and the ICC

Precisely the same problem of finding an appropriate regulatory technique to carry out the goal of deterring unfair discrimination without sacrificing other important values exists in other major areas of discrimination. At first glance, railroad regulation appears to have little relation to civil rights, but, as we will see, the underlying justifications are very similar.

While a variety of motives led to the enactment of the 1887 Act to Regulate Commerce—more commonly known as the Interstate Commerce Act—it is clear that "unfair" discrimination was at least one important consideration. Three of the statute's major substantive provisions concerned discrimination. The second section forbade different charges for the same service; the third section broadly outlawed discrimination favoring particular persons, companies, or localities; and the fourth section declared as unlawful the charging of higher rates for shorter hauls than for longer ones, except where these could be justified in terms of cost savings. Even the first section, which asserted that rates should be "reasonable and just," applied in part to discriminatory rates.

Not only the substance of most of the 1887 act but also its legislative history indicate that discrimination was a paramount concern. For example, the extremely influential 1886 Cullom Report, which followed an extensive investigation and listed 18 grievances against the railroads, concluded that

> [N]early all of the foregoing complaints are based upon the practice of discrimination in one form or another. This is the principal cause of complaint against the management and operation of the transportation system of the United States.[23]

The essence of an unjust discrimination, the Cullom Report argued, was the fact that different customers or regions, which are equally costly to serve, must pay different rates.

But why should bargaining and contracts be different in the case of railroads than in the cases of other products, such as toasters or cement, where hard bargaining over contract terms is generally expected? During the period that railroads constituted the sole means of long-distance transport in the United States, that answer was based on the railroads' considerable impact on the ability of different firms to compete effectively. Shipping charges constituted a substantial portion of total delivered price for many commodities. As we noted earlier, welfare is maximized when firms vigorously compete in price, quality, and other ways. Their strategies and decisions in these respects—and not fortuitous factors—should determine firms' relative degrees of success.

Thus, if a firm's ability to compete effectively depended in large part not on the way that it planned or managed but on nothing more than its ability to secure a preferential rate from a railroad (which, in turn, reflected nothing more than the shipper's size), a fundamental rule of the competition game would be violated in conflict with the goal of economic efficiency. A shipper located where a higher rate was charged at the whim of a railroad would be at a severe disadvantage compared with a more favored shipper, even though the former's quality might be higher and production costs lower.

This same reasoning does not apply in the case of the toaster or cement manufacturer obtaining supplies; they have a choice of suppliers and often raw materials as well. Furthermore, these manufacturers can develop methods to utilize alternative materials if they are dissatisfied with present ones. Thus was steel replaced by aluminum, which was in turn replaced by plastic in many manufacturing industries. In contrast, when railroads constituted the sole practical mode of shipping to distant markets, no alternatives existed. And even when several railroads existed between two points, they each would probably act alike— favoring certain regions and large customers.[24]

The foregoing argument concerning railroad regulation no longer necessarily applied when truck carriage became a viable mode of transport, but it did have a certain plausibility before that alternative was developed. While some analysts would disagree, in the case of railroads—as in the instance of discrimination based on race, sex, religion, or other personal characteristics—the discriminatory contract is in apparent conflict with the benefits that the system of free contract is supposed to effect. A plausible, even if not wholly convincing, case can be made for regulation in these types of situations.

BARGAINING POWER DISPARITY

The limitations of the concepts of common law contract, fraud, duress, and capacity have led to another equity justification for public intervention in the process of contract formation. Under some circumstances, the state through regulation will seek to redress party disparities in bargaining power. Minimum wage regulation, for example, seeks to redress a glaring disparity in bargaining power as do the safety and health rulings of the Occupational Safety and Health Administration.

So, too, the 1887 Interstate Commerce Act was legislated *partly* because of the perceived glaring disparity in bargaining power between some shippers and railroads (although, as we saw, discrimination was an important consideration in that law).

The Notion of Duress

But why are wages of workers with a low degree of bargaining power assisted by government regulation but not the wages of workers with a greater degree of bargaining power, such as electrical engineers, for example? A close look at the notion of duress will help to clarify where the line should be drawn. If a person is forced to enter into an agreement, there is no contract in a legal sense because the most fundamental principle of contract has been violated: there has been no *freely* agreed upon meeting of the minds. But duress may come about in more subtle ways than holding a gun to someone's head or threatening blackmail.

Duress may result from gross bargaining power inequality. Some would maintain that an unskilled worker in a high unemployment area cannot bargain about the dangers posed by the machinery with which he will work; the alternative is starvation. Similarly, a small farmer, seeking to transport his goods to market or otherwise go bankrupt, was at the mercy of one or two giant railroads serving his area during the period when railways were the sole viable mode of freight transportation.

From such considerations, the courts and legislators concluded that some contracts that ostensibly were free of duress were, as a practical matter, not very different than if force, duress, or fraud were involved in their formations. The Supreme Court in 1889, quoting the Earl of Chesterfield, declared as an unconscionable contract one which "no man in his senses and not under delusion would make on the one hand, and ... no honest and fair man would accept on the other." [25] Translated into operational terms, two considerations are paramount in determining whether the legislature should intervene through regulation or whether the courts should not enforce a contract as valid.

First, is there *gross* inequality of bargining power between the parties? Since some differences in bargaining power almost always exist, such regulation might be appropriate if very wide disparities of bargaining power are apparent. This disparity may stem from relative bargaining position and/or from relative ignorance. Thus, very unskilled workers are not only in weak bargaining positions but are also apt not to even recognize the dangers posed by machines which they must use pursuant to their contracts of employment. In contrast, an engineer accepting a job with a very large company is likely to have far greater bargaining power as well as considerably greater insight and knowledge of his or her working conditions.

The second consideration is more objective and allows us to test whether gross disparity of bargaining power exists. Based on relatively objective market criteria, is the contract commercially reasonable? For example, if a buyer should agree to purchase for $5,000 a new television set that ordinarily retails for $500, the contract would not be commercially reasonable. The same kind of judgment can be made with respect to labor or other types of contracts. The problem is particularly acute with respect to contracts-of-adhesion, which are printed forms carefully drafted by one party and offered on a "take it or leave it" basis to the other. Leases and installment sales contracts are examples of these very common agreements, most of which contain carefully worded, lengthy statements written in complex legalistic language that the typical purchaser cannot understand. Nor is it practical for a purchaser to hire a lawyer to explain the language or its consequences in many of these cases. For example, it would be irrational for a person contemplating the installment purchase of a television set for $400 to hire an attorney for $200 to explain the agreement. Thus, statutes such as the Truth in Lending Act, which requires credit extenders to set forth full and accurate information concerning true rate of interest and repayment terms, were enacted to handle the needs of poor purchasers who must acquire consumer durables on an installment basis.[26]

Similarly, municipal multiple-dwelling regulation—concerned with such things as defective faucets, the frequency with which the dwelling is painted, rent control, etc.—is based on the legislative judgment that prospective tenants cannot bargain effectively for better living conditions relative to what they must pay. Wealthier persons, on the other hand, have a wider variety of options (home ownership, renting in suburbs, etc.), while the poor must rent in a fairly compressed section of an urban area.

But why does the market not work under these circumstances to provide reasonable housing for the poor? The issue, again, is rife with controversy. Many economists argue that the market would work but that it is distorted by government regulation such as interest-rate controls and rent controls. But those who seek to justify such regulation argue that there are circumstances in which market adjustments contribute to considerable human suffering because they take a long time to work. These advocates point to situations where there is an enormous increase on the demand side relative to the ability to increase supply, as was the case during the great immigration wave of the 1890s and the first two decades of the 20th century. The same thing happened when the nation was suddenly thrown into a wartime economy, with large numbers of people moving to areas in which war-related industrial plants were located while scarce materials were diverted from peacetime construction to war preparation. Under such circumstances, freedom of choice is so narrow and negotiations so absent that the situation approaches duress. And if duress is present, an incentive to efficiency is absent.

Labor Contracts

Regulation of the labor contract is often justified on grounds of duress, because the relatively unskilled worker would be at the mercy of the employing class if the basic structure of labor contract regulation were to disappear. To many observers in the 19th century, the duress involved in the impairment of free choice through the use of an overt threat and the "duress" stemming from a significant difference in bargaining power were identical in impact. Thus, my threatening to starve you if you do not sign a contract—thereby removing your free choice—would constitute duress; the contract so signed would have no legal effect. But is this also true of a laborer faced with the threat of starvation if he does not accept the "take it or leave it" wage offer of a prospective employer? Yes, because in both instances free will and judgment—cardinal attributes of the contract system—are removed.

After a protracted struggle, this kind of rationale was used to justify state intervention in the labor contract. The notion of duress justified regulation of the minimum wage that must be paid, the right of workers to join together in unions that bargain collectively on their behalf, and working conditions. Oliver Wendell Holmes, noting the growth of large corporations through merger and combination in the late 19th century, once stated:

> Combination on the one side is patent and powerful. Combination on the other is the necessary and desirable counterpart, if the battle is to be carried on in a fair and equal way.[27]

These kinds of considerations led to enactment of the 1935 Labor Relations Act protecting the right of workers to organize and bargain in good faith with employers. To assure this right, the act established the National Labor Relations Board (NLRB) with the power to monitor a number of unfair labor practices and to assure the right of employees to organize and bargain collectively. The 1938 Fair Labor Standards Act, also enacted during the Great Depression, established minimum wages and maximum work weeks as well as constraints on the use of child labor for many occupations. These provisions have been regulated by the Department of Labor. During this same period and subsequently, state laws have been enacted—with considerable variation from state to state—covering the same subjects for occupational groups not embraced by federal laws.

Such were the basic regulatory principles governing the labor contract until Congress intervened in the contractual relationship between the individual employee and his trade union with the 1959 Landrum-Griffin Act. That law was premised on the inequitable relationship between the now-powerful unions and their members. After finding that the membership had almost no control over organizational affairs in several corrupt unions—while the officials virtually ruled with a free hand—Congress enacted the 1959 law requiring detailed union financial disclosure and requiring secret ballot elections of officers whose terms were restricted by law.

Critics have questioned the necessity of an enormous body of rules and decisions devised by the agencies with jurisdiction over the labor contract. They point to the fact that unemployment rates in the post-World War II era have been far lower than those that prevailed during the Great Depression, with the result that almost every worker's real wages—whether a member of a union or not—have risen dramatically. Thus, the principle of collective bargaining has been established, and workers may choose it if they so desire. These critics conclude that the market, operating through free contract, has operated and will continue to operate efficiently without government intervention.

Occupational Safety and Health

These pleas for legislative reform of labor regulation have fallen on deaf ears, however. Indeed, federal regulation of the labor contract took a dramatic turn in 1970 with the Occupational Safety and Health Act that established work-place safety and health standards to be enforced by a new agency—the Occupational Safety and Health Administration (OSHA).

Two events occurred in the coal mining industry in 1968 that indicated unions insufficiently represented worker interests in health and safety and that the worker lacked sufficient bargaining power in the relationship of the worker to union and company (notwithstanding the great power of the United Mine Workers (UMW), one of the oldest and most powerful in the country). The first event was the November 1968 Farmington, West Virginia, mine blast that killed 78 miners; the second was the growth of a grass-roots movement to aid victims of black lung, a disease common among coal miners.[28]

Generalizing from the coal mining experience, advocates of the 1970 OSHA statute argued that the low cost to business of workmen's compensation (which granted awards to workers *after* the damage had taken place) made it more expensive for employers to prevent mishaps in advance than to pay after they occurred. In the words of Democratic Representative Phillip Burton of California: "Therefore, unless and until the basic economics of these disasters are changed, nothing in the working place may change." [29] Accordingly, Congress concluded, government once again must intervene in the labor contract to protect worker safety and health.

But why do not unions or the market provide incentives for health and safety or encourage it? In some respects, the regulation of coal mining safety during the Progressive Era illustrates the difficulty of relying upon market mechanisms. During the early 1900s, mine operators encouraged safety on the ground that it encouraged work-place efficiency. After all, when an accident occurs, work is disrupted; if the accident is of major proportions, as is a mine blast, the company also sustains a substantial loss because of the disruption in operations. But the economic argument cuts both ways, as William Graebner, a student of Progressive Era regulation, has indicated:

> Because of the competitive structure of the industry and the marginal performance of many of its firms, commercial efficiency most often meant cost-cutting, trimmed expenditures for wages and safety.[30]

And labor in many cases is easily replaceable. Thus, the market, while providing incentives for safety, also provides disincentives and is, in any event, an unreliable mechanism to ensure a reasonable level of safety.

With respect to unions as a means to ensure worker health and safety, first, they do not exist in many—indeed, in an increasing number—of work places. In addition, undemocratic unions often do not adequately represent worker interests. But more important, unions frequently are badly informed about the complexities of health and safety issues, while the workers also are likely to be misinformed about long-range or subtle health and safety effects and relatively incapable of articulating the risks involved. Finally, unions themselves have conceded that they have a weak bargaining posture relative to managements on such issues.[31]

In summary, bargaining power disparity as a justification for regulation is controversial. In theory, it is possible to draw a line between duress and its absence, and the common law of contract has no problem in applying relevant principles in most cases. But it is a different matter in other areas that the regulatory technique is expected to cover—areas that are not quite duress yet that fall somewhat short of the freely-entered-into-contract ideal.

INFORMATION DISPARITY

We begin this topic with an example that illustrates one of the defects in the contract and market systems, indicating the plausibility of information disparity regulation. Suppose an unregulated market exists in the sale of drugs employed to cure or alleviate an illness. A firm devises a product that can have serious side-effects in a few patients, or perhaps it learns that the drug can have widespread serious side-effects in many users 15 years after ingestion but shows no contemporaneous adverse effects.

Having expended considerable sums in developing the new drug, the company is going to be reluctant to reveal damaging information that might reduce—or even destroy—sales. Rather, the firm will probably tend to hope for the best: that both the immediate side-effects in the few patients in the short-term and the long-range side-effects will not be shown to be causally related to the drug. The firm will, of course, provide vast amounts of information to both physicians and pharmacists indicating the therapeutic benefits of the drug and how it should be administered, including cautionary information about its use.

This example does not suggest that the pharmaceutical firm will deliberately ignore discovered side-effects during the development process, nor does it suggest that such firms will not do a great deal to rid the newly developed drug of its adverse side-effects. The point is that most products have the potential for both harm and good; and when the decision has been made to market a new product because of its benefits, there is a strong incentive not to disclose the kind of defects that buyers cannot discover without incurring substantial information costs. Of course, if an ordinary consumer's inspection could reveal defects or difficulties—or if consumer information costs were otherwise low—the firm would be irrational to conceal the potential harm.

The case for pharmaceutical regulation has been succinctly stated by a vigorous opponent of the particular laws and regulations that currently govern the subject:

> But the firm has less incentive to provide information that is full and accurate because doctors and patients cannot independently check its reliability or adequacy, at least not in the short run. Word may eventually get around, but until it does, manufacturers operating in an unregulated market are generally free from the consequences of providing misleading information.[32]

Another factor, stemming from the complex nature of modern business organizations, reinforces this point.[33] Modern corporations tend to be highly decentralized decisionmaking bodies in which responsibility over particular products or processes is usually vested well below the top management level. Profit maximization is, however, the principal criterion by which middle managers are judged, and to a great extent their future careers depend on how well they meet this goal. Thus, from one perspective, a modern corporation may be viewed as a collection of decentralized profit-maximizing centers.

Suppose that an ambitious middle manager discovers some concealable flaw in a product under his supervision, which might have an impact on purchaser safety or health—but, on the other hand, might not. For example, suppose he was charged with producing a new automobile and discovers that the design of the fuel tank might make it much more vulnerable to explosion than those used in most other cars. Obviously, the aspiring middle manager is in a difficult position. If he brings the defect to the attention of his superiors, his career will be seriously jeopardized. Such failure, costing the corporation a considerable sum of money, is not a good way to assure career advancement. The manager's strong incentive will be to conceal information that might degrade his work and then hope for the best. If injury results in a few cases or some time thereafter as a result of the defect, the causal chain will be insufficiently clear to prove liability; the firm likely will be able to point to other factors and deny responsibility.

The wide information disparity between buyers and sellers of increasingly complex goods and services coupled with the incentives that sellers sometimes have to conceal, mislead, or deceive has led to rising concern about whether the protections afforded by contract are sufficient. How, for example, can a prospective purchaser—or even his hired mechanic—determine that a particular car might have an undue propensity to explode on impact when the information costs of making that determination are staggering? It is not enough that an auto buyer can obtain a warranty against explosion or that a drug purchaser can obtain a warranty against harmful side-effects. In both cases, buyers would more likely not purchase the product if appropriate information was available.

Thus, the fraud and mistake conceptions of contract law are insufficient to assure rational bargaining in cases of information disparity. A mechanism must be found to permit those who are inequitably disadvantaged by the traditional contract relationship to bargain intelligently. Regulation of some sort can redress the inequitable disparity in information. This inequity stems not so much from a disparity between the parties to a contract in resources or information—these always exist—but rather that the disparity is so great *in some instances* that one party is unable to make rational judgments.

With the increasing complexity of products and the increasing extent of occupational specialization, it is not surprising that there has been more and more intervention by all levels of government that is based on the information disparity justification. Medical doctors and lawyers are licensed by states; the Federal Trade Commission prohibits false advertising of products; the Securities and Exchange Commission requires those offering new issues of stock to provide certain information in formal statements to potential purchasers; and the Food and Drug Administration requires pharmaceutical manufacturers to perform certain tests before marketing new drugs.

Although different regulatory techniques have been used in each of these cases, they are all bound together by one underlying objective: curing the problem of information disparity. Unaided by government, few of us can incur the costs or gather the expertise necessary to judge reasonably the quality of doctors, the financial soundness of a stock issue, or the safety of drugs. Indeed, most people are relatively helpless in evaluating almost any of the many advertising messages that confront us daily. The problems involved in information disparity are determining: (1) whether the justification applies in any particular case and (2) the appropriate regulatory method.

Regulation over the Person

The first major issue of information disparity regulation is whether such regulation should focus on the person or the activity. For example, regulation of medical practice is centered on the determination of who shall and shall not be allowed to practice medicine legally. In contrast, anyone may open a restaurant in most communities, but activities relating to cleanliness and public health standards are usually regulated. Of course, the two categories are not mutually exclusive, and the state may regulate both the right to enter and practice a trade or occupation as well as the actual practice of it. Nevertheless, regulation usually focuses on one or the other.

Six principal factors are involved in determining whether regulation should be imposed at all and, if so, whether it should be over the person rather than the activity:

(1) the degree of skill or training embodied in the practitioner;

(2) the breadth of discretion and judgment customarily exercised by the practitioner in the usual course of his or her trade or occupation;

(3) the difficulty of imposing explicit standards;

(4) the risk of harm to person or property from improper practice;

(5) the reversibility of harm once imposed; and

(6) the cost or difficulty of obtaining sufficient information to make a reasonable judgement.

A few examples will illustrate the application of these variables, beginning with the licensing of physicians. First, it is unquestionably true that the degree of skill and training required of a physician relative to most other occupations and trades is very high. Second, it is also clear beyond doubt that physicians exercise extremely wide discretion both in diagnosing and treating illness.

Third, because of the high degree of judgment involved, it is extremely difficult to draw explicit performance standards. Each patient's condition and history are so different that it would be next to impossible for the state to prepare standards that either specify ends to be attained (performance standards) or the means that must be employed to achieve those ends. For example, could the state reasonably specify how a physician should treat a patient with pneumonia who also suffers from heart disease? A performance standard such as "to cure the patient" is nothing more than a meaningless generalization and is often incapable of attaining even with the best of care.

Fourth, the risk of harm from improper practice is obviously high, and, fifth, the harm once imposed under such circumstances—either because of the practitioner's active malfeasance or because the patient expended valuable time seeing a quack during which time his condition worsened—is frequently irreversible. Finally, without the provision of information about the quality of a physician, most patients would have to expend huge sums of money to obtain information about the physician's training and knowledge and then evaluate it.

From the foregoing application of our six variables to the purchase of a physician's services, it follows that regulation over the person is warranted and that regulation over the activity would be far more cumbersome in redressing information imbalance. But it does not follow that the present system of physician licensure is the most effective and least costly way to redress that imbalance.

But these six factors must be applied to each case individually, and results may vary from case to case. A second example will illustrate this point. California was the first state to require testing and licensing of real estate brokers in 1917; today all 50 states require a license to sell real estate.[34] Is the procedure warranted? Looking briefly at our list of factors, real estate brokerage would appear to fall far short of justifying regulation: the skill and training required are not enormous; the discretion and judgment involved are not great; and ultimately housing buyers and sellers make their own decisions. General standards regarding fraud and deception as they apply to all contracts in private law appear sufficient to cover the occupation.

Considering the last three variables, while there is a risk of financial loss, the sales decision in this case certainly is not irreversible—what is bought may be sold—and the cost of obtaining an inspection of the premises relative to the cost of purchasing property is not substantial. Moreover, this information is generally within the ability of a prospective purchaser to make a reasoned judgment concerning the price and product—e.g., the air conditioner is very old, or the basement floods. Nor does the real estate broker usually play any role in obtaining or evaluating the information. For these reasons, some have argued that there is little justification for licensing of real estate brokers.

Techniques of Regulation over the Person

When occupational regulation based on information disparity is justified, we must determine the appropriate form. Three regulatory techniques may be instituted over persons practicing a trade or occupation: licensing, certification, and registration.

Under licensing, a license is required *before* one may lawfully practice a trade or occupation. Usually the license is granted only after an applicant fulfills certain training requirements and passes a test that is administered and graded by a state authority composed of persons already practicing the trade or occupation. Practicing without first obtaining the requisite license subjects the person or firm so doing to civil or criminal penalties as well as an injunction preventing further unauthorized practice. Physicians and lawyers are subject to licensure requirements on information disparity grounds. (As we have seen, however, licensing also may be justified on efficiency grounds—as in electric utilities—or on externalities grounds—as in nuclear power generation or automobile drivers.)

As we noted in Chapter 4, licensing may be categorized in another way: qualification or restriction. In the former case, anyone who meets the qualifications set by the licensing standard may practice the trade or occupation, whereas the number of those practicing is explicitly restricted in the latter case. This distinction may be more meaningful in principle than in practice; the licensing standard may be designed so as to exclude virtually everyone except a few practitioners and in that way greatly reduce supply relative to demand.

Some observers have argued that certification, rather than licensing, would be a superior way to regulate the practice of medicine. Under a certification system, anyone may practice a trade or profession, but only those persons who have fulfilled certain educational and/or testing requirements may be certified with a particular designation. For example, anyone may practice accountancy in many states, but only those persons who have fulfilled certain educational and testing requirements may legally hold themselves out as certified public accountants (CPAs).

In contrast to licensing, under certification the number of persons who may practice a trade or occupation is not limited by state intervention. Accordingly, one clear benefit of certification is that supply of a service will most likely be greater than under licensing. And if we assume constant demand in both licensing and certification, prices should be lower in the certification case. Of course, one can argue that the costs of certification relative to licensing outweigh the benefits (which will be explained later in this chapter).

The third category of information regulation over persons is registration, which is of limited utility compared with licensing and certification. Under registration, individuals or firms are required to list their names in an official register if they wish to engage in a certain activity. They may not be denied the right to undertake the activity if they are registered, but failure to register can subject them to civil and/or criminal penalties.

Registration therefore conveys no information about the qualifications of the practitioner. However, registration can convey information that can help to prevent or detect fraud or theft and the perpetrators of such acts. For this reason, stores that sell firearms must register themselves as well as register each gun sold. Taxicab operation is a good example of a service that is frequently licensed but perhaps more properly should be registered. The principal justification for municipal regulation of taxicabs has been summarized by economist Milton Friedman:

> A taxicab driver picking up a person at night may be in a particularly good position to steal from him. To inhibit such practices, it may be desirable to have a list of names of people who are engaged in the taxicab business, to give each a number, and to require that this number be put in the cab so that anyone molested need only remember the number of the cab.[35]

This justification was recognized in the case of Chicago taxicabs by the Illinois Supreme Court.[36] But occupational licensing is certainly not justified in this case: the skill and education required of a taxicab driver are no different from those required of any other driver. Restrictions on entry and rate regulations, which are common in many jurisdictions and which have the effect of enhancing prices above competitive levels, cannot be justified.[37]

Registration would appear to be an appropriate technique when the level of additional information required in a contractual arrangement is low. Its principal use is in conjunction with preventing force or fraud. But when the information necessary to make an informed judgment is more costly and purchasers are incapable of understanding such information (as in the case of physicians), licensing or certification is the more desirable regulatory technique. The principal cost of licensing is, as we have noted, the higher-than-competitive price—known as a monopoly rent—that purchasers of the service must pay because supply is less than it would be if the certification technique were used instead. Economic evidence strongly indicates that the very high incomes of physicians and dentists are attributable to their collecting monopoly rents.[38]

But how are we to evaluate the choice of regulatory technique? Clearly no definitive answer can be made with respect to every occupation that is subject to licensing. But considering the clear economic drawback of licensing because of its restrictions on entry, it would appear that certification is to be preferred unless the minimum quality level that would prevail under certification does not increase the welfare of some purchasers. Concretely, if minimum quality levels allowed quacks to practice medicine with resultant harm or no welfare benefit to consumers, certification would be insufficient.

Certification regulation would not be justified in cases where three of the six factors that we set forth earlier appear: (1) information costs are very high and information is beyond the ordinary competence of purchasers to evaluate; (2) the reversibility of harm once imposed is impossible or extremely difficult; and (3) the risk of harm under conditions of low-quality practice is very high. Clearly, a strong case can be made under these criteria that physicians should be licensed, while much weaker cases can be made for most other occupations. Therefore, in most occupational situations, the presumption—albeit rebuttable—is that certification (or registration or no public intervention) is sufficient.

Regulation over the Activity

While regulation over the person through licensing, certification, and registration is largely confined to the state and local levels of government, the principal focus of information disparity regulation over the activity is at the federal level. Without even considering state and local laws and ordinances, the number of federal statutes that seek to redress the information disparity between contracting parties is vast.

Consider the following list of agencies and their principal regulatory missions intended to solve the information disparity problem:

— The Federal Trade Commission (FTC) regulates false and deceptive advertising of most products, makes specific rules covering the labeling and advertising of fur and textile products, and regulates the truthfulness of consumer credit agreements.

— The Consumer Product Safety Commission (CPSC) is empowered to regulate the design, labeling, and instructions accompanying consumer products in order to reduce injuries.

— The National Highway Traffic Safety Administration (NHTSA) regulates the safety features of automobiles in order to reduce the number and severity of automobile accidents.

— The Securities and Exchange Commission (SEC) regulates publicly traded securities and stock exchanges.

The common thread in these cases is that government has interposed itself through regulation in the affairs of contracting parties. One of the parties presumably suffers from a substantial information gap because: (1) information costs are very high and/or (2) the information is beyond the capability of most consumers to evaluate reasonably.

There are two main reasons for regulating the activity rather than the person. First, and most obvious, the mission of the regulation may embrace activities undertaken by a large number of trades and occupations. For example, the FTC is principally interested in false and misleading advertising whether undertaken by cabinet manufacturers, milk distributors, book publishers, etc. Similarly, the CPSC is concerned about safety in most products. It makes little administrative sense to license, certify, or register every U.S. manufacturer, distributor, and retailer with respect to every product or service offered. But some agencies do have narrower jurisdictions over specific industries or groups of industries, such as the Food and Drug Administration (FDA)—responsible for the safety and efficacy of drugs—and the NHTSA—with jurisdiction over automobile safety. Regulation that covers the activity and not the qualifications of the person is appropriate in such cases of narrow jurisdiction.

A comparison of two closely related activities—the practice of medicine and the manufacture of drugs—illustrates these points. The critical difficulty in regulating the activity of physicians is the inability to articulate with any precision the standards that should apply. It is of little use to state that a physician should exercise "due care" or that a surgeon should exercise "reasonable precautions in performing an operation." Such ambiguous language provides no useful guidance for the practitioner or the other contracting party, the patient. The range of judgment that the physician may reasonably exercise is still wide. Consequently, some regulation over the persons who may practice based on training and examination coupled with remedies under the private legal system is considerd a better technique.

In contrast, a set of more explicit standards may be imposed on drug manufacturers. The requirement that drugs should be safe at first seems equally ambiguous but upon closer examiniation is susceptible to more concrete formulation. For example, a manufacturer may be required to undertake a set of tests for a new drug that will show whether it has harmful side-effects and whether it cures a disease or alleviates a symptom in an animal population and an experimental human group. Similarly, the NHTSA can institute specific standards as to how well an automobile should be able to withstand a crash at a speed of 40 miles per hour.

In summary, information regulation over an activity rather than the person is more likely when: (1) the focus is on an activity that is undertaken by many trades and occupations, and/or (2) explicit standards are more easily articulated and imposed. This latter reason is, of course, a relative concept that ranges over a continuum of explicitness so that there likely will be close as well as clear cases where such regulation is justified.

When information costs are low and a purchaser can readily evaluate a product or service, regulation is less likely to be justified. For example, a paint manufacturer who for many years has offered a second can of paint "free" with the purchase of the first can has made a claim that prospective purchasers may readily evaluate since they may easily compare prices and they should know that businesses do not give products away.[39] But, on the other hand, a prospective buyer cannot be expected to determine and evaluate effectively whether a particular drug will alleviate the symptoms of hay fever as claimed by the manufacturer. Nor can a prospective purchaser of an airline ticket readily know whether the aircraft in which he will fly is safe; the Federal Aviation Administration must make that determination.

Arguments Against Information Regulation

At this juncture, advocates of minimum regulation are apt to argue that competition under many circumstances will operate to raise quality or at least supply what consumers desire, especially in the cases of larger or established companies. As Richard Posner has stated:

> A seller cannot expect a false claim to go undetected indefinitely. If the profitability of his business depends upon repeated sales to the same customers as is true of most established sellers, a policy of false advertising is bad business: customers will take their business elsewhere after they discover the fraud. Even if the seller does not depend on repeat customers, prospective customers may hear about his fraud from his former customers and be deterred from patronizing him.[40]

And what is true of deceptive statements is, according to the same logic, true of information not revealed about safety, health, or product quality. For example, an airline company would be irrational, from the most coldblooded business perspective, to skimp on safety; one or two crashes could ruin the company. Similarly, a drug company would be irrational to market a product that has dangerous side-effects; the resultant fear would carry over to their other products.

According to this argument, sellers have strong incentives to meet consumers' reasonable expectations of safety, health, quality, and performance. The first factor mitigating against regulation is the force of competition. Insofar as the products of one firm attract business away from another's products, the injured firm has a strong incentive to expose any defects in its rivals or their products. Again, the threat of private litigation and recoveries of great sums deter firms from making false claims or not meeting acceptable standards of safety, health, quality, or performance.

Furthermore, numerous private and governmental organizations disseminate information about products and services; news broadcasts

are full of adverse claims about companies or their products. Penulti-
mately, many products are warranted by manufacturers or sellers, and
in many instances buyers can demand additional warranties in negotiating a purchase. Finally, the good sense and skepticism of buyers should
not be underestimated. Purchasers are not forced to buy products and
services and may compel sellers to provide information that answers
questions to their satisfaction. If prospective buyers' questions are not
reasonably answered, they may decide not to make the purchase.

Arrayed against these arguments is that in many instances manufacturers and sellers may not exercise the degree of care that they
should or that they often deceive buyers—a fact to which the many
volumes of orders entered by the FTC and other agencies attest. Such a
situation may result from: (1) an employee trying to conceal a mistake
that he hopes will never be traced to him; (2) a rational calculation that
the probable benefits outweigh probable losses, taking risk of discovery
into account; or (3) simple laxness in considering safety, health, etc. The
advocates of information regulation therefore maintain that government-imposed requirements supported by the threat of sanctions will
prod manufacturers and sellers into exercising greater care by increasing both: (1) the costs of deception or making products relatively unsafe,
unhealthful, or unreasonably low in quality or performance and (2) the
likelihood of discovery.

Techniques of Regulation over the Activity

Of course, there are costs to regulation, with greater benefits
usually resulting from the market system. Consequently, the regulatory
hand should be applied as lightly as possible consistent with the
indicated ends. Three techniques for regulation over the activity are
available to attain this compromise solution: (1) information regulation,
(2) performance standards, and (3) specification standards.

Information regulation over the activity consists simply of either
requiring a minimum informational standard (such as truthfulness in
advertising) or requiring the provision of certain information disclosing
hazards, problems, or matters of pertinence that otherwise would be
very costly for consumers to obtain. The mandatory warning on
cigarette packages, which states that consumption of the product can
lead to grave consequences, is one of the better known examples of
information regulation. The information disclosure approach has the
merits of minimizing government interference in the market and
preserving the free choice of potential purchasers instead of using a
paternalistic approach where government imposes its presumably superior judgment through standards upon both buyers and sellers.

Information regulation is inadequate under certain circumstances,
however. First, it may be extremely difficult (if not impossible) to

convey sufficient information briefly to prospective purchasers in a form that can be readily understood. For example, consider the number of parts and the complexity of the modern automobile as well as the large number of potential hazards. A book is necessary to convey the requisite information to consumers that would go into making informed judgments. Or consider the enormous number of side-effects to which consumption of a prescription drug could lead, either alone or in combination with some other pharmaceutical product. These complicated situations contrast with the simplicity of the cigarette warning. In brief, whether information regulation or a mandatory standard is more appropriate is *in part* a function of the cost or difficulty in imparting sufficient information required to make a reasonable judgment.

The choice between information regulation or imposing standards is also *in part* a function of the severity of the risk involved and the reversibility of the harm. In general, the greater the risk of harm and the less likely that it is reversible, the more likely that standards rather than information regulation will be the chosen technique. The underlying theoretical assumption is that consumers would have shown a want of sufficient intellect to make an informed judgment if they entered into a contract for a product or service below the minimum or explicit standard with respect to risk and reversibility.

Of course, this principle conflicts with the value of freedom of choice. Various people prefer diverse solutions; some would ban a high-risk product, the serious harm from which is irreversible, while others would give priority to free choice, provided consumers are sufficiently informed. Still others consider as an important factor whether risks could be reduced to more acceptable levels at prices most consumers would be willing to pay. Under these circumstances, standards—rather than information regulation—are indicated.[41] Of course, this technique would apply only if the market does not operate to make such calculations itself.

In practice, however, regulations and laws appear to be inconsistent. For example, cigarettes are subject to information disclosure, but the 1958 Delaney Amendment to the Food, Drug and Cosmetic Act bans (with certain exceptions) any food additive that is found to induce cancer in animals or humans, even though most analysts of food and drug policy see "no reason to ban an additive used at safe levels in foods consumed by man simply because much larger amounts of the same substance induced cancer in animals."[42]

Efficiency is an important consideration that should tilt policy in the direction of information regulation rather than mandatory standards in close cases (even though this argument may be rebutted). Of course, market incentives operate best when purchasers can make reasonably informed judgments on matters of quality and performance, just as they do on price. Only under such circumstances will firms routinely compete in quality and performance. Thus, information disclosure of a type that purchasers can reasonably use in making an informed judgment (and many information requirements are not useful in this way) aids efficiency.

In contrast, mandatory standards may lead to inefficiencies in both the technical and welfare senses by making inputs more expensive relative to outputs and requiring scarce resources to be used in a less productive alternative use. Information, of course, always carries a price tag, but the costs of standards almost always exceed those generated by information regulation.[43]

Nevertheless there are instances in which information regulation may be inappropriate and mandatory standards required. As we saw in Chapter 4, standards may be framed in rigid terms or in terms of minimum requirements. For example, the Food and Drug Administration has instituted regulations requiring minimum safety and efficacy standards for drugs, while the Delaney Amendment imposes a minimum standard regarding cancer-producing effects of drugs. On the other hand, the 1966 Vehicle Safety Act rigidly required automobile manufacturers to install seatbelts for all occupants, padded instrument panels, and dual-braking systems in all new cars.

Standards also may be divided into performance and specification categories. Performance standards demand the attainment of a specified result, permitting the firm to select the least costly means designed to attain that result; under specification standards, the regulator selects the means to attain the result. While not necessarily always the case, it is generally true that performance standards are minimum standards while specification standards are considered rigid ones.

As we saw in our discussion of externalities in Chapter 4, performance standards are generally preferable to specification standards since performance standards allow a firm's managers to choose the cheapest means available to attain a given end. Additionally, performance standards are usually cheaper to enforce, encourage technical change to achieve performance goals at less cost, and reduce the risk of sanction. In contrast, specification standards involve considerable loss of flexibility and act as a disincentive to technical change because of their rigidity. In some cases, however, all but one of the alternative means to a health or safety end may be ruled out, leading to the imposition of a specification standard. Except in these unusual instances, however, performance standards are considered superior to specification standards, just as minimum standards are superior to explicit, rigid ones.

CONCLUSION

The contract is one of the principal legal instruments associated with the free market system; indeed, without free contract there can be no free market, and market failure would be the standard condition, not the unusual one. For this reason, we began this chapter with a close look at the nature of the contract and its underlying assumptions. We saw that there are circumstances in which these assumptions may be unwarranted or in which regulation of contract might be otherwise justifiable. Situations exist in which the operations of contract might hinder, rather than help to attain, efficiency. This judgment gave rise to four subcategories of regulation under the aegis of equity: government agreements, discrimination, bargaining power disparity, and information disparity. But as we saw in the examination of each subcategory of equity regulation, considerable controversy exists with respect to whether the free market or regulation leads to better economic and social performance.

NOTES

1. "Stilling The Voice of Firestone," *Wall Street Journal*, July 22, 1980, p. 28.
2. For Pareto's full explanation, see Vilfredo Pareto, *The Mind and Society* (1935, New York: Dover, 1963), pp. 1456-1477.
3. Richard A. Epstein, "Unconscionability: A Critical Reappraisal," *Journal of Law & Economics* 18 (October 1975):293.
4. George Stigler, *The Citizen and the State* (Chicago, Ill.: University of Chicago Press, 1975), p. 36.
5. The best discussions of the history of contract are S. J. Stoljar, *A History of Contract at Common Law* (Canberra: Australian National University Press, 1975); and Frederick Pollock and Frederic Maitland, *The History of English Law*, 2 vols. (1898, Cambridge: Cambridge University Press, 1968), 2:184-239.
6. Adam Smith, *The Wealth of Nations* (1776, New York: Random House Modern Library, 1937), p. 423.
7. Max Weber, *Economy and Society*, trans. E. Fischoff et al., 3 vols. (New York: Bedminster Press, 1968), 1:26.
8. See Stigler, *The Citizen and the State*, pp. 178, 179.
9. Generally, see Stella Kramer, *The English Craft Gilds* (Oxford: Oxford University Press, 1928).
10. See William Robert Scott, *The Constitution and Finance of English, Scottish and Irish Joint Stock Companies to 1720*, 2 vols. (1912, New York: Peter Smith, 1951), 1:chaps. 1, 2.
11. *McCulloch* v. *Maryland*, 4 Wheat. 316 (1819); and *Trustees of Dartmouth College* v. *Woodward*, 4 Wheat. 518 (1819).
12. *Proprietors of the Charles River Bridge* v. *Proprietors of the Warren Bridge*, 11 Pet. 420 (1837).
13. The landmark article on certificates of public convenience and necessity is William K. Jones, "Origins of the Certificate of Public Convenience and

Necessity: Development in the States 1870-1920," *Columbia Law Review* 79 (April 1979):426-518.

14. Alfred E. Kahn, *The Economics of Regulation*, 2 vols. (New York: John Wiley & Sons, 1971), 2:3.

15. George W. Hilton and John F. Due, *The Electric Interurban Railways in America* (Stanford, Calif.: Stanford University Press, 1960), chap. 5.

16. Federal Communications Commission, *Policy Statement Concerning Comparative Hearings Involving Regular Renewal Applicants*, 22 FCC 2d 424 (1970), quoted in Douglas H. Ginsburg, *Regulation of Broadcasting* (St. Paul, Minn.: West Publishing Co., 1979), p. 118.

17. See Martin Glaeser, *Public Utilities in American Capitalism* (New York: Macmillan, 1957), pp. 197-205.

18. *Munn* v. *Illinois*, 94 U.S. 113 (1877).

19. *Nebbia* v. *New York*, 291 U.S. 502 (1934).

20. Walter E. Williams, "Preference, Prejudice and Difference—Racial Reasoning in Unfree Markets," *Regulation* (March/April 1979):40.

21. Ibid., p. 41.

22. Among the many articles on the subject of affirmative action, a particularly valuable collection is found in *Regulation* (September/October 1978):15-41.

23. Reprinted in *The Economic Regulation of Business and Industry*, ed. Bernard Schwartz, 5 vols. (New York: Chelsea House, 1973), 1:63; see also 1:42.

24. See the discussion in William Z. Ripley, *Railroads: Rates and Regulation* (New York: Longman, 1913), chaps. 6, 7.

25. *Hume* v. *United States*, 132 U.S. 406, 411 (1889).

26. See Alan Stone, *Economic Regulation and the Public Interest* (Ithaca, N.Y.: Cornell University Press, 1977), pp. 240-246.

27. Quoted in Charles O. Gregory and Harold A. Katz, *Labor and the Law*, 3d ed. (New York: W. W. Norton & Co., 1979), p. 62.

28. For details, see John Mendeloff, *Regulating Safety* (Cambridge, Mass.: MIT Press, 1979), pp. 15-20.

29. Quoted in Michael Levin, "Politics and Polarity," *Regulation* (November/December 1979):36.

30. William Graebner, *Coal Mining Safety in the Progressive Era* (Lexington, Ky.: University Presses of Kentucky, 1976), p. 160.

31. Mendeloff, *Regulating Safety*, pp. 16, 17.

32. David Seidman, "The Politics of Policy Analysis," *Regulation* (July/August 1977):23.

33. The following argument is based on Paul J. Halpern, "Corporate Power and Consumer Politics: The Case of Automobile Safety" (Unpublished Ph.D. dissertation, Department of Government, Harvard University, May 1972); and Paul J. Halpern, "The Corvair, The Pinto and Corporate Behavior: Implications for Regulatory Reform" (Paper presented before the Symposium on Regulatory Policy, November 1979).

34. Peter Meyer, "Entangled Freedoms," *Harper's* (June 1980):44.

35 Milton Friedman, *Capitalism and Freedom* (Chicago, Ill.: University of Chicago Press, 1962), p. 146.

36. *Farwell* v. *Chicago*, 71 Ill. 269, 272 (1874).

37. Edmund W. Kitch, Marc Isaacson, and Daniel Kasper, "The Regulation of Taxicabs in Chicago," *Journal of Law & Economics* 14 (October 1971):285-350.

38. Keith B. Leffler, "Physician Licensure: Competition and Monopoly in American Medicine," *Journal of Law & Economics* 21 (April 1978):165-186; and Lawrence Shephard, "Licensing Restrictions and the Cost of Dental Care," ibid., pp. 187-202.
39. See *Mary Carter Paint Co.*, 60 FTC 1786 (1962).
40. Richard Posner, *Regulation of Advertising by the FTC* (Washington, D.C.: American Enterprise Institute, 1973), p. 5.
41. National Commission on Product Safety, *Final Report of the National Commission on Product Safety* (Washington, D.C.: Government Printing Office, 1970), p. 11.
42. Rita Ricardo Campbell, *Food Safety Legislation* (Washington, D.C.: American Enterprise Institute, 1974), p. 4.
43. A particularly good study of the costs imposed by mandatory standards is Thomas M. Lenard, "Lawn Mower Safety," in *Benefit-Cost Analysis of Social Regulation*, ed. James C. Miller III and Bruce Yandle (Washington, D.C.: American Enterprise Institute, 1979), pp. 61-74.

PART III

The Politics of
Regulation

I n the following three chapters, we will focus on the behavior of those involved in the regulatory process. Most Americans and their public officials at every level of government hold to an ideology that roughly corresponds to the structure developed in the preceding chapters; that is, they generally believe that the free market offers the best alternative in most situations but that in others the free market needs to be supplemented by regulation or some other policy technique. This is not to say that most Americans or their public officials have a clearly articulated grand theory of when such supplementing should be undertaken. Rather, often the reasons for regulation in a particular case may be translated into one of the regulatory justifications—efficiency, externalities, and equity—discussed in Part II.

Firms, industries, legislators, and regulatory administrators often seek to advance policies not for the general interest but for some special one that benefits them. However, the likelihood of success is greater if a special interest can reasonably be portrayed as a general one. The process of doing this is politics.

But this is not always the case. Chapter 6 provides a framework for understanding legislative processes in the regulatory arena. Whereas Part II helped us to *evaluate* legislative action, Chapter 6 will help us to *understand* legislative behavior. In understanding the legislative role in regulation, however, one point is critical: the legislative role is not discontinuous. Congress does not simply create an agency and then forget about it.

Although Congress is the birthplace of regulatory activity at the national level, it frequently monitors and attempts to influence the behavior of those who administer its statutes. In Chapter 7 we will see that while in major respects the administration of regulatory programs is an independent process primarily guided by formal law and procedure, in other respects it is an interactive process. Regulatory administrators also must be attentive to Congress, the president, interest groups, and other actors in the political process.

Since regulation is an interactive process, it is not surprising that the not infrequent failure of regulatory programs to fully achieve performance goals has resulted in proposals for reform. In the final chapter, we will look at the reasons for widespread support of the regulatory reform movement that began in the late 1970s and will critically examine some of the most important reform techniques that have been advanced.

In undertaking this examination, we will look at the connections between regulation and other major societal concerns. Often, as we observed in Chapter 1, significant changes in regulatory direction occur not because defects in the substance or process of regulation are found—these always exist—but rather because other societal changes demand a re-examination of the way regulation impinges on them. We will see in Chapter 8 that problems such as inflation and the United States' changing place in the world economy are playing these kinds of roles in the 1980s.

6

Regulatory Legislation

The legislative process in regulatory legislation is similar to that in other policy areas, but regulatory laws also tend to have certain peculiarities. This chapter is intended to explain why. After listing some of the major characteristics of regulatory legislation, we will examine what activities Congress undertakes in the realm of regulation and the processes and structures by which it engages in these regulatory tasks. Using the law-and-economics approach that assumes legislators behave rationally in attaining goals, we will examine the legislative incentive structure—the political behavioral rules that are akin to rules governing economic behavior such as profit maximization. Then we will look at probable legislative behavior within this legislative incentive structure.

After this journey through the regulatory process, we will understand why regulatory legislation usually reflects compromise among a variety of interest groups, why it is likely to contain both symbolic language as well as language with substantive impact, and why such legislation usually devolves much interpretative authority to regulatory agencies.

WHAT IS DIFFERENT ABOUT REGULATORY LEGISLATION?

In certain respects, regulatory legislation is similar to legislation concerning any topic. It is subject to the same institutional and informal legislative rules and procedures as other types of legislation. But there are three peculiar tendencies of regulatory legislation that are different from other types of statutes in ways that affect the shape of regulatory legislation.

First, regulatory legislation involves relatively low *direct* costs to the taxpayer, although, of course, *particular* enactments in other policy areas may also involve low direct costs. For example, a particular military appropriations bill may not require much budgetary outlay; but as a class of policies, military and foreign policy activities do involve substantial sums of money. In contrast, the direct costs of all regulatory programs constitute only approximately 1 percent of the federal budget, although many analysts have argued that the indirect costs that result from business compliance with regulatory programs and forgone investment opportunities are much greater (as we will see in Chapter 8).

The second distinctive tendency of regulatory programs is that they are usually of concern to a variety of interest groups and are usually susceptible to *substantive* bargaining and compromise over subject matter. Of course, other categories of legislation may also be subject to bargaining and compromise, but often—as tax, transfer payments, and defense policies illustrate—their bargaining and compromise negotiations *usually* concern sums of money expended or taxed, not the substantive shape of the program. When controversy over the substance of such nonregulatory programs does occur, the dispute usually stems from ideological differences involving the proper role of government. In contrast, the dispute in regulatory policies usually stems from perceptions of relative costs or benefits to particular interest groups affected by the legislation.

Third, because of this substantive bargaining, the language of regulatory legislation generally can be reshaped to reflect such compromises but often only with considerable difficult negotiation. For example, an environmental statute may require the Environmental Protection Agency to take marginal costs and marginal benefits into account in making policy; or such language may be absent in the legislation, allowing the agency considerable discretion in that regard; or the language may forbid the EPA to consider costs and require it to consider only benefits; or the language may contain still some other variation. Of course, the particular language chosen will relatively please or displease groups with vested interests in the legislation, such as steel companies, environmentalists, medical groups, etc. In brief, there are frequently several—sometimes many—interest groups concerned about the particular substantive outcome of regulatory legislation, and the resultant legislative action reflects substantive bargaining and compromise.

Legislative Functions

Before discussing legislative behavior in the regulatory area in more detail, we must look at the specific tasks that Congress undertakes in connection with regulation. It is important to realize that the legislative process with respect to any regulatory area is dynamic; Congress does not simply create an agency and forget about it. Second, it is important to understand the informal and formal legislative rules of the game, for they can have a major impact on the shape of legislative regulatory action.

Congress is concerned with regulatory legislation at many different levels. First, of course, Congress creates agencies and decides how they will fit into the structure of the executive branch, choosing among three basic types of regulatory agency. Congress may decide to create an independent commission consisting of five or more commissioners, one of whom chairs the agency. Such agencies may act *relatively* more independently of the president than the second and third types of agency. Commission members are appointed by the president and confirmed by the Senate for staggered terms and can be removed by the president only for good cause. The Federal Trade Commission is an example of this type of regulatory agency.

Second, Congress may create an independent agency outside the structure of the formal cabinet posts, whose administrator serves at the pleasure of the president. The Environmental Protection Agency is this type of regulatory agency. Third, Congress may create an agency headed by an administrator and place it within a cabinet department so that the administrator is formally responsible to a department secretary. The administrator, after appointment and confirmation, serves at the pleasure of the president. The Occupational Safety and Health Administration, located within the Department of Labor, is an example of this type of regulatory agency.

Unfortunately, no one has yet devised a theory covering the range of regulatory agencies created since 1887 (the date of the Interstate Commerce Commission's creation) to explain why Congress chooses particular types of agencies in different instances. In any event, while an agency's organizational form clearly makes a difference in operating style, the best evidence indicates that form is not an impediment to performance.[1]

As discussed in Chapter 1, Congress creates a new agency and provides it with an *organic statute* that sets forth its responsibilities, procedures, sanctions, etc. Thus, the FTC was created in 1914, and its organic statute establishing its responsibilities was the Federal Trade Commission Act. But that organic statute, like most others, has been amended by Congress on several occasions—sometimes adding new responsibilities, sometimes fashioning new procedures. Indeed, amendments may cover virtually any matter contained in the organic statute. An agency's responsibilities and activities may be changed not only through an amending statute, however, but by a new statute as well. Congress usually chooses to enact a new statute when it enlarges or changes an agency's jurisdiction in an important way. For example, at various times, Congress has granted the FTC new responsibilities over the labeling of various products, such as furs or textiles. These statutes not only expanded the agency's jurisdiction but also established new and detailed procedures and sanctions.

Thus, Congress interacts with regulatory agencies frequently. But when we consider other important legislative functions, it is clear that regulatory agencies must always perform their tasks with legislative response in mind. First of all, they must consider each chamber's annual appropriations process. Congressional appropriations subcommittees examine the annual proposed budgets of agencies in extreme detail. While this does not imply that these subcommittees do their jobs well or comprehensively, they do focus on many particulars in their questioning of agency officials. Congress is apt to cut budget requests not only on efficiency or priority grounds but on substantive grounds as well. That is, if Congress determines some agency program or proposed program is not justified, it may decline to grant funds for it or attach restrictive conditions to the use of appropriated funds.

Congress also performs oversight and investigative functions. Committees and subcommittees with appropriate oversight jurisdiction investigate an agency's activities—or nonactivities. For example, in July 1980 the House Government Operations Committee's Subcommittee on Environment, Energy and Natural Resources conducted an oversight hearing on EPA activities in the area of ground water contamination from industrial pits and ponds. While hearings followed by a report is the traditional way Congress conducts oversight, committees and subcommittees may also require agencies to submit periodic reports, which are examined by legislative staff. In contrast to the oversight function, Congress's investigative function involves looking at policy problems rather than agency performance. For example, both the Senate and House Small Business committees have examined such questions as the cumulative impact of regulations upon the operations of small business. Proposed legislation is frequently associated with such investigations, although this is not always the case.

The final formal congressional function that we will discuss is the newest and the least developed—the legislative veto. The Federal Trade Commission, with its changing level of support within Congress, has been the central focus of this development. Swept along in the tide of consumerism, in 1974 Congress greatly enlarged FTC enforcement powers, goading the agency to more vigorous action. By 1977, the mood of Congress had changed, and the FTC was subjected to intensive legislative criticism for some of its actions. In the course of its activities during the three-year interval, the FTC had affronted many businesses that maintained agency actions were unfair and injurious to their operations. What is more, the mood of Congress by that time had begun to change to the extent that some regulations were perceived as too costly or inflationary or otherwise adversely affecting productivity. Nevertheless, the FTC did not retreat and defended its activities despite sharp legislative criticism.

Among the legislative proposals advanced in Congress was one allowing either the Senate or the House to veto any trade regulation rule promulgated by the agency. While Congress had already enacted more than 200 legislative veto provisions, this was the first time this device had ever been applied to a regulatory agency. The compromise that ultimately was reached in May 1980 allowed Congress to veto many FTC rules if both houses of Congress approved, and the precedent of a legislative veto over regulatory activity had been established.[2]

This incident also illustrates the informal powers of Congress. Simply because of the formal congressional powers that we have examined, regulatory agencies must be attuned to the mood of Congress and its general concerns. An agency, to avoid being threatened by Congress, at least should not conflict with this prevailing mood. Thus, in the FTC legislative veto case, the agency failed to read the mood of Congress and thus almost invited Congress to "clip its wings." Agencies, including the FTC, do not usually respond this way. To the contrary, they are usually attentive not only to the general mood of Congress but also to the particular views, whims, and interests of the legislators, especially powerful figures on committees with jurisdiction over agency activities. The FTC, for example, at one time expedited almost any request from a legislator, especially if it arose from a complaint of a constituent in whom the legislator took a particular interest. The FTC opened a field office in Oak Ridge, Tennessee—a small city that was the home of a powerful legislator, Democratic Representative Joe Evins— even though its other field offices had been located only in the largest commercial centers. In these ways as well as others, agencies have usually sought to cultivate and maintain good relations with Congress.

Regulators thus must be continuously attentive to Congress, but it does not follow that they are nothing more than the dutiful servants of legislators. There is a wide range between such a posture and agency attentiveness to Congress. Indeed, as we will see in the next chapter, concern about legislative response is only one factor that affects agency behavior. This stems in part from the problem of information costs, which have been important in many of our discussions. Regulatory agencies undertake a vast number of individual actions each year. Until recently their number had expanded. At the same time, the number of nonregulatory matters Congress considers also increased. Accordingly, it is virtually impossible for any legislator to be reasonably familiar with even a small fraction of the subjects upon which Congress is expected to act.

Rules and Structure

Congress has responded to the information cost problem in the same way that other organizations have—through specialization and the division of labor. Formally, each chamber is divided into committees, each with its own specialized jurisdiction. In turn, each committee is divided into various subcommittees with specialized jurisdiction within the wider committee framework.

Almost every committee has some regulatory jurisdiction. The House Energy and Commerce Committee's regulatory jurisdiction is extremely widespread. Among the committee's subcommittees are: (1) Telecommunications, Consumer Protection and Finance, (2) Health and the Environment, and (3) Commerce, Transportation and Tourism. Thus, most matters dealing with the Securities and Exchange Commission would fall within the jurisdiction of the first of these, most Food and Drug Administration matters under the second, and most Interstate Commerce Commission activities within the third subcommittee's jurisdiction.

Except for appropriations matters (which are sent to the appropriate Appropriations Committee subcommittees), all other matters are handled by committees and subcommittees with substantive jurisdiction. Some matters fall within the jurisdiction of two or more committees, however, and decisions about which committee has jurisdiction over a bill are made by the leadership in each chamber. While only a small percentage of the bills introduced in each session of Congress are even considered by either chamber, the "lucky ones" are usually accorded a committee hearing. In this process, witnesses from interested groups and affected agencies, others in the executive branch, and concerned legislators are granted an opportunity to testify and present documents in support of their respective positions.

These congressional rules and structures have responded in a very rational manner to the enormous information problem posed by the size and scope of contemporary American government. First, the hearings are intended to inform legislators, and it is customary for all viewpoints to be presented and considered. Second, committee and subcommittee staffs are conversant with the subjects that must be considered, and they inform the committee and subcommittee members in the course of both on- and off-the-record conversations. Third, it is not uncommon for legislators to serve on the same committee through many terms, thereby accumulating much knowledge about and experience in a particular subject. The reports prepared on the bills considered and acted upon by committees are intended to inform other members of Congress about the reasons for policy decisions in much the same way that memoranda from lower officials in corporations to top policymakers are intended to summarize a substantial amount of information.

One should not infer that this decisionmaking system *necessarily* always supplies sufficient information to make a reasoned judgment, only that the rules and structure are a rational response to the information problem. Nor should one infer that Congress acts on any regulatory matter it considers only upon rational deduction from the information developed. Rather, in making their decisions on whether to act and how to do so, legislators engage in a complex calculus. They often—but hardly always—consider policy issues within a framework that can be translated into our regulatory justifications. But even when legislators do think in such terms, they consider many other factors, including interest group pressures, impact on future election prospects, impact on constituents or important segments of them, and the favorable or unfavorable publicity value that will come from taking a strong stand on an issue.

THE ENVIRONMENT OF REGULATORY LEGISLATION

We will now examine some of the factors involved in legislative behavior in the regulatory arena. First, we will consider two factors that circumscribe legislative behavior in the regulatory area and weigh heavily on the probable success of regulatory bills: the public philosophy and the element of crisis. Then we will discuss legislative behavior in the regulatory area to determine what factors facilitate enactment of regulatory legislation.

The Public Philosophy

Typically, inaction in any situation is an easier course to take than action. Indeed, only 5 to 10 percent of the bills introduced in each session of Congress ultimately become law. Yet there have been certain periods during which a large number of important, ground-breaking regulatory proposals did become law. As we noted in Chapter 1, these periods constitute the great waves of regulation between which few novel proposals are enacted and the pace of regulatory activity slows down considerably.

Our first problem is to provide some suitable generalizations about these peculiar patterns of intense regulatory activity followed by relative dormancy, followed by another burst of activity, etc. Each period is characterized by a change in the prevailing public philosophy—a set of general themes concerning the appropriate role of government, its limits, and the best ways to attain desired performance. In some periods, such as the New Deal, the public philosophy has called for an active, highly interventionist government role, while at other times the prevailing public philosophy has mandated a relatively passive government role or urged government to disentangle itself from activities in the economic and social spheres.

Of course, it is outside the scope of this book to determine why the public philosophy changes over time. The important point here is that legislation is more likely to be enacted if it is consonant with the prevailing public philosophy than if the proposal is either at variance with that philosophy or outside its scope. Thus, during the recent era when many regulatory laws were enacted because of their purported benefit to consumers, a new proposal likely would have fared better if it was based on its alleged gains for consumers. At times the public philosophy merges with one of our regulatory justifications—for as John Maynard Keynes observed, the writings of theorists do have ways of filtering through to policymakers. At other times, however, the two do not merge.

An example will illustrate these points more concretely. Prices during the Great Depression sank to extreme lows relative to their high levels during the 1920s. At the same time, the severe economic conditions generally affected smaller firms more severely than larger ones whose reserves permitted them to withstand adverse national economic conditions more effectively. The predictable result was that a large number of small and medium-sized firms failed. Consequently, part of the public philosophy during the New Deal called for the development of measures that would increase—or at least stabilize—prices and stem the tide of business failures.

Taking advantage of this sentiment and the concomitant fear of monopoly, business groups successfully sponsored legislation in Congress that: (1) forbade suppliers from charging large customers lower prices than small ones under many circumstances and extending the antidiscrimination principle to advertising allowances and the furnishing of services (the Robinson-Patman Act); (2) permitted manufacturers to set the retail price of trademarked goods (and thereby prevent retail price competition) if a state enacted enabling legislation; and (3) stabilized agricultural prices under many statutes. While not every group was able to take advantage of this part of the New Deal public philosophy, one of the major histories of the period concluded:

> Generally, the prizes . . . went to the groups with the greatest cohesion, the strongest political organization, and the *most plausible arguments for linking their own special interests with the current conception of the public interest.*[3] (Emphasis supplied)

More recently, an antibusiness public philosophy developed during the 1960s. Its call was for curbing "business excess" in the name of the consumer through stringent governmental regulation. But while this public philosophy (most closely associated with consumer activist Ralph Nader) is clearly different from that which prevailed during the New Deal, the underlying principle has remained the same. From the perspective of both legislators and interest groups, the problem is linking a special interest with the public interest. The new social groups in the consumerist era were not solely concerned with advancing the public weal because of some abstract commitment to virtue; rather, the presumed benefits that the "new regulation" would bring were seen as increasing their individual welfares through environmental purity, safer drugs, etc., in the same way that higher prices were supposed to increase the welfares of advocates of New Deal regulation. In both cases, special interests were linked to a prevailing public philosophy.[4]

As we will see in Chapter 8, the public philosophy recently has changed again. The early 1980s have been characterized by an attempt to "deregulate" and reduce some government regulations. But while the public philosophy may change, once regulation that has been enacted in part because of its linkage to a public philosophy is in place, agencies created have a *tendency* to persist. But the prevailing public philosophy is only one of several factors important in the regulatory process; and unless other factors are also present, it may be insufficient for enactment of legislation.

Crisis and Regulation

Political scientist James Q. Wilson has observed that the enactment of some regulation—especially those policies that confer general benefits at a cost borne by a small section of society—is aided immeasurably

> by the efforts of a skilled entrepreneur who can mobilize latent public sentiment (by revealing a scandal or capitalizing on a crisis), [and] put the opponents of the plan publicly on the defensive by accusing them of deforming babies or killing motorists.[5]

Clearly, common sense and a great deal of evidence indicate the truthfulness of Wilson's perception, not only in cases that confer general benefits at the expense of a small group but in other regulatory situations as well. Of course, this does not mean that a crisis is a *necessary* condition for the enactment of regulatory legislation, for there are numerous cases of regulatory enactment without a concomitant or preceding crisis. But a crisis greatly enhances the likelihood that a bill on the subject will be enacted.

At one level, the reason for the greater attention to crisis associated with legislation is clear. Legislators are confronted with a much larger number of demands for action than they can handle effectively. Moreover, workload tends to increase with each session of Congress because legislators must not only attend to new matters but must also exercise oversight over existing legislation. Since the number of members of each legislative body remains relatively constant over time, this implies an ever-increasing difficulty for any particular proposal to claim the attention of a sufficient number of legislators to force action on it.[6]

Given this problem, the most effective way for a group to force legislators to devote attention to its favored legislative project is to heighten legislators' perceived costs if they ignore the situation. Legislators are concerned about their chances for re-election and/or their party's future prospects. If they can be persuaded to reasonably believe that their prospects or those of their parties will diminish considerably by ignoring a matter, they are more apt to pay attention to it. Similarly, legislators tend to take a strong interest in a bill if they feel they can receive a benefit from such action. Once again, the prospect of obtaining support for themselves and/or their party provides the strong incentive.

What is a crisis? Crises commonly involve the perceived threat or actual imposition of greatly increased costs and/or the long-term irreversibility of such costs. Thus, in one of the most serious post-World War II crises—the 1962 Cuban missile crisis in which the Soviet Union surrepticiously placed missiles with nuclear warheads in Cuba—the United States was faced with the large potential cost of enormous destruction at the hands of the Soviet Union. Recent oil crises stemming from attempts of the Organization of Petroleum Exporting Countries (OPEC) to foreclose the shipment of petroleum to western nations involved the threat of severe economic costs ensuing from an oil shortage.

These cases are dramatic illustrations of the crisis phenomena. But while a sharp dividing line between crisis and noncrisis situations is clearly difficult (if not impossible) to draw, many situations can be reasonably described as crises without reaching the scale and scope of potential cost entailed in the Cuban missile crisis or a worldwide oil shortage. A crisis is a situation that involves an actual or perceived increase in costs or their risk to a government or firm, industry, sector, or group. Sometimes the crisis erupts suddenly, while at others it mounts incrementally until the gravity of the situation is finally perceived. The sudden enormous losses sustained by the Chrysler Corporation in the late 1970s, for example, constituted a crisis, as did the gradual decline of the American textile industry in the face of Asian competition. Finally, a crisis need not be as cataclysmic as the Cuban missile crisis; significantly lower cost imposition can still result in a crisis situation.

The Thalidomide Crisis

A crisis can trigger intensive action on the part of interest groups and government officials to give high priority to appropriate public policy. An almost classic illustration involves the 1962 Amendments to the Pure Food and Drug Act, which imposed more stringent testing standards before new drugs could be marketed.[7]

In 1958, Democratic Senator Estes Kefauver of Tennessee, chairman of the Senate Antitrust and Monopoly Subcommittee, and his staff initiated an investigation of prescription drug prices, with formal hearings beginning in 1960. Whereas medical researchers tended to support the critical thrust of the Kefauver inquiry while drug companies resisted it, the general public was largely indifferent, both at the beginning and after 26 months of hearings that ended in February 1962. Nevertheless, Kefauver and his supporters maintained that the evidence demanded a bill directed toward drug pricing, advertising, marketing, and testing practices. A carefully drafted bill, rewritten to replace a loosely worded one, was introduced in March 1962. It drew little support in Congress, lukewarm support from President John F. Kennedy and his advisers, and vigorous opposition from pharmaceutical manufacturers and other business groups.

The likelihood that the bill would be enacted was very low at that point. In April 1962, however, a Johns Hopkins University professor of pediatrics read a paper before the American College of Physicians in which she reported that a presumably harmless sleeping pill, known as thalidomide, taken by women in the early stages of pregnancy had resulted in more than 35,000 deformed babies, mainly in West Germany. The resultant widespread publicity led to sharply heightened public awareness of the problem and a strong fear that the existing law concerning the marketing of drugs was inadequate to protect public health. The Kefauver bill suddenly jumped to the top of the legislative agenda and was soon enacted, although in a form far different than initially proposed.

Analyzing this incident, we see that the costs to legislators of losing public support rose significantly after the thalidomide "crisis." Due to the widespread publicity, the issue became sufficiently salient to constitute an important issue to legislators. Legislators perceived that they could employ support of a new drug bill to illustrate concern for their constituents and thereby increase the likelihood of future electoral success.

The pharmaceutical manufacturers reacted to the thalidomide crisis in a significant way. They clearly could not appear to be smugly indifferent to the incident and the danger of a public overreaction. Therefore, the drug producers switched their tactic from outright opposition to one in support of a weaker regulatory bill—without the patent and price regulation that Kefauver and his supporters had deemed equally as important as the new testing procedures. And by greatly facilitating legislative negotiation necessary to enact a new law quickly, the manufacturers obtained, in their opinion, a far less objectionable statute than what might have resulted from continued opposition. Finally, the thalidomide crisis also illustrates that human agents must manipulate a crisis, bringing whatever resources that they can command to bear on the situation. An academic paper presented to a small medical convention might have gone unnoticed, but the forces aligned with Senator Kefauver translated the findings into a simple, grim story and skillfully publicized it.

As we observed earlier, a crisis does not *necessarily* lead to the enactment of new regulatory legislation. Although a crisis situation clearly facilitates enactment, that opportunity must first be seized. In the thalidomide case, the mustering of public opinion through widespread media dissemination was a crucial intervening variable, but it is hardly the only one used in response to crisis. There are some cases in which political actors view the crisis as so *objectively* important that they feel compelled to act without the intervention of public opinion or interest group action. The widespread failure of banks during the Great Depression, which led to banking regulation, provides a good example of this role of crisis. A crisis for a particular interest group can also trigger that group to reconsider a political strategy previously employed, resulting in a new, innovative one that will simultaneously alleviate the crisis conditions and draw sufficient support from other groups to enhance the likelihood that legislation favorable to it will be enacted.

Crisis and the Economic Order: Banking

In the banking industry, crisis constituted the critical spur that a group needed to devise an effective legislative strategy. In this case, legislators were not the prime movers of legislative proposals but rather responded to the activities of interest groups. Whereas the crisis in the thalidomide case arose from a sudden, unforeseen event extraneous to the plight of a producer group, in the case of banking regulation political actors felt compelled to respond to crises because of the intrinsic importance of the economic sector. Banks and other lending institutions provide credit throughout the economy, channel spare funds into investments, provide means of payment, and create money. No demonstration is required to show that banking is not just another industry among equals; rather, the malfunctioning of this important sector can affect the entire economy.

Every *major* piece of banking regulatory legislation was ultimately enacted in response to a crisis. The two principle Civil War statutes stemmed from the government's financial crisis during that war; the 1913 Federal Reserve Act followed the financial panic of 1907; the Emergency Banking Act of 1933 was associated with the catastrophic bank failures during the early part of the Great Depression; and the 1980 Depository Institutions and Monetary Control Act stemmed from the impact of high and accelerating rates of inflation on financial institutions.

Rapid rates of inflation during the years preceding the 1980 statute made some features mandated by the 1933 law very undesirable from the perspective of banks and other lending institutions. The unattractiveness to depositors of noninterest-paying checking accounts and the interest-rate ceilings on time deposits mandated by the 1933 law compelled banking institutions to search for ways of evading these requirements in order to attract deposits that would sustain strong loan demand. This motivation led to the development of devices such as certificates of deposit, negotiable-orders-of-withdrawal (NOW) accounts, and pay-by-phone systems—all involving not only ways of circumventing existing interest regulations but also invasions by each type of institution into services and functions that were traditionally associated with and limited to other institutional types. After a considerable delay attributable to the difficulty of resolving the complex issues without seriously displeasing contending interest groups, Congress enacted the 1980 statute in a move toward freer competition among financial institutions, albeit still within a pervasive regulatory framework.

Crisis and Legislative Incentives

Crisis, then, is one of the more effective ways to move regulatory issues to the top of the legislative agenda. Crisis leads to this result either because of the inherent importance of the issue, as in banking regulation, or because it greatly increases the saliency of the issue to the public and/or affected interest groups. Looked at in a different way, crisis raises the costs of inaction relative to the costs imposed by political action. The spur to action by one interested group spurs, in turn, mobilization and action by others affected. Thus, the thalidomide incident at first mobilized only those interests seeking drug law reform. But because of their action and the potential harm of adverse legislation, the potential costs of inaction to the pharmaceutical manufacturers—who originally opposed reform—were also increased. Nevertheless, we must remember that crisis is only one factor—although an important one—that can lead to regulatory legislation. Statutes can be enacted without the intervention of a crisis, and some crises never lead to the enactment of a statute.

In addition, it is important to appreciate that legislators are not simply passive agents who react to crises. They are very often political entrepreneurs who have prepared legislation far in advance of a situation's full-blown development into a crisis. Senator Kefauver, in the thalidomide case, had proposed new pharmaceutical regulation well before 1962; moreover, he actively contributed to publicizing the medical findings. Similarly, banking reform bills had been incubating for many legislative sessions prior to their enactments. In each successful case of enactment—as well as other regulatory cases not involving crisis—the political entrepreneurs were able to utilize their skills in bargaining and otherwise operating within the framework of legislative motivation.

THE ENVIRONMENT OF LEGISLATIVE MOTIVATION

Economic and Legislative Incentive Structures

Can we make certain assumptions about legislative motivation in the area of regulation? This question leads to two distinct inquiries. First, we must look at the environment of legislative motivation, and, second, we must analyze motivation itself. Then we will be able to determine what factors lead to success in enacting regulatory legislation. What must groups interested in new legislation do to induce legislative action—or, for that matter, inaction?

Our starting point is the legislative environment, with particular attention paid to the differences and similarities in incentives between the legislative and the economic realms. In the economic realm, the motivation assumption follows from the nature of business. Unless a firm seeks to maximize profits, it will exit from the competitive race; even a monopolistic firm must do the same in order to attract new capital.

Many attempts have been made to employ economic categories and principles to the political activities of affected interests, legislators, and regulatory administrators. Clearly, there is much to be said for such attempts, but there are significant differences between the economic and political realms that preclude a mechanical application of the more precise formulations developed in the economic realm to politics.

James Q. Wilson has pointed out three ways in which the political arena differs from the economic.[8] First, while in the economic realm one can assume that each person's goals are identical—wealth maximization—this is not true of the political arena for two reasons. Given the principal resource employed in the economic realm—money—one is compelled to rank-order preferences and make choices. Given one's income and assets, a person must choose, for example, between a boat or a new car. But in the legislative realm, legislators can choose cheap energy prices as well as a 100 percent environmental cleanup without any disciplining agent—such as money—that compels them to consider trade-offs: they need only pass laws requiring both.

Put a different way, the economic realm virtually compels a person or firm to make rational assessments in selecting alternative means and competing ends. But this is not true of the political realm because nothing *compels* rational choice (even though it sometimes may be more realistic). Additionally, nothing compels us to quantify goals in the political realm, whereas each goal in the economic realm—e.g., the boat and the new car—has a price tag.

The second principal difference that Wilson observed between the economic and political realms lies in the nature of choice. In the economic realm, one can make *individual* choices, the only condition being economic viability—does it make a profit? Thus, I can be among a very small minority that collects records of Burundi folk music and not one of a vast majority that collects rock records.

But this is not true in the political realm, for political action requires majority approval before it is instituted. This fact has several implications for the political realm. First, in the political realm, minorities are bound by the action undertaken in the name of the majority, whereas majority and even small minority preferences may be satisfied simultaneously in the economic realm. Second, in the economic realm we may reasonably assume that, if the production and sale of a product are economically viable, some entrepreneur will undertake to supply it. This is not necessarily the case in the political realm, for, as we have noted, only a small percentage of the total number of bills introduced in Congress are acted upon—at least in the short run. Consequently, our wants in the political realm may not be acted upon even though they are viable in the sense that they *could* be acted upon and instituted.

The third principal difference between the economic and political realms is more a matter of degree than kind. Wilson has asserted that while preferences in the economic realm are given and come into being outside it, this is not true of the political realm. He wrote: "What people want is thought to arise from outside the market ... only how much they purchase is affected by the market." [9] In contrast, the very essence of politics, Wilson argued, consists of attempting to change preferences. This argument is overdrawn, however, for a great deal of economic activity in the forms of advertising and promotion is devoted to changing intraproduct and interproduct preferences. Furthermore, political candidates often are promoted and advertised in the same manner as products; in both cases, the intention is to seduce consumers to desire that which is offered.

Nevertheless, there are significant differences in the preference structures. In the economic realm, producers often must be careful to design products that meet the claims made about them. The baked beans must taste "good"; the small automobile must provide high gas mileage; the ethical drug must cure the disease. Failure to meet such claims is irrational if repeat sales are important (the typical situation) because customers would switch to other brands or away from the product entirely. This is not to suggest that deception and exaggeration do not take place—far from it. Rather, I am emphasizing that a considerable body of information must be provided about a product in order to induce a purchase in the first instance, and sellers have considerable incentive to assure that the product meets the induced expectations in order to assure repeat sales.

Is the same equally as true in the political realm? No, for a variety of reasons, the most important of which are: (1) the costs of not meeting a preference are not as high in the political realm, and (2) there are strong disincentives to providing extensive information about "products" (which translate into policy preferences and accurate reasons for desiring particular preferences). Legislators are in the fortunate position of being able to demand the production of the best possible product—a 100 percent cleanup of the environment, for example—and then to shift the blame on administrators or regulated firms if these goals are not met. In the economic realm, this would be analogous to a case where a firm produced automobiles of Rolls-Royce cost and quality and then complained about the failure of the sales force in marketing large quantities.

In other words, legislators can often evade bearing the costs of not making a rational decision on a regulatory matter that would weigh the trade-offs and alternative means carefully. Instead, they have a strong incentive to demand the highest possible goal and leave the problem of means to administrators and regulated firms so that the latter can be blamed for failures. In so doing, legislators have an incentive to provide ambiguous, unclear—or even no—information on the means by which to achieve policy goals.

Symbolic Politics and Interest Group Liberalism

This dynamic may in part account for what political scientist Murray Edelman has termed "symbolic politics." In a work replete with case studies, Edelman concluded that "mass publics respond to currently conspicuous political symbols: not to 'facts' ... but to the gestures and speeches that make up the drama of the state." [10] Since it is virtually costless or at least much cheaper for legislators to deal in grand gesture and symbolic ambiguity rather than in the difficult and costly process of accumulating data, weighing costs and benefits, and assessing alternative means, they have a clear incentive to choose the symbolic path.

This dynamic may also account for one of the consequences of what Theodore J. Lowi has described as "interest group liberalism": ". . . the shift from explicit legislative standards toward general instructions to administrators." [11] Lowi has argued that this trend became more pronounced after the 1930s—an undeniable assertion—but some of the best examples antedate that decade. For example, well before the 1930s the Interstate Commerce Commission was charged with approving reasonable rates and the Federal Trade Commission was charged with declaring "unfair methods of competition" unlawful. But at the same time—as well as since—Congress enacted legislation containing much more explicit standards. Can the same set of motivations explain the fact that Congress has simultaneously enacted symbolic, discretionary, and explicit legislation?

An example of explicit legislation will illustrate how this can be done. In December 1970, Congress enacted a law imposing very stringent emission standards upon automobile manufacturers. [12] The strict time schedule, obvious disregard for cost or technical feasibility, and the substantial fine of $10,000 for each car not meeting the standards were all quite explicit. The statute was prepared: (1) without any significant evidence in the hearings that reducing or even eliminating auto emissions would have any detectable effect on the nation's health and (2) without regard to cost or technical feasibility. As Howard Margolis explained: "The issue was almost entirely perceived as the auto industry versus the public interest in a cleaner environment." [13]

The two principal politicians involved in the legislation, President Richard Nixon and Democratic Senator Edmund Muskie of Maine, had strong incentives to produce a tough bill:

> Senator Muskie (then the most probable Democratic nominee for President) was Mr. Environment in Congress. Nixon had every incentive to try to seize the auto-pollution issue from him; Muskie in turn had every incentive to try to outdo whatever Nixon proposed. [14]

The automobile industry did not vigorously resist the enactment of the law, an *apparently* surprising fact. But from its perspective, the bill was the best one for which the industry could have hoped. As Margolis shrewdly observed:

> The bill merely demanded that industry do what it felt to be impossible. But there is a certain comfort in being asked for the impossible: you know you will not actually have to do it. And to the extent that the Muskie standards could in fact be approached, automobile owners, not the automobile industry, would have to pay the price. From the standpoint of the auto industry [this goal] . . . was clearly preferable to . . . developing a nonpolluting engine . . . to replace the internal combustion engine. . . . [15]

This example illustrates that the legislative incentive to evade bearing the costs involved in statutory enactment can apply to explicit as well as symbolic and discretionary legislation. In each case, political gain can be expected for advocating the best solution, regardless of cost, and the inevitable costs that result can be deflected upon administrators or—as in the auto emissions example—the regulated firms. The costs to these firms, as Margolis noted, were low relative to those that could have been imposed under other real alternatives, while the gains to environmental groups were significant to the extent that the auto emission abatement goals would be met.

Similarly, discretionary regulatory legislation achieves for legislators the semblance of having done something yet being able, again, to deflect costs upon others. Symbolic legislation rarely exists as a pure type in the regulatory arena because a set of commands coupled with sanctions is an inherent part of regulation. Yet as the automobile emission case illustrates, symbolism is an important component of both explicit and discretionary regulatory legislation. Indeed, inflated claims about what legislation will accomplish are a vital component of the legislative incentive structure.

Putting all of this in perspective, we can see that these legislators are confronted with strong incentives to provide the appearance of having given maximum benefits because they can deflect the burden of bearing the costs onto administrators or regulated firms. Thus, in the regulatory-political as well as the economic realm, producers both respond to given consumer preferences and try to create new preferences—if they perceive potential benefit from such activity. In the economic realm, however, a firm is disciplined by the need to obtain correct information, make instrumentally rational decisions based on cost and trade-off considerations, and coordinate decisionmaking between the production, sales, and other departments under the direction of a central authority focused on the overriding goal of profit maximization. Similarly, a firm's decision whether to undertake a function internally or contract for its performance with another firm is based on the same considerations.[16] In contrast, although there are overall budgetary constraints, a legislator looking at individual regulatory programs—each of whose costs are but a minor part of the whole budget—has a strong incentive to advocate or support new legislation if it will yield political benefit. And the costs to legislators for "contracting a function" to administrators are zero.

Notwithstanding the implications of the relatively costless environment of legislative motivation to produce symbolic and/or "interest group liberal" legislation, there are particular incentives at work in the regulatory-legislative arena that have a counterthrust. At the simplest level, legislators do want to produce what they conceive to be "good" public policy. And they do respond to the cross-pressures of interest groups that seek not mere symbolism but policy outputs that will benefit or at least minimally harm them. Balancing what we have described in this section with these motivations is the essence of the legislative art. It is important to appreciate that regulatory statutes are usually quite malleable; rarely does the bill introduced in either chamber closely resemble the one that emerges for the president's signature. Legislative motivation is what we must focus on in order to understand the gap.

In summary, regulatory legislation will contain a great deal of substance that has real impact upon affected interests. But at the same time, much interpretive authority devolves to enforcing agencies, and the statute, especially the preamble, usually contains material that can be described as symbolic language.

LEGISLATIVE MOTIVATION

Cross-Pressures and Cross-Incentives

Each statute, of course, has its own unique legislative history; nevertheless, some general observations can be made. First, legislators and the president are concerned with achieving popular support for electoral purposes. Such motivation may stem from concern for their own future electoral chances or, even if they plan to retire from electoral politics, because as political men and women they are concerned about their parties' or their successors' electoral chances. Accordingly, they may introduce new legislation not only at the behest of interest groups seeking some benefit but also in an entrepreneurial role without any strong interest group pressure, when they sense that their sponsorship will yield a political benefit. When crisis does not force—or at least exert strong pressure to force—the proposal onto the legislative agenda, some other compelling political reason can play a substitute role. Because regulatory legislation is such a slight drain on the overall budget, it can be a favorite in this respect.

Some critics have charged, for example, that President Lyndon Johnson sponsored much consumer regulation during the costly and unpopular Vietnam war for this reason. But, on the other hand, as we will see shortly, regulatory proposals usually involve several interest groups with conflicting interests, and a legislator has an incentive to support compromise legislation that will not dissatisfy most of these interests. This task is often not an easy one and can lead to inaction, delay, and long incubation periods for regulatory legislation.

Further complicating this task of producing compromise legislation is that legislators respond to other actors in the political process. In an important study, political scientist John Kingdon hypothesized that legislators respond to seven sets of actors: (1) their constituency, (2) interest groups, (3) the presidential administration, (4) their staffs, (5) suppliers of written information on a topic, (6) fellow legislators, and (7) party leadership.[17] Kingdon concluded, largely based on interviews, that constituency, fellow legislators, and interest groups are most important, with constituency the most important influence on issues. Thus,

> if there is a piece of legislation pending that would help a district industry in a direct way, or especially one that would hurt it, nearly all congressmen defend that industry's interests. They do it because they see the whole economy of their area at stake....[18]

Consequently, Michigan legislators seek the enactment of laws that will aid the automobile industry, while North Carolina legislators exert efforts on behalf of the tobacco industry. Therefore, an interest group's best strategy is to convert its narrow benefit interest into a statement of general interest both to a particular legislator's jurisdiction and to the nation as a whole.

While Kingdon concentrated on to *whom* legislators respond, political scientist Richard Fenno focused on *what* the goals of legislators are, listing three: (1) getting re-elected, (2) achieving influence within Congress, and (3) making "good" public policy.[19] The last goal can, of course, embrace a wide range of policy proposals since rationalizations can readily be conjured up to support virtually any preference as "good" policy.

To these concerns, political scientist David Mayhew added another dimension:

> The average voter has only the haziest awareness of what an incumbent congressman is doing in office. But an incumbent has to be concerned about actors who do form impressions about him, and especially about actors who can marshal resources other than their own votes.[20]

These resources include money and the ability of a group or an influential person to sway significant numbers of other voters. But one should not therefore assume that diffuse public opinion counts for naught in legislative decisionmaking. Public opinion or taste might be vaguely formed with little conception of the appropriate—or even reasonable—means desired, yet it is extremely important. Public opinion wants legislators to "do something" about high prices, consumer protection, etc., which provides an incentive for solutions that will relieve legislators of blame for costs.

These general principles based on the keen observations of political scientists present a quandary in the area of regulatory legislation, however. As we noted, a regulatory statute usually results in a very small claim on the public budget, yet the political payoff to legislators and interest groups may be substantial. Thus, within the confines of the public philosophy, legislators have a strong incentive to further such legislation.

On the other hand, however, most regulatory bills are of considerable concern to many interest groups, including government agencies, each with a somewhat different desired outcome. For example, five federal agencies, large and small commercial banks, savings and loan associations, the housing industry, money market funds, credit unions, and many more interests have sought different and conflicting goals in regulatory proposals in the banking industry. This is why printed committee hearings usually contain statements from the many interest groups seeking different objectives from the proposed legislation. Typically, any particular House district—and certainly states in the case of the Senate—contains a number of these conflicting interest groups. Legislators often have an incentive to avoid making regulatory policy for fear of affronting an important district interest.

Thus, regulatory legislation—like legislation in other areas—provides an apparenty anomalous situation in which there are not only incentives to action but also incentives to inaction. But legislators may—and indeed usually do—engage in a bargaining process, both among themselves and with conflicting interest groups, in which the terms of a proposed statute are modified as a solution to the cross-incentive problem. Compromises often are not easy to reach, however; for this reason, the time between the first introduction of a bill and its signing into law may be extremely lengthy.

Minimum Winning Coalitions and Minimax Marginalism

But exactly how do legislators usually determine what the optimum position should be? How do they respond to the pull of different, often competing, motivations? We will discuss two alternative solutions.

One response, of course, is to do nothing, although this sometimes can lead to antagonizing every group involved. When no group's feelings on a matter are particularly intense, or when no acceptable conciliation can be worked out, inaction may be an appropriate response. But otherwise we can assume that something will be done. In so doing, legislators are *prone* to adopt what we will call a "minimax" strategy, which is designed to minimize their possible losses.

The minimax strategy accords with Kingdon's observation that legislators tend to look for consensus, either generally or within the field of forces with which they share an electoral connection—party, constituent interest groups, etc.[21] For example, a representative from New York City will strive for consensus among labor and industrial groups, but the interests of wheat farmers probably will be of little or no concern to him.

A simple demonstration will illustrate a minimax strategy. Consider a case where there are five interest groups in a constituency, each with equal strength. Assume further that there are only two issues and that a legislator wishes to adopt what is called a "minimum winning coalition"—a coalition *barely* sufficient to win a vote—rather than a minimax strategy. A legislator's coalitions on the two issues may then be:

$$\text{Issue 1}: A + B + C > D + E$$
$$\text{Issue 2}: A + D + E > B + C$$

By arranging matters in this way, however, the legislator may have succeeded in antagonizing B, C, D, and E and only pleasing A, unless he is nearly certain that B and C value the gain in Issue 1 more than they value the loss in Issue 2. But in the real world of costly information, a legislator likely will not or cannot know exactly how salient or important each issue is to each interest group. This difficulty is multiplied as we include more issues into the legislator's considerations.

Additionally, from the perspective of B and C the cost of losing on Issue 2 is even greater than the specific costs occasioned by that particular decision, for they can no longer assume that the legislator will fulfill their requests in the future and must therefore make costly alternative plans to cope with adverse decisions on future issues. Consequently, a minimum winning coalition strategy *in situations in which there are conflicting views* is an extremely high risk enterprise from a legislator's perspective.

A minimax solution is a much more rational strategy in such situations. The legislator seeks to achieve a policy solution that will not dissatisfy any of the interests involved or at least only very few of them. In banking regulation, for example, the legislative response was to reach a solution that somewhat satisfied each group as well as fulfilled the aspirations of legislators to make "good" public policy. It is for this reason, as economist Gary Becker has noted, that

> empirically, even small but vocal minorities often have to be appeased: minority opposition is not automatically muted simply because the majority has 51 or 75 percent of the vote.[22]

But does this mean that the minimax strategy requires that the policy advocated by a legislator must embrace every interest? No, it does not, for the same marginal concept that applies to the externalities problem is also appropriate here. In a word, marginalism guides the minimax strategy.

Returning to our original example of five interest groups and two policy issues, why should the legislator seek to satisfy somewhat all five interests, rather than just four of them in each issue? The likely answer, as Becker noted, is that a legislator is apt to use the same kind of marginal analysis used in connection with externalities. A legislator will determine what the additional benefits will be by satisfying an *addi-*

tional interest compared with the *additional* losses incurred by so doing. Thus, he may find in Issue 1 that adjusting the policy proposal so that A, B, C, and D are satisfied and only E is dissatisfied minimizes his loss (E), because adding E might require a policy adjustment that will necessarily displease A and B. Again, in Issue 2 the legislator might be able to arrange a policy proposal through compromise that will allow him to add both B and C without endangering the loss of A, D, or E.

Obviously, there are several possible hypothetical outcomes to any given situation, but they all point to the use of marginalism as the better way to maximize interest group support while employing the minimax solution. To be sure, this mode of decisionmaking also involves risks associated with imperfect information about the intensity of interest groups concerning regulatory proposals and possible compromise solutions. But it clearly is a better way to attract and retain support than simply building minimum winning coalitions, issue by issue.

Of course, the minimax strategy operates within constraints including: (1) a legislator's conception of the public philosophy; (2) the need to take a position triggered by crisis and/or the intensity of desire for some action to be taken; (3) the tendency to take action that will evade blame for costs while maximizing public support; (4) the difficulty of finding a solution that will maximize interest group support; and (5) the resources that interest groups possess such as funds or votes. In addition, in order to assure sufficient interest and support in a particular piece of legislation, concerned legislators must logroll or vote-trade with other legislators who might otherwise be indifferent to the matter in question.

In summary, compromise, subject to the constraints mentioned, characterizes government regulation, especially at the national level. But in order for this bargaining and compromise to occur, interest groups cannot sit back and passively await an outcome that takes their interests into account. Rather, they must organize and actively participate in the legislative process. Thus, before environmental groups organized, there was no significant environmental regulation. Similarly, many interest groups are often inattentive to the activities of the much less visible state legislatures and city council chambers, who can be expected only to respond to those groups that are active—usually producer rather than consumer groups. Thus, many occupational groups have sought and obtained from government at these levels restrictive licensing statutes that preclude entrants or otherwise protect members of the occupation to the detriment of consumers.[23] The lesson is plain: to be successful in regulatory legislative politics is to be active in the political process.

CONCLUSION

We began this chapter by looking at the unique characteristics of regulatory legislative politics. We found that low cost to the public, many interests active in the area, and bargaining were the most important characteristics. After describing legislative functions, rules, and structure, we discussed what factors most likely facilitate the enactment of a regulatory bill. Adherence to the extant public philosophy and the element of crisis are two of the most important. By examining the motivation and probable response of legislators in shaping the provisions of regulatory statutes as they move though the regulatory process, we saw why regulatory legislation contains both symbolic and substantive material, why such statutes can be explicit in their commands to regulators (but yet why much interpretive authority often is left to these same regulators), and, most important, why regulatory legislation usually reflects the spirit of compromise.

NOTES

1. See especially David M. Welborn, *Governance of Federal Regulatory Agencies* (Knoxville: University of Tennessee Press, 1977).
2. Tom Alexander, "It's Roundup Time for Runaway Regulators," *Fortune* (December 3, 1979):126-132; and Ernest Gellhorn, "The Wages of Zealotry," *Regulation* (January/February 1980):33-40.
3. E. W. Hawley, *The New Deal and the Problem of Monopoly* (Princeton, N.J.: Princeton University Press, 1966), p. 190. See also Kenneth Elzinga, "The Robinson-Patman Act: A New Deal for Small Business," in *Regulatory Change in an Atmosphere of Crisis*, ed. Gary Walton (New York: Academic Press, 1979), pp. 64-65.
4. See the interesting discussion in William Tucker, "Environmentalism and the Leisure Class," *Harper's* (December 1977):49-56, 73-80.
5. James Q. Wilson, "The Politics of Regulation," in *The Politics of Regulation*, ed. James Q. Wilson (New York: Basic Books, 1980), p. 370.
6. An excellent study of the implications of the volume of business upon which policymakers are requested to act is Isaac Ehrlich and Richard A. Posner, "An Economic Analysis of Legal Rulemaking," *Journal of Legal Studies* 3 (January 1974):257-286.
7. Full details are provided in Richard Harris, *The Real Voice* (New York: Macmillan, 1964).
8. Wilson, "The Politics of Regulation," pp. 362, 363.
9. Ibid., p. 363.
10. Murray Edelman, *The Symbolic Uses of Politics* (Urbana: University of Illinois Press, 1967), p. 172.
11. Theodore J. Lowi, *The End of Liberalism* (New York: W. W. Norton & Co., 1969), pp. 144-156.
12. Details on the politics of this statute are contained in Howard Margolis, "The Politics of Auto Emissions," *Public Interest* 49 (Fall 1977):3-21.
13. Ibid., p. 19.

14. Ibid., p. 10.
15. Ibid., p. 13.
16. See R. H. Coase, "The Nature of the Firm," *Economica* 4 (New Series) (November 1937):394-398.
17. John W. Kingdon, *Congressional Voting Decisions* (New York: Harper & Row, 1973).
18. Ibid., p. 36.
19. Richard F. Fenno, Jr., *Congressmen in Committees* (Boston: Little, Brown & Co., 1973), p. 1.
20. David R. Mayhew, *Congress: The Electoral Connection* (New Haven, Conn.: Yale University Press, 1974), p. 40.
21. Kingdon, *Congressional Voting Decisions,* chap. 10.
22. Gary Becker, "Comment on Sam Peltzman's 'Toward a More General Theory of Regulation,'" *Journal of Law and Economics* 19 (August 1976):245.
23. See especially Thomas G. Moore, "The Purpose of Licensing," *Journal of Law and Economics* 4 (October 1961):93-117.

7

Regulatory Administration

The central function of this chapter is to establish what principles guide regulators in administering the programs under their jurisdictions. Our first task in this endeavor is to place regulatory administration within the wider context of regulation. We have already examined the legislative role in regulation. But the courts and the executive branch also impinge on agency administrators' activities and decisions, although in varying ways depending on the organizational form of the particular agency.

Following our look at the institutional structure of regulation, we will examine regulatory administrative behavior, the first step of which is to dispose of the false charge that regulators are for some unexplained reason lazier or less competent than other professionals. To the contrary, no evidence exists to show that regulators are, as a class, less concerned about doing a competent or thoroughly professional job than people in any other profession. With this in mind, we will look in some detail at the two principal formal tasks of regulators—adjudication and rulemaking—noting the difficulty and cost in each as well as the incentives regulators have to engage in informal rather than these formal proceedings.

The graphic description of adjudication and rulemaking will illustrate that applicable law, procedures, and regulators' perceptions of sound public policy are the most important influences in regulatory behavior. But these influences may be modified by groups and institutions that impinge upon regulatory administration. We will see that industry groups, the executive branch, and others play important roles in regulatory decisionmaking but that their roles are secondary to the agency's perception of its mission to enforce its laws.

THE REGULATORY SYSTEM

Analytically, legislation may be viewed as the first step in the regulatory process. The second step is the implementation of a regulatory statute by an administrative agency through formal rules and decisions, as well as through informal procedures that vary considerably from agency to agency and even within an agency over time. As noted briefly in Chapter 6, agencies my be divided into three organizational types. While agency effectiveness is not affected by agency type, according to most research certain consequences in terms of responsibility do result from organizational type.

The first agency type is an independent regulatory commission, which consists of five or more members appointed at staggered intervals for fixed terms of years. Commissioners may be removed only for cause and not at the discretion of the president. Thus, the president may not remove a member of the Federal Trade Commission, an independent agency, even though the commissioner opposes the president's program. In contrast, the president may remove an Environmental Protection Agency administrator at his discretion because that agency is *within* the executive branch. The peculiar structure of the independent regulatory commission suggests one of the principal legislative goals intended for it—relative independence from the executive branch. For this reason, the independent regulatory commissions have often been called the "fourth branch of government."

Although not a regulatory agency in the sense used in this book, the Civil Service Commission (CSC) provides the best example to illustrate what Congress intended in the independent regulatory commission concept. Created in 1883, the CSC was charged with developing rules for government hiring decisions, which would supplant political reward with tested competence as the principal criterion for public employment. Accordingly, Congress created the CSC to operate independently of the potential political influence of the president and his top officials.

In a similar manner, four years after the CSC had been created, the Interstate Commerce Commission was established and accorded independent regulatory commission status. Congress's concept was that railroad regulation should be a matter for the continuing application of technical principles affecting such questions as proper rates and should not be a matter of politics. Over the years, Congress has created many such agencies, almost always on the theory that the agencies' problems were technical and not political in nature and should be handled accordingly. During legislative debates about creating the independent regulatory commissions, a persistent theme has been that experts and not political favorites should be appointed as commissioners.

There are obvious costs to the independent regulatory commission idea, however. Foremost among them is the fact that, unlike the case of legislators or the president, public responsibility is very tenuous within administrative agencies. Regulators make decisions that affect the lives of the American public, but citizens cannot exercise their displeasure at bureaucratic performance by voting these officials out of office. Nor will regulators even respond to the public's preferences or objections by modifying their policies as will the president and legislators. For this reason (and a second to be stated shortly), Congress has sought to impose restrictions upon the ways that regulatory officials may operate to ensure that they abide by "fair" practices and supply reasons for their actions based on an agency's authorizing legislation.

The 1946 Administrative Procedure Act is the Magna Carta of this legislative undertaking. Section 557 of the act illustrates its control over regulatory proceedings. That section requires all administrative decisions to include findings and conclusions of fact and law and reasons for each of these. In a word, Congress's solution to the responsibility problem was to assure that regulators behaved like judges so that, like judges, they would be responsible to justice and reason through formalized procedures.

The second cost of the independent regulatory commission concept is that in its original form neither the president nor Congress could bend an agency's policies to their general policy preferences. This might not have been very important before Franklin D. Roosevelt's administration when centralized economic management became important, but it has been vital since. For example, if we assume a general economic policy dedicated to fighting inflation through wage and price restraint, should the ICC be allowed to approve transportation rate increases in defiance of that policy? Because of this problem the independence of these regulatory commissions has been eroded in several ways.

The executive branch's Office of Management and Budget (OMB) reviews agency budgetary requests not only in accounting terms but also in terms of whether individual items accord with the president's general program. During the annual appropriations process, Congress is apt to focus—often quite critically—on agency budgetary requests that are perceived to be in conflict with congressional views of sound public policy. But these congressional responses, of course, fall far short of coordinating each agency's policies with a general economic program before they are implemented.

For this reason, most of the regulatory agencies created since the 1960s—as well as many before then—are either independent agencies or bureaus in existing executive departments (see Table 7-1). In these cases, the chain of command to the president is direct, as in the case of an independent agency such as the Environmental Protection Agency,

Table 7-1   Federal Regulatory Agencies, 1980

Independent Commissions

Civil Aeronautics Board
Commodity Futures Trading Commission
Consumer Product Safety Commission
Federal Communications Commission
Federal Energy Regulatory Commission
Federal Maritime Commission
Federal Reserve Board
Federal Trade Commission
Interstate Commerce Commission
National Labor Relations Board
Nuclear Regulatory Commission
Securities and Exchange Commission

Independent Agencies

Environmental Protection Agency
Equal Employment Opportunity Commission
Federal Deposit Insurance Corporation
Federal Home Loan Bank Board
Federal Mediation and Conciliation Service
National Mediation Board
National Transportation Safety Board

Bureaus in Executive Departments

Agricultural Marketing Service (Agriculture)
Agricultural Stabilization and Conservation Service
   (Agriculture)

Animal and Plant Health Inspection Service
   (Agriculture)
Federal Grain Inspection Service (Agriculture)
Food Safety and Quality Service (Agriculture)
National Bureau of Standards (Commerce)
Army Corps of Engineers (Defense)
Economic Regulatory Administration (Energy)
Food and Drug Administration (Health and Human
   Services)
Office of Interstate Land Sales Registration (Housing
   and Urban Development)
Office of Surface Mining Reclamation and Enforcement
   (Interior)
Antitrust Division (Justice)
Drug Enforcement Administration (Justice)
Mine Safety and Health Administration (Labor)
Occupational Safety and Health Administration
   (Labor)
Office of Federal Contract Compliance (Labor)
Wage and Hour Division (Labor)
Federal Aviation Administration (Transportation)
Federal Railroad Administration (Transportation)
National Highway Traffic Safety Administration
   (Transportation)
Bureau of Alcohol, Tobacco, and Firearms (Treasury)
Office of the Comptroller of the Currency
   (Treasury)
U.S. Customs Service (Treasury)

or indirect through a cabinet secretary, as in the case of the Occupational Safety and Health Administration, which is part of the Labor Department. From Congress's perspective, there is an additional benefit: the executive branch cannot hide behind agency "independence" to evade responsibility for regulatory action. But one should not draw the erroneous conclusion that independent agency and bureau decisions are "political" in the same way that foreign policy decisions are. Such regulatory decisionmaking must be understood in a different way, as we will see.

Regulatory Decisionmaking

One simple statement, so often repeated that it has become a cliché, is the starting point for understanding regulatory decisionmaking or, for that matter, informal regulatory action: ours is a government of laws. In brief, no regulator—from the top level of an agency to the bottom—may undertake an action unless it is authorized by statute and rules. Thus, not only may an agency not do something forbidden by the Constitution, statute, or rule, but it also may not do anything unless specifically authorized by statute or rule. Failure to abide by this prescription assures that an agency's order will be reversed by the courts. Consequently, an agency seeking to undertake some novel action must point to statutory authorization. To this extent, then, regulatory decisions are not "political" in any sense of the word.

What is more, the decisions of regulatory agencies must provide reasons for actions taken. In specific decisions affecting individual firms or in rulemaking proceedings, an agency is obligated, like the courts, to show why its particular orders are an appropriate way to achieve statutory results. It must discuss the path chosen as well as those proposed and rejected and show why it is a reasonable one to secure statutory objectives. Regulators must do this not only because of their adherence to the maxim stated above but also because otherwise courts will reverse their actions. In most cases, those adversely affected by a regulatory agency's actions may appeal an agency's order to a U.S. Court of Appeals. That court will scrutinize the record to determine whether the agency scrupulously abided by the Constitution, pertinent statutes, and the agency's own rules. It will also determine whether the agency's conception of its statutory powers is consistent with the court's view of what Congress intended and whether there is sufficient evidence to support the agency's findings of fact upon which its order is based. Courts may reverse the agency's decision, remand it for further administrative proceedings, or affirm it.

What we have said thus far indicates that agency decisionmaking is largely legalistic, which to a great extent is true. But, as we discussed in

Chapter 6, regulatory statutes frequently contain discretionary language. Those who make policy based on such language may, obviously, impose their own values and priorities upon agency activity (but always only within statutory confines). In that sense, agency decisions are "political," but they are not necessarily political in the sense of responding to bribes, legislative pressures, interest group pressures, etc. Rather, as we will see in this chapter, regulators respond in certain ways to their conceptions of what their respective agencies should do. We begin a closer examination of regulatory behavior by clearing away certain misconceptions.

The Question of Regulatory Mismanagement

One would be foolhardy indeed to assert a set of general rules applicable to all agencies or even to assert general rules applicable to the behavior of a single agency over time. However, we may readily dispose of certain popular prejudices and misconceptions about regulatory behavior. To make a sweeping categorical assertion that regulatory agencies operate in the public interest, or that they are subservient to the interests that they regulate, or even that they are consistent is dangerous in the extreme. It is equally absurd to suggest that regulatory agencies are efficient or that they are inefficient. The occasional anecdote told about an administrator who is asleep at his desk during business hours is no substitute for a comprehensive study of regulatory efficiency. Nor does the occasional indictment of a regulator for accepting a bribe tell us anything about the general level of morality or professionalism that prevails in the regulatory bureaucracy.

Even the fact that a high percentage of regulators leave government to work for the industries that they previously regulated does not prove anything about their motivations or conduct while in public service. One would expect, for example, a lawyer who obtained Civil Aeronautics Board experience to seek outside employment in aviation law, not environmental law about which he has obtained no marketable experience. In fact, regulated companies and their law firms, seeking to hire government regulators, will more likely try to secure the services of a zealous, hard-working public employee who has diligently done his job rather than a lazy or careless employee whose lack of effort may have been more beneficial to the regulated firm's interests. The loyalties of professionals such as lawyers, economists, and accountants are viewed as transferable whether from company to company or government to private enterprise. It is primarily ability and experience that business firms seek.

Richard Posner has perceptively written:

> the evidence that has been offered to show mismanagement by the regulatory agencies is surprisingly weak.... The common argument

that the employees of regulatory agencies must be less able than their counterparts in the private sector, since they are paid lower salaries, ignores the fact that service with an agency frequently increases the later earning capacity of the employee in the private sector.... The motivation of the agency employee to work diligently and honestly is similar to that of the employee of a business firm. Both want to obtain advancement (not necessarily within the same employing firm or agency) and to avoid being fired, demoted or humiliated.... [T]he agency head's incentive is [also] clear. He derives few benefits from the slackness of his staff—not even the famous "quiet life".... Furthermore, the agency's head is answerable both to the legislative and (if he desires promotion or reappointment) to the executive branches.... There is competition among agencies for the largest possible slice of the appropriations, and the agency that has a reputation for economy and hard work enjoys an advantage in the competition....[1]

This is not to suggest that the mission of any particular agency is justifiable nor does it suggest the motivations or incentives of regulators. Clearly, there must be a difference between the motivations of those who work in government and the motivations of persons employed by business corporations, whose activities must be measured against the company's overriding goal of long-range wealth maximization. Rather, the point is that the "evidence" that regulatory agency employees are lazy or incompetent is extremely flimsy. The occasional anecdote supplied in a shallow Ralph Nader report or by some disgruntled business executive cannot support a theory of regulatory agency behavior.

Our task, then, is to determine the incentives of regulators (other than to perform competently). To some extent, regulators are entrepreneurs, capable of selecting regulatory opportunities, emphasizing some issues, and rejecting others. But to a greater extent, agencies and their employees conduct themselves in response to a variety of structural and political factors. Structurally, they are bound by their appropriations, procedural and substantive statutes, and internal rules. Constraints are also imposed by their different abilities to obtain information as well as the fact that the time of their employees is a scarce resource that must accordingly be rationed in some way. Politically, too, as we will see, regulators are subject to considerable pressures, often in conflicting directions.

Before looking at the question of political pressures and then trying to evaluate agency performance, we will examine how two particular agencies—the Federal Trade Commission and the Consumer Product Safety Commission—work, tracing hypothetical proceedings from inception to conclusion. The purpose of these examinations is not to suggest that these hypothetical matters illuminate the way other agencies operate nor does it follow that they proceed in precisely the same manner today or even that there are not different procedural methods that can be used at the same time. Rather, the purpose of these examinations is to point to common problems that confront regulators in many agencies.

Formal and Informal Procedures

We will look at the two most important *formal* functions of regulatory agencies—adjudication and rulemaking—in case studies. Adjudication can involve a formal trial of a firm or person charged with a violation by the agency or a proceeding in which various participants seek some benefit from an agency, such as a television license proceeding. The defining point in adjudication is that *named* individuals or companies are charged with a violation or may receive some benefit. Did X violate the statute; should A, B, or C be granted the television license? In contrast, rulemaking is concerned about a general activity regardless of who engages in it. Thus, if the Consumer Product Safety Commission requires glass to be made pursuant to certain standards, the identity of specific firms involved is not important to the proceeding.

Several points will emerge from these case studies. First, we will see that there is a place for both types of formal proceeding. There may be a few overlapping instances in which one type may be substituted for the other, but rulemaking is no blanket substitute for adjudication. Second, in each type of proceeding, information is a costly good. Obviously the amount of money and resources expended on obtaining information will vary from matter to matter, as a function of complexity and detail. But, again, the type of proceeding employed (adjudication or rulemaking) does not assure low information costs. Other parts of these processes are also costly, such as information evaluation.

Third, the processes involved in a proceeding are apt to consume a great deal of time as well as money. The type of proceeding does not necessarily decrease the amount of time that must reasonably be employed in a proceeding. Much legislative and public criticism of agencies is misplaced because the critics fail to appreciate the expenditure of time necessarily required in a proceeding. Fourth, we will see that in typical administrative proceedings "politics" in the sense described in connection with legislation plays virtually no role, certainly not a major one. Rather, regulators focus on the laws and procedures that govern their conduct and the choice of specific actions that in their views best promote statutory goals.

An important point follows from these difficulties inherent in formal procedures: regulators have a clear incentive to develop *informal* mechanisms for negotiating with affected interests and securing promises of compliance that will save considerable funds, time, and manpower. Contrary to what some critics of regulatory behavior argue, the choice of informal rather than formal techniques by regulators does not necessarily imply that they have "sold out" or that they are "soft on business." Rather, informal techniques, such as voluntary agreements or informal conferences, are more often than not rational responses to the fact that agency resources are scarce and limited. Therefore, these resources must not be squandered when lower expenditures may achieve reasonable results.

ADJUDICATION: THE FEDERAL TRADE COMMISSION

Among the many statutes that the Federal Trade Commission enforces is the Federal Trade Commission Act, Section 5 of which declares, in part, that "deceptive acts or practices in commerce are declared unlawful." The statute then grants the FTC jurisdiction to enforce this substantive provision over all "persons, partnerships, or corporations" except those regulated by other agencies, such as railroads, over which the ICC has jurisdiction, or banks, which are regulated by several agencies.

At the outset, then, regulators must be aware of their agency's jurisdictional limits. In cases where jurisdictional limits are not clear, the agency's Office of General Counsel makes a legal determination, after researching the question, whether the agency has jurisdiction. The relevant statutes must not only grant jurisdiction over the person or firms but over the activity as well. Thus, the FTC regulator, receiving a complaint about a bank, must reject the matter because the agency has no jurisdiction over the person or firm. On the other hand, the FTC may receive a claim about a drug company's testing procedures. While the agency has jurisdiction over many activities undertaken by drug companies (advertising, pricing arrangements, etc.), it has no jurisdiction over the subject matter of testing, which is under Food and Drug Administration jurisdiction. The point is a simple one but is sometimes overlooked. The starting place for any agency is a determination whether jurisdiction lies over the person and the subject matter.

Now we will look at what appears to be a simple matter. A letter is written to either the FTC Washington, D.C., headquarters or a regional field office complaining about a series of advertisements placed in newspapers and on television by the X Company, a manufacturer of a personal deodorant spray. These advertisements claim, in substance, that no other spray can equal the safety and effectiveness of X's product. The letter continues by complaining that sprays marketed by the Y and Z companies are at least as safe and effective and far cheaper than X's product. Consequently, the letter concludes, X's advertising is deceptive and leads consumers to expend a great deal of money that could have been used in alternative ways if they knew the truth.

At this point, two of the most important problems confronting a regulatory agency are raised: (1) how to obtain information that enables it to fulfill its mission and (2) how to rank-order priorities among many possible tasks. Specifically, no FTC staff member is likely to be so familiar with the chemistry and physiological effects of various deodorant sprays that an evaluation of the claims in the advertising can be made quickly. And, as we have seen on many occasions, such information is costly. But the second problem is an equally serious one. The FTC receives many similar complaints about a variety of different products. In addition, the agency may decide on its own initiative to evaluate still other advertising claims. Given the limitations of time and financial appropriations, the question is very simply: why should the FTC expend resources on the deodorant matter rather than in some other way?

Reactive and Proactive Approaches

Every agency has some formal or informal manner of determining which matters to pursue or not. If the decision is made to pursue a matter, the next question is whether to handle it at the outset through informal procedures that will utilize few resources or whether to pursue it through a full-scale effort that might exhaust considerable resources. Consequently, a letter of complaint goes first to a policy evaluation office that will make the initial judgment of probable disposition and transmit the matter to the appropriate office. Such preliminary dispositions are often made pursuant to a formal collection of agency policy statements to which the evaluation office will refer. But the initial disposition may also be made pursuant to an articulated oral sense of what types of matters the agency considers important at that time or simply to a "feeling" based on experience about the probable importance of the matter. A variety of other factors—such as congressional or executive pressures or simply that the agency has gained considerable information about the problem from other matters, thereby reducing information costs in the present situation—are important in the initial policy evaluation decision.[2]

The matter that we have been examining is subsumed under what has been termed the "reactive approach."[3] In the reactive approach, matters are initiated by outsiders bringing information about possible transgressions or investigative opportunities to the attention of the agency. In the case of the FTC, reactive matters are usually brought to the agency's attention by competitors or other businesses who feel that they are placed at a competitive disadvantage because of the actions of the party against whom the complaint has been registered. Although others, such as consumers or other government agencies, are also sources of reactive complaints, disgruntled businessmen, who combine high degrees of knowledge and self-interest, supply the largest number of reactive complaints.[4] Thus, in our hypothetical deodorant spray example, the Y and Z companies are experts on spray deodorants and have an obvious incentive to complain about advertising claims that they feel will injure their profit expectations.

But matters may also originate in a "proactive" manner pursuant to which an agency assumes the initiative and examines matters that it feels are important without any outsider complaint being received. Every agency employs both methods but in considerably varying degrees. The ICC, for example, tends to operate primarily in the reactive manner, while the Consumer Product Safety Commission generally uses hospital accident reports without any formal requests for action in operating proactively. But both of these regulatory agencies as well as most others employ both styles.

Returning to our deodorant spray example, the policy evaluation office has several options at this point. It may write a letter to the informants stating that it would not be in the public interest to expend further resources on the matter and formally close it. Or the office might feel that the matter warrants action on an informal basis and turn it over to an office specializing in informal procedures that will notify the party against whom the complaint was made with a view to arranging an informal settlement that has no force of law. For example, the informal procedure office might extract a promise from the X Company that it will no longer make advertising claims unfavorably comparing competitors' products with its own. Or the policy evaluation office might decide that the matter warrants a full-scale investigation with a view toward instituting formal proceedings. In so doing, it might rank-order the particular matter according to some scale of importance and priority. We will assume that the deodorant spray matter is sent to an operating bureau that handles deceptive practice matters with instructions to give it very high priority.

Information Costs

The letter is then transmitted to the director of the Bureau of Consumer Protection for further action. At this juncture, the critical questions are the specific personnel who should actively pursue the matter and the resources that should be expended upon it. Again, information cost is the critical variable in these decisions. Bureaus in virtually every agency are divided, either formally or informally, into divisions that specialize in particular types of matters or industries. For example, the Bureau of Consumer Protection might include a division that specializes in drug and cosmetic product claims. Information costs can be reduced through this division of labor since there will already be personnel who are experienced in evaluating matters in the general category, even if not in the precise claims under consideration. Such personnel will almost certainly have a better sense of what additional information to obtain and how to evaluate it than will someone with no experience in drug and cosmetic matters. And the appropriate division chief, in turn, will seek to utilize the personnel with the closest experience for the matter under consideration—perhaps someone who has already undertaken an investigation of deodorants.

The matter is then formally docketed for investigation, a number assigned to it, and a regulator (usually a lawyer) assigned to supervise investigation of the matter pursuant to a set of instructions and guidelines provided by the bureau and/or division. The principal investigator may, for example, be instructed to conduct the entire investigation from Washington or may be requested to utilize the services of one or more field offices. In any event, the principal investigator must obtain permission from the bureau and/or division chiefs to undertake any part of the investigation outside the framework of his or her guidelines or instructions.

Investigation and Evaluation

The investigative phase now begins.[5] The chief investigator sends letters to the party under investigation and others who might supply relevant information, subpoenas documents, conducts an investigatory hearing, and/or requires the party under investigation to prepare a special report on the subject matter. He or she may personally interview persons, such as chemists who might be able to shed light on the safety and effectiveness of X's product and those of its competitors. The chief investigator may want to obtain permission to use FTC funds to obtain an independent laboratory test assessing X's claims. Or the regulator may transmit the entire matter to a field office with instructions to obtain specific information and prepare a report with recommendations. During the investigative phase, it is very important for all agency personnel to adhere strictly to constitutional and administrative law requirements as well as the procedural rules of the FTC, for a serious procedural deviation may result in the dismissal of even the strongest and most carefully developed substantive case. By the end of the investigation, the chief investigator will have accumulated a substantial file consisting of interview reports, documents, and correspondence.

The next step is the evaluation of this accumulated material. The principal investigator must assemble this information in a coherent fashion and prepare a report discussing the material pertinent to possible violations of law, evaluating the quality of the evidence, and recommending disposition of the matter. The principal investigator may recommend, for example, that the matter be closed, that it be settled informally, or that formal action should be taken by the agency. The formal actions that may be proposed include the issuance of a formal complaint against the party under investigation or the issuance of a proposed substantive rule. The latter course will be undertaken if the investigation reveals that not just the X Company but virtually everyone in the spray deodorant industry is making similar deceptive claims or that conditions can only be corrected if the entire industry is bound and guided by a set of substantive rules.

We will assume that the deodorant spray situation is unique and does not require the promulgation of a substantive rule. The principal investigator forwards the file recommending issuance of a complaint up the administrative ladder where it must be approved by the division, the bureau, and a majority of the commissioners. The test at this point is not whether the case against the X Company is proved but whether there is reason to believe that the respondent has violated the law.

The Administrative Trial

The steps that follow in adjudication closely resemble a court proceeding. A complaint is prepared setting forth the principal facts upon which a violation of law is premised and is served upon the charged party (the respondent) who has a designated time in which to prepare and serve a written answer. The case is formally docketed and an agency administrative law judge (ALJ) is assigned to preside over the matter. The ALJ places the case on his or her calendar, indicating to both sides when the pretrial conference will take place. But during this early period, as well as afterward, it is not uncommon for FTC and respondent attorneys to try to work out a compromise consent order so as to avoid the time and expense of formal litigation. Indeed, most matters are settled through the consent order procedure without a formal trial.

Pretrial conferences originated in the federal court system but have been widely employed in the regulatory agencies that use litigation. The functions of these informal conferences, in which the ALJ and attorneys representing the contesting parties participate, are to narrow the issues to those involving a real dispute of fact or law and to structure the forthcoming trial in such a way as to reduce procedural delay, trial time, and expense. A wide variety of procedures is employed to achieve these ends, including: (1) exchange of documents that will be used in evidence; (2) informal interviews of witnesses who will be called by adverse parties; (3) preparation of summaries in place of numerous individual documents; and (4) scheduling the order of trial.

Thus, in our hypothetical case the parties might be ordered to exchange scientific studies bearing on the safety and efficacy of X's product, interview each other's witnesses, etc. At the end of the pretrial proceeding, the ALJ prepares a statement setting forth the essential issues in the case, the facts that are accepted by both sides, and the trial schedule. While the pretrial process does save time in many matters, it can also be used by one of the contesting parties to interpose a variety of procedural objections and resist efforts by the ALJ to narrow the issues and speed up the proceedings. Indeed, there have been many cases where the pretrial procedure has actually delayed proceedings beyond what might have occurred if the procedure had not been available. Procedural issues that can sometimes arise during the pretrial hearing under the Administrative Procedure Act or the Constitution ultimately may have to be resolved by the courts, resulting in substantial delay before the trial on substantive issues can begin.

At some point, however, the trial on the disputed issues commences and generally is conducted in a manner similar to that which prevails in a court of law. The rules governing the trial are determined by the Administrative Procedure Act, agency statutes, rules and precedent, and, of course, constitutional requirements. In general, however, agencies are far more flexible in admitting evidence than are courts of law, in part because ALJs, in contrast to juries who determine facts in court proceedings, are far better prepared to evaluate the quality of each piece of evidence. But while an administrative tribunal is apt to be much more lenient in admitting evidence, ALJs must not base their decisions solely on rumor or uncorroborated hearsay.[6] In other words, unless there is some evidence that would stand up in a court of law, the ALJ's findings and decisions stand a reasonable chance of being reversed. Implicit in this standard—known as the residuum rule—is a cardinal principle of American justice. Furthermore, except as a statute otherwise provides, the party proposing a rule or order must bear the burden of proof. In the deodorant spray case, the FTC staff attorneys must first prove that X's statements concerning safety and quality are untrue or misleading. Only after this showing does X have the obligation to rebut the evidence offered by the agency.

Administrative trials, like trials in courts of law, vary considerably in the amount of time they consume. The complexity and number of issues, number of witnesses, disputes between the sides during the course of trial, and other factors contribute to how long a trial will take. But at some point, of course, the record is closed. At that time, the ALJ requests that each side prepare within a designated time *proposed* findings of fact and a memorandum on the applicable law. Each side is usually granted an opportunity to respond to the proposed findings and memorandum of the other sides. The ALJ then has the task of reviewing the record of the proceeding and the documents filed by each side. From these a report is written containing, first, the findings of fact and explaining with respect to each disputed issue of fact why the ALJ has decided what the probable truth is.

Second, the ALJ's report contains a discussion of the applicable law. The ALJ attaches great importance to the legal discussions of the agency or the courts on similar matters. Finally, the ALJ drafts a proposed order, the purpose of which is to remedy the wrong or create new conditions that will prevent future transgressions. Thus, in our example, the ALJ might order the X Company not to make unsubstantiated claims about the comparative advantage of its deodorant sprays, or the X Company might be required to issue advertisements correcting the false or misleading impressions created by the original deceptive advertisement.

Appeals

The matter has hardly reached the stage of its final determination when the ALJ publishes and serves a report on the contesting parties, however. The case may be appealed to the full commission or, in the case of single-headed agencies, to the administrator. Agencies differ widely on the scope of review of ALJ decisions. Some agencies will review the entire record and substitute their assessments of the facts for those of the ALJ. Other agencies may adopt a more limited form of review, only reversing the ALJ's findings of fact when, on the basis of the record, there is clear and unmistakable error. In some cases, review may be cursory while in others it may be extremely thorough. In any event, any party to the original proceeding that considers itself aggrieved by the ALJ's proposed order may appeal to the agency pursuant to procedures spelled out in the agency's procedural rules. Both parties involved may be theoretically dissatisfied with the ALJ's proposed order and may appeal, but typically only one party appeals. Most agencies will schedule a date for oral argument by the sides to the controversy, examining the record beforehand. After considering the arguments and the record, the agency will begin the preparation of its decision and final order. The agency may affirm or reverse the ALJ, or sometimes it will remand the matter to the ALJ for further proceedings to obtain information deemed necessary to make an appropriate final decision.

The matter is not necessarily closed at this point, however, for a private party aggrieved by the agency's order may appeal to a court (usually one of the U.S. Circuit Courts of Appeal) as well. And in a few instances the case may even reach the dizzying heights of the Supreme Court.

THE SUBSTANTIVE CONSEQUENCES OF PROCEDURE

Information Costs and Social Costs

As we have noted: (1) there are substantial procedural variations from agency to agency; (2) some agencies such as the Nuclear Regulatory Commission must grant permission before private sector activity may commence, while others such as the FTC usually operate after the private sector activity has occurred; and (3) some proceedings are more susceptible to rulemaking than litigation; but this description of agency activity does illustrate certain problems common to almost every regulatory activity. Each agency is faced with the problem of information gathering and evaluation and making a decision based upon decision rules—a costly and time-consuming process. Of course, the costs and fact-gathering activities may be displaced upon the regulated firm, as the Food and Drug Administration does, although the government evaluation problem still remains. But it is difficult to see what this accomplishes since the attendant costs will, in turn, be shifted from the regulated firms to the consumers of the product or service. Additionally, the overall social costs resulting from such delay *may* exceed the social benefits, as several examples will illustrate.

Pharmacologist William Wardell has studied FDA procedure in the approval process before new drugs may be marketed, finding that the average time required from filing an investigational new drug application to gaining approval for marketing was nine years in 1976. The average cost for a U.S. firm to bring a new drug to the domestic market was $54 million. As a result, the number of potentially useful drugs marketed in the United States is considerably lower than in countries, such as the United Kingdom, that have less demanding testing and information cost requirements. The result may be that more lives are lost because of the unavailability of potentially useful drugs and procedural delay than are saved because of the stringent cost requirements imposed upon regulated firms.[7]

Consider also the FDA's intense hearing in the 1960s concerning peanut butter. It took nine years and an 8,000 page record to resolve the question of whether a product must contain 90 percent or 87 percent peanuts to be labeled peanut butter. The proceeding, which involved numerous parties including farmer and consumer groups—a major reason for the time consumed—is an obvious example of information overkill.[8]

This is not to suggest that the costs of gathering information, together with other costs, necessarily exceed or are less than the benefits obtained. There are clearly instances of both. Rather, regardless of whether information costs are *initially* borne by the agency or imposed upon individuals or firms in the private sector, they ultimately impose social costs. Second, whether the agency or the private sector is involved in the process of information collection, the problem of delay and the costs imposed are inherent in the processes of most regulatory agencies, no matter how different their specific operating procedures may be. And the problem persists during the information evaluation phase. Obviously, the numerous pieces of information gathered by an agency are of varying degrees of reliability. This is true whether, as in the case of a state public utility commission, information must be supplied in advance of action or whether, as in the case of the FTC, information is supplied after action. It is true whether most information comes from outsiders or from the agency's own investigative facilities, and it is true whether the burden of coming forth with evidence is placed upon the agency or upon the person or firm charged.

A well-documented (although old) example will illustrate this point—the thorough study of the life insurance industry by the Temporary National Economic Committee (TNEC). The TNEC was a special committee, composed of officials and staff of both houses of Congress and the executive branch, from 1939 to 1941. It was charged with investigating the concentration of economic power in the United States. The TNEC investigation is widely considered to have been the most comprehensive governmental investigation of the structure and conduct of American business ever, and among its most important topics of inquiry was the life insurance industry. The study established that the rate structures for life insurance were set as follows:

> a committee of the [life insurance] association considers the combined experience of its six largest member companies ... and reaches an agreement as to the interpretation of that experience. A rate recommendation is approved at a meeting of the association and is transmitted to the superintendent who invariably adopts the recommendation ... official action is practically automatic.[9]

Why should the superintendent of insurance operate this way? One possible explanation is that he is bribed or beholden to the regulated interests. Yet evidence of this is extremely slim, usually based on innuendo rather than fact. A far more plausible explanation is that the ultimate rate structure rests upon a veritable mountain of documentation, which is under the control of the regulated firms who prepare summaries from it, that the superintendent is virtually unable to evaluate independently without examining each and every underlying document. And obviously such an independent process of fact-gathering and evaluation would be both extremely time-consuming and expensive. It is for this reason that regulatory agencies, when confronted with a substantial volume of data that must be evaluated in order to reach a conclusion, will often rely largely upon the efforts of the regulated firm or firms, which, of course, will tend to build their favored evaluations into the presentation. Of course, an agency does not necessarily have to operate in this manner, but to the extent that it does not, it makes a trade-off between additional delay and cost, on the one hand, and the benefit of independent evaluation, on the other.

The more complex the subject matter and the more voluminous the information required, the less likely that an independent agency evaluation will take place. Conversely, other factors provide the agency with incentives to incur the additional costs and delay. First, if the regulated firm's conduct could lead to great harm to public health or safety or substantial economic loss to the group the agency is charged with protecting, responsible regulators will have an incentive to incur those extra costs. An incentive similarly exists when that harm is irreversible. For these reasons, both the Food and Drug Administration and the Nuclear Regulatory Commission are often willing (indeed, expected) to incur the substantial costs and delay involved in independently collecting and evaluating complex information. Finally, the threat of agency embarrassment occasioned by adverse publicity also provides an incentive to engage in independent data collection and evaluation. Thus, when an agency or some of its activities are being watched carefully by public interest groups or others capable of generating adverse publicity, we would expect the agency to investigate and evaluate information more scrupulously.

Decision Rules

Agencies not only must gather information and evaluate its quality but they must also have a set of decision rules covering both substance and procedure. Thus, the Federal Trade Commission, as we saw, has a set of rules founded in its organic statutes, the Constitution, and the Administrative Procedure Act. These decision rules pertain to such topics as the way in which a complaint is to be written, the time that a respondent has to answer, pretrial conferences, etc. The overriding purpose of such procedural rules is sometimes forgotten by zealots anxious to speed up proceedings. Our system of justice, whether being dispensed by courts of law or administrative agencies, adversely affects some people. A person charged with false advertising or a firm that will be bound by a proposed EPA rule may be adversely affected. Our cardinal principles of justice deplore the ability of government to act arbitrarily in the manner of an absolute monarch or dictator. Accordingly, we require government officials to restrict their activities to those permitted under law and seek to assure that a person or firm may not be deprived of life, liberty, or property without a reasonable opportunity to challenge official action. Procedural rules are intended to guarantee that opportunity.

Substantive rules serve a similar purpose. Many statutes, of course, charge the regulatory agencies that will administer them with fairly vague standards. For example, rate-setting agencies such as the ICC are expected to set rates that are "just and reasonable," and the FTC is charged with thwarting "unfair methods of competition." Nevertheless, an agency can usually point to statutory language and legislative history that guides it in limiting discretion and performing its regulatory mission. Agencies therefore try to devise substantive rules and regulations that can be shown to relate to the legislative purposes and confines of the statutes they administer, while those adversely affected are afforded an opportunity to show otherwise. And once reasonable substantive rules and regulations are adopted, they are generally followed by the agency in subsequent proceedings of a similar nature, unless sound reasons can be shown to change course. But, again, those who might be adversely affected should be afforded, at some stage, the right to present their points of view.

Although the specific constitutional rules concerning what constitutes an unacceptable exercise of agency discretion have grown increasingly complex, the underlying principle set forth by the Supreme Court in 1886 still prevails. In *Yick Wo* v. *Hopkins,* a laundry operator was convicted of violating a municipal health and building code that was being administered in a prejudicial way so that only Chinese laundries were guilty—and therefore eliminated as competitors. The Court stated:

> When we consider the nature and the theory of our institutions of government . . . we are constrained to conclude that they do not mean to leave room for the play and action of purely personal and arbitrary power. . . . For, the very idea that one man may be compelled to hold his life, or the means of his living, or any material right essential to the enjoyment of life, at the mere will of another, seems to be intolerable in any country where freedom prevails.[10]

Decision rules vary from agency to agency and frequently change within a particular agency. Within the requirements of the fundamental values that we have just noted, Congress and agencies seek to adjust their rules so as to expedite matters and prevent delay. Thus, agencies tend to prefer rulemaking covering a large number of persons and firms rather than the process of individual litigation. But this is not always possible, especially in complex and unique matters. Moreover, many persons charged with violating a rule seek to show that their circumstances are outside its scope, a question the agency must examine to the extent warranted by the specific facts. Additionally, many lawyers practicing before agencies are adept at utilizing procedure, constitutional objections, and appeals in order to delay proceedings when that strategy is in their clients' interests.

In brief, if there is a will to delay, there is usually a way to do so. And while delay may be (and often is) abused, the great value that we place on fairness principles compels us to tolerate a certain degree of delay. The best that can be done is what regulators constantly do: try to devise new procedures consistent with fairness that will speed up matters. But lawyers intent on delaying can ingeniously use the new procedures in the same manner that they employed the older ones to effect delay. And if an agency goes too far in streamlining procedures, the courts may find a fundamental constitutional objection to them.

One important inference that must be drawn from this discussion is the basis of an important regulatory theory developed by Bruce Owen and Ronald Braeutigam. They concluded:

> Parties with superior resources have an advantage in being able to sustain heavy litigation costs, but even parties with few resources can use them strategically to delay resolution of the issue. The advantage lies with those who gain from the status quo which can in many cases be perpetuated for years.[11]

The general tendency of regulation to preserve the status quo, or at least to retard change, must not be confused with a simplistic notion advanced by some commentators that regulation usually helps big business or the wealthy. For there are many times that business interests seek change, while others who think of themselves as representing the meek and humble have successfully delayed it. Nuclear Regulatory Commission proceedings, for example, usually pit utilities and reactor firms on one side seeking rapid disposition of the licensing issues and environmentalists, on the other, seeking to maintain the status quo. But consider the way in which the Federal Communications Commission has retarded widespread commercial application of cable television to the great benefit of the three major networks and the UHF stations.

Of course, we must not overstate what is a clear *tendency* stemming from the structure of the regulatory process. The status quo can be overcome and procedural matters can be speeded up, although it is difficult. We will look later at political factors and behavioral considerations that can lead to change—or retard it.

RULEMAKING:
THE CONSUMER PRODUCT SAFETY COMMISSION

It is important to realize that Congress and agencies are well aware of the difficulties inherent in the procedural process and have sought remedies, the most important of which is to replace adjudication with "legislative rulemaking," which we will simply call rulemaking.

The Consumer Product Safety Commission, a five-member independent commission, was created by Congress in 1972 with the widespread support of consumer groups. The agency was provided with the authority to set safety standards for approximately 11,000 consumer products and to ban those providing an unreasonable risk of injury. The only consumer products not covered were those governed by other regulatory agencies such as aircraft, automobiles, food, drugs, and pesticides. The CPSC has been provided with a substantial budget to undertake its legal and administrative processes, test products, gather medical statistics pertaining to product-related injuries, and disseminate information to consumers.

Aware of the information gathering and evaluating difficulties that confront many agencies, Congress included a provision in the agency's authorizing statute (Section 15(b)) that requires manufacturers and sellers of covered consumer products to report to the CPSC the existence of any substantial product hazards. Rulemaking, rather than administrative adjudication, was to be the principal means by which the CPSC would ensure rapid decisionmaking. Stiff penalties imposed upon violators of the standards set forth in the rules were intended to ensure effective compliance.

Yet, notwithstanding the conscious attempt by Congress to assure quick and effective decisionmaking and without any hint of dishonesty or individual incompetence, the CPSC was soon under attack. A respected Washington investigative reporter claimed in 1977 that the CPSC "has been such an abysmal failure that it is at least as responsible as any other government agency for the plummeting popularity of consumer protection." [12] A 1978 *New York Times* report on the agency claimed it was uniformly regarded as feeble and extremely slow in issuing rules. The *Times* article noted, for example, that the agency had not issued flammability standards for upholstered furniture—a leading source of fire-related death—more than four years after receiving the relevant information.[13] Finally, the General Accounting Office, after a careful study, sharply criticized the CPSC in 1977 for its tardiness, pointing out that during its first four years the agency had issued standards for only three products. The report observed that the CPSC took an average of 834 days to establish a standard, notwithstanding the fact that Congress in the legislation establishing the agency had set 330 days as the maximum.[14]

Problems in Developing Standards

The almost universal disappointment at the Consumer Product Safety Commission's performance compels us to inquire what went wrong. Was it the personnel or some other bureaucratic factor? Or was the rulemaking process relative to the task to be undertaken largely at fault? When we look closely at the task and measure the rulemaking process against it, we must conclude that rulemaking is hardly the panacea to reduce consumer accidents that Congress thought it had devised.

First, consider the enormous scope of the problem that the Consumer Product Safety Commission has been charged with solving. We have already observed that the agency has jurisdiction over more than 11,000 different consumer products—and the number is increasing annually. Obviously, most of these products come in a variety of different designs with considerable variation in characteristics, and any particular product may pose a large number of different consumer hazards. Complicating the problem is the fact that the notion of a hazard is considerably more ambiguous than might be apparent at first blush.

The problem is that the inherent risk of any product must be considered together with the conditions of use and the environments of use. For example, the hazard posed by an automobile is dependent upon its particular use (i.e., driving at normal speeds or very rapidly) and the environment of use (a densely traveled freeway or a deserted rural road). And there is at least some (debatable) evidence that reducing the inherent hazardousness of a product often leads users to take greater personal risks in more dangerous environments. Ironically, making some products inherently safer may actually lead to greater numbers of accidents because many people overestimate, or even disregard, conditions of use and environments.[15] For example, mandatory safety belts *may* actually have led to an increasing number of automobile accidents and injuries.[16]

In establishing a standard the CPSC must also consider the marginal benefits that may be obtained with each increment of marginal cost devoted to safety, a difficult problem made more complex by the fact that many people compensate for a perceived reduction in risk attributable to one variable by increasing risk with respect to other variables. Furthermore, decreasing the risk inherent in the product must be weighed against the possibility that the product's quality may also be reduced. Additionally, the CPSC is expected to assess the new hazards that might be imposed by adopting the new standards. Finally, all of the above considerations must be related causally to the adopted standard. Failure to do so may lead a court of appeals to strike down a standard, compelling the agency to retrace many of its earlier steps.[17] Clearly, then, the information gathering and evaluating activities that the CPSC must undertake with respect to each product are apt to be costly and time-consuming, regardless of how efficient agency staff might be.

CPSC Standards for Architectural Glass

We will examine rulemaking in the case of architectural glass—one of the first products for which the CPSC issued product standards—to show that, contrary to Congress's fond hope (and delusion), rulemaking is no simple road to speedy decisionmaking in complex matters. Prior to the CPSC's 1977 standard, architectural glass (principally glass doors and similar fixtures) was subject to a large number of local and state building codes and regulations.

Consequently, manufacturers and distributors of these products advocated a single set of standards that would supersede the myriad of standards that prevailed before the CPSC rule. The point is significant because it indicated that the industry's attitude toward CPSC activities would be cooperative, although, of course, it does not follow that all members of the industry would be pleased with the national standards ultimately adopted. Yet, under these circumstances we would expect the architectural glass industry voluntarily to supply much of the information required for determination and generally to help speed up proceedings. In addition, product injuries—even minor ones—invite lawsuits. Glass doors accounted for approximately 73,000 injuries in 1973—although only 2 percent required hospitalization—and it was thought that adopting a national standard *might* help manufacturers and builders to defend against these.[18]

The story begins before the creation of the CPSC when the Consumer Safety Glazing Committee (CSGC)—consisting of industry representatives, members of safety organizations, and government officials—was formed in 1968.[19] Its initial purpose was to press the states to enact a uniform law covering safety features of the subject products. But with the creation of the CPSC, the CSGC's strategy changed. Obviously, it is much easier to achieve national standards through administrative action by a federal agency than to persuade 50 state legislatures to adopt them. Consequently, on June 20, 1973, the CSGC petitioned the CPSC to commence a proceeding for the promulgation of a rule. The petition was not granted until November 1, 1973, because the CPSC, like any organization with scarce resources, preliminarily had to decide that architectural glass was a high priority item among the vast number of products under its jurisdiction in terms of: (1) frequency and severity of injuries; (2) costs and benefits of agency action; (3) unforeseen nature of the risk; and (4) other factors. Architectural glass was one of 29 projects accorded high priority status at the time.

The next step was the publication, required by law, of a notice of proceeding in the *Federal Register,* a periodical published by the government that serves as the source of notice to the public of all agency rules, hearings, proposed rules, and other administrative matters. The notice of proceeding for architectural glass outlined the steps that would be taken in conjunction with the ultimate rule that would be promulgated. During this period, the CPSC Bureau of Epidemiology was conducting an in-depth investigation of injuries associated with architectural glass. The bureau's report, printed in July 1974, summarized the circumstances of a large number of such injuries. For example, one of the cases studied reported: "Victim was angry and started throwing things around kitchen. She tripped over coffee pot thrown on floor and fell forward into window." [20] The purpose of this inquiry, of course, was to provide the agency with information about the various kinds of injuries associated with the product so that the standard eventually adopted would respond to the most common and dangerous of these.

One of the more interesting innovations of the CPSC's organic statute is the "offeror" process, designed to reduce delay and obtain high-quality information. The CPSC is required to employ the services of a professional testing organization, such as Underwriters Laboratories Inc.—the offeror—whose function is to test a product with respect to its potentially harmful properties and write a first draft of the proposed standard. Since such organizations were already in the highly technical business of testing products and materials for industrial concerns and others, Congress decided that considerable time and savings would be effected by using their resources rather than starting a rival government department within the CPSC from scratch.

Of course, such testing organizations are also busy doing nongovernmental work. The CPSC statute imposed one requirement, however, that distinguishes contract work for the CPSC from the testing organizations' private arrangements. Industry and consumer groups were to be represented on the standard-developing committee. This requirement was included within the law at the insistence of consumer groups, who felt that the principal focus of testing for the CPSC was different from the principal focus involved in testing for industrial concerns—the testing organizations' traditional clients—and that consumers needed this additional protection.[21] But there is a price to be paid for such additional protection and input during the information gathering and evaluating process—procedural delay. The offeror in the architectural glass case was selected on August 5, 1974, and its recommended standard was submitted to the CPSC on January 24, 1975.

The next step is CPSC evaluation of the standard developed by the offeror. The offeror's proposal is placed on a review calendar together with other pending matters, and particular agency staff members are assigned the detailed task of review. This process consists, first, of looking at the proposed standard's effect on the cost, utility, and availability of the product in question. Second, the proposed standard must be evaluated in terms of its probable effects. For example, it is possible that a production change in the manufacture of architectural glass could result in safer products but that the additional environmental or energy costs imposed by the new process would be substantial. In a word, the agency must consider a large number of trade-offs. Finally, the agency must consider alternatives to the specific proposed standards in order to see whether these might better satisfy goals. In this case, the evaluation process took until January 16, 1976, when the CPSC voted to publish a proposed standard for architectural glass.

The proposed safety standard for architectural glass was published in the February 11, 1976, *Federal Register*—ten pages of closely printed, three-column material. The proposed standard first provided background information and then delineated the standard itself, including desired breakage characteristics, environmental durability, and impact tests. A brief recital of economic and environmental considerations was then followed by a long section defining certain key terms used and explaining the scope of the rule.

Detailed testing procedures, together with appropriate engineering drawings, were then set forth. The next section listed a number of prohibited acts under the standard. Finally, the proposed standard invited interested persons to submit on or before March 12, 1976, written comments on technical and economic aspects or implications of the rule. Parties were invited to submit supporting data and documentation in conjunction with their comments. Additionally, the proposed standard announced that a public hearing would be held on March 8, 1976, and that any persons wishing to make an oral presentation should notify the CPSC secretary before February 26, 1976.

The agency received a substantial number of memoranda, written statements, letters, reports, test data, and other material; a legislative type hearing rather than the more formal adjudicatory proceeding was held; and the proposed standard was then evaluated in light of this additional material. Not until January 6, 1977, was the final standard for architectural glass published in the *Federal Register,* with an effective date of July 6, 1977. Petitions regarding amendments to the final standard were not disposed of until September 21, 1977.

But the story does not end there, for affected firms frequently—and sometimes successfully—petition courts of appeal on the grounds that standards are not supported by substantial evidence. In the most important case to date involving the CPSC, the Fifth Circuit Court of Appeals ruled that the agency must show that standards adopted improve safety and that they would have prevented prior accidents.[22] Thus, it is not uncommon for a court to remand rule-making proceedings to an agency for further consideration—and further procedural delay.

Rulemaking vs. Adjudication

As this case study indicates, rulemaking is not a magic formula for the rapid dispatch of the public's business or a universal substitute for the more formalized procedures of case-by-case adjudication. While there are clearly situations in which an agency may choose either procedure to transact its business, there are many instances when an agency inexorably must choose one or the other. Rulemaking is more applicable when there are many parties and broad policy questions must be settled and when it is relatively unimportant to place blame for an event on a particular party or parties.

Adjudication is appropriate when one or a small group is charged with undesirable conduct or seeks certain relief specific to it (such as a rate request instituted by a public utility) and when the issues in question relate to specific facts about who did what, where, how, when, why, and with what motive. Furthermore, adjudication is also more appropriate when the impact of a specific company's practice is in question, while rulemaking is more appropriate when the practice in question is general throughout an industry.[23] Both processes, however, require the costly generation of information to resolve issues fairly and reasonably. And while legislators and self-appointed guardians of the public interest may costlessly carp at agencies for taking considerable time in resolving problems, the only real alternative is arbitrariness and disregard of the duty to make reasoned choice—an alternative more appropriate to a totalitarian regime than a democratic society.

This is not to suggest that agencies cannot make their procedures more efficient or effective. They constantly try to do just that. But there is no simplistic shortcut to the difficult process of gathering information, evaluating it, and making decisions. Both rulemaking and adjudication involve these costly undertakings, and both manifest the same tendency for delay and preservation of the status quo because of these difficulties. One must not, however, confuse a tendency with an ironclad law. The status quo can be overcome, although it is difficult. Among the factors that can lead to change (or retard it) are what might be termed the "politics" of the regulatory process and the persistence and behavioral patterns of the people who operate within a regulatory agency.

THE BEHAVIOR OF REGULATORS

The Nature of Bureaucracy

Since the important writings of Max Weber, certain characteristics of bureaucracies, both regulatory and otherwise, have been recognized.

The activities and duties of bureaucracies are circumscribed by rules and laws. Bureaucracies are structured hierarchically so that superiors are held responsible for the actions and inactions of those under their command. Actions must be undertaken on a regular and consistent basis in which appeal is made to laws, rules, precedent, or reason. Except in situations that must be kept secret, decisions affecting persons or firms in the private sphere must be made in a written form that provides a basis for understanding the disposition of a matter.[24]

Yet while Weber's widely accepted perceptions tell us much about how regulators behave—especially their continual need to point to laws, rules, or reason to justify action—they do not help us to understand how agency discretion is exercised within these constraints. Why is one matter pursued rather than another? Why are substantial resources employed in one case and few in another? Of course, politics can play a role in exercising discretion, as we will see in the next section. If a senator who chairs an important committee overseeing the work of an agency takes an interest in a particular proceeding, this will affect the way the matter is handled.

Such political considerations have played major roles in the activities of many agencies. Yet it is far more common for regulators to go about their business without fearful concern about what legislators, public interest groups, or others will think about *specific* results. And even when politics plays a role in a particular matter, usually a regulator will think of the matter *primarily* in the way he or she would consider any other case: How does the result fulfill the agency's mission? Only after considering a matter in this way will a regulator look over his or her shoulder, so to speak, to determine the political implications. Only when the result is patently unrealistic politically will the proposed course of action be altered—and, even then, not always. How do regulators respond when exercising discretion in allocating resources? What are the factors that they weigh and consider?

Law and Policy

A regulator's first consideration—and it cannot be restated enough—is whether a proposed course of action can be justified by the laws administered by the agency and the decisions made thereunder. The second preliminary judgment is whether the particular matter under consideration fits into the agency's current plans or priorities. The plans and priorities in any agency can change considerably when the agency's leadership changes.

For example, during the 1960s, FTC chairmen explicitly called for vigorous enforcement of the laws regulating price discrimination. Yet no explicitly drafted policy statement announced this goal—the staff simply knew it and accordingly gave high priority to such cases. By the mid-1970s, however, FTC chairmen explicitly de-emphasized price discrimination matters, and the staff responded accordingly. At certain times, FTC chairmen have stressed voluntary procedures for settling matters while vigorous legal enforcement has been emphasized at others. And the staff takes its cues from the preferences of its leaders whose own judgments are often based on differences about where priorities should lie and how best to employ limited agency resources.

During the first year of his administration, for example, President Jimmy Carter appointed several former associates of Ralph Nader and others associated with the consumerist, environmentalist, and public interest advocacy movements to leadership positions in a number of regulatory agencies, including the CAB, FTC, OSHA, EPA, NHTSA, and EEOC. These individuals shared a belief that corporate power and behavior must be strictly controlled and that without such strict control, business firms could be expected usually to operate contrary to Naderites' conception of the public interest. Accordingly, they called for the development of many new, innovative regulatory programs and were relatively unsympathetic to business claims that the costs stemming from such programs frequently would outweigh the probable benefits.

For example, the NHTSA administrator "proposed a massive federal program to set up about 600 auto-inspection centers at which consumers could get before-and-after evaluations of repair work done on cars by private repair shops." [25] Although that expensive program was rejected by the secretary of transportation, the message translated to agency staff by such regulatory leadership is clear: be innovative and tough on the firms regulated and unsympathetic to the business argument that probable costs will outweigh public benefits. In other words, both explicit planning goals as well as the general views of those who head regulatory agencies at any particular time play important roles in determining priorities and methods of proceeding as well as allocating resources among an agency's many tasks.

This general guidance from law and policy priorities thus constitutes the first two factors in understanding an agency's internal decisionmaking processes. These considerations are usually far more important than the impact of external institutions such as Congress, the executive branch, and interest groups. The first point that follows from this observation is that in some instances an agency does not have the discretion to reject a matter for serious consideration. For example, when the American Telephone and Telegraph Company (AT&T) proposes a major interstate rate increase to the Federal Communications Commission or a motor carrier applies to the Interstate Commerce Commission for operating rights to haul plywood between two points, the agencies by law must seriously consider the proposals. In this respect, some agencies resemble courts; but, like the courts, this fact does not guarantee a particular outcome.

As these examples illustrate, when a matter must be considered because of statute or internal rules, the amount of resources that an agency will employ largely depends on the scope and complexity of the matter, regardless of the wishes of the agency. The ICC must devote more resources to considering an application for the merger of two large railroad systems than it usually will to a small trucker's application for the right to haul commodities. Although there is considerable variation from agency to agency, all agendas are to some extent controlled and to some extent open.

Rational Decisionmaking

To the extent that regulatory agencies are free to choose matters upon which they will concentrate and to allocate resources among them, what principles can we discern? Unfortunately, no ironclad rule can be provided, which is not surprising in view of the large number of persons who make and have made regulatory decisions.

Nevertheless, a valiant attempt to describe the process of *rational* decisionmaking has been undertaken by Richard Posner.[26] His insights provide the basis for much of what follows. Posner noted that an agency's goal is assumed to be to maximize the utility of its activities, with utility defined as the probable public benefit discounted by the probability of success in instituting the policy. Thus, the agency will probably not seek to institute a policy through rulemaking or adjudication if the probability of success is extremely low, even though the probable public benefit is fairly high; it will prefer to bring a matter with somewhat lower probable public benefit if the likelihood of success is somewhat higher.

To illustrate, assume that $U = BP$ where U is utility, B is probable public benefit, and P is probability of success. Thus, where B ranges from 1 to 10 and P ranges from 0 to 1, utility will be greater when B is 7 and P is .5 than when B is 10 and P is .2. The critical point is that simply considering probable public benefit without taking into account the likelihood of success results in a flawed picture of rational regulatory behavior. It fails to comprehend the *rational* behavior of many regulatory agencies that invest their resources in a large number of small matters with high probabilities of success rather than in a few large matters with low probabilities of success.

According to Posner, the above formulation constitutes only a first approximation of agency behavior. An agency's resources are limited both by its budget and the time of its personnel (usually lawyers) that must be consumed in a matter. Thus, a budget constraint factor must be added to the model. Additionally, the time and money that the agency can expect to use up in the matter is to some extent a function of the time and expense that firms and persons who will be affected by the decision or rule wil! probably expend in the matter.

In other words, if all other factors are held constant, it is less likely that an agency will consider a matter if the resources that will be used are higher than if they are lower. And the resources that the agency will probably use up are roughly proportional to the probable resources that affected parties will bring in contesting the proceeding. Of course, in reality the other variables—public benefit and probability of success—must also be brought into consideration; although there are important exceptions, in general the higher the probability of an agency's success in a particular matter, the less likely that an affected interest will wish to use up scarce resources on that matter.

But what considerations will make it more likely that an affected firm or person will probably use up its resources to battle the agency rather than quietly comply with the agency's proposed rule in rulemaking proceedings or proposed order in adjudication? The most important factor to the firm or person is the differential in its wealth position without and with the entry of the rule or order. For example, a firm might decide that an order will have no impact on its wealth position. Under these circumstances, it would not be rational for the firm to expend the resources necessary to contest the matter effectively. Many respondents against whom the FTC issues complaints quickly sign consent orders for this reason. Agency personnel have a fairly good idea about what the respondent's likely response will be in advance of bringing such matters and use this judgment in projecting the probable resources that the agency will expend.

On the other hand, there are situations in which the affected firm's wealth position will decline substantially because of the promulgation of an agency rule or order. Under these circumstances, it is much more likely that the firm will employ its resources to contest the agency's proposal. For example, early in the FTC's career, the agency concluded that selling goods through a lottery device, such as a punchboard, constituted an unfair method of competition under its organic statute. Notwithstanding the clear principle holding that lottery selling was an unfair method of competition, respondents invariably employed considerable resources in battling the agency. Since these firms tended to make all of their sales using the lottery device, they would go out of business when the order was enforced; they therefore invariably fought the entry of an order because their stake in the issue was so high.[27]

The lottery case also illustrates another principle posited by Posner—asymmetry. The utility of a matter to an agency may not be the same as the disutility measured by an affected firm. When an affected firm's perceived disutility is greater than the agency's perceived utility, the likelihood of a resource-consuming contest is greater. In the lottery case, from the agency's perspective: (1) the resources expended were relatively low even though the defendant would almost certainly contest the matter; (2) the probability of success was extremely high; and (3) the probable public benefit was perceived to be moderate—say, 4 on a range of 1 to 10. But the respondent's calculation was based on the differential wealth positions and the resources that it would have to expend, which also were low. Because of the disparity between perceived utility to the agency and perceived disutility to the respondent, we would expect the matter to be contested. Similarly, two firms subject to the same proposed rule or order might respond quite differently. An EPA rule forbidding the continued operation of an exhaust-emitting device would be considered differently by a firm that had just made a substantial investment in such a device than by one that had an option of installing that device or one that the EPA would approve at about the same cost.

Another important consideration that helps to predict whether a matter will be expensively contested or settled at relatively lower cost to the public stems from the different ways in which the regultory agency and the affected firms can measure probable public benefit. Particularly important in that regard is the precedent value of a proceeding, which is often very high to an agency but very low to an affected party. Suppose the Antitrust Division of the Justice Department discovered, from the legal perspective, an ideal test case that would establish an important principle in antimonopoly law to clarify and simplify future actions it contemplated bringing. Suppose also that the product in question contributed a very small amount to the aggregate profits of a large conglomerate corporation. The asymmetry once again is quite clear and in this situation would probably lead to the signing of a consent decree by the defendant corporation rather than an expensive court battle.

Even within the limitations of this model—which excludes, for the moment, political considerations—additional factors will influence whether an agency brings a matter, the resources it will employ, and the probable type of disposition. For example, an agency must consider each matter relative to other ones within the constraints of its budget. Thus, an agency may decide to settle a matter that we might otherwise predict would be bitterly contested because too many resources would be used up relative to its total budget. Or it might do so because this technique allows it to conclude a larger number of matters, each with some precedent value.

As this discussion indicates, the questions of which matters to bring, the resources to expend on each of them, and the appropriate way to resolve each of them are highly complex—even before we consider the important problem of political pressures. The simplistic recommendations that agencies should bring only important matters or the complaint that they devote inordinate amounts of effort to "trivial" matters turn out, upon closer examination, to be very superficial. So, too, does the self-righteous complaint of would-be reformers that many agencies frequently enter into compromise settlements with affected private interests that should have resulted in far more stringent public relief. As we have seen, allocating resources is no easier matter in the administrative realm than it is in private economic conduct. And this is true even before we consider the fact that groups extraneous to an agency's internal decisionmaking can intrude into the process.

REGULATORY POLITICS

The Life Cycle Theory

Few areas embraced within the subject of regulation have generated so much heat, yet so little light, as the politics of regulation, conceived as the impact upon decisionmaking of forces and groups extraneous to the formal administrative processes. Typically, sweeping assertions based on precious little evidence seek to show that such extraneous impact is powerful, indeed. Consider, for example, economist John K. Galbraith's statement endorsing what has been termed the "life cycle" theory:

> Regulatory bodies, like the people who comprise them, have a marked life cycle. In youth they are vigorous, aggressive, evangelistic and even intolerant. Later they mellow, and in old age—after a matter of ten or fifteen years—they become, with some exceptions, either an arm of the industry they are regulating or senile.[28]

According to the life cycle view, then, regulatory agencies move away from concern about the public interest to concern about the well-being of the firms that they regulate—which is presumably reflected in their decisionmaking.

But the life cycle theory is deficient in several respects. First, agencies are frequently innovative during many stages of their lives, developing new approaches and attacking new problems. The FTC, for example, acting on its own initiative 50 years after its creation, issued a novel trade regulation rule that required the disclosure of possible harmful effects on cigarette packages.[29] There are innumerable examples of innovation occurring in regulatory agencies long after their birth. In addition, regulatory agencies develop bodies of precedent, which enable subsequent matters to be treated in a manner similar to that taken when the problems were first looked at and decided. This behavior is properly described as relying upon experience and not as engaging in timid or passive policymaking.

The second difficulty inherent in the life cycle theory is the view that when public attention in an agency begins to wane, the agency becomes captured by the interest that it is charged with regulating. Initially, there are, of course, many regulatory agencies whose jurisdiction extends over a large number of interests, such as the Federal Trade Commission or the Environmental Protection Agency. The theory claiming that such agencies are captured by the industry they are required to regulate is simply inapplicable. But the theory is equally suspect when applied to agencies that focus on one or a few industries. Of course, as we have seen, Congress or a state legislature may draft a statute in such a way that an agency has little choice but to protect a trade or industry. But the administrators should not be blamed for examples of statutory cartelization such as medical or taxicab licensure; they are simply carrying out a legislative mandate.

And there are agencies that have fairly consistently favored one group over another. The FCC, for example, had tended to favor over-the-air broadcasters in their disputes with cable operators (although this, too, has been changing). But on the other hand, the FCC has also upheld the claims of upstart telecommunications companies against the Bell System. There are many instances, especially in the public utility area, in which business interests complain loudly about agency decisions. In brief, little evidence supports the life cycle theory. Although there are clearly some cases that it describes, there are too many cases that it does not fit.

The Capture Theory

A similar theory of regulatory politics with widespread popularity is capture. According to this theory, regulatory agencies behave in ways that persistently serve regulated industries to the harm of the public at large. Thus, the agency sees its role as one of industry protection: the FCC protects AT&T, the ICC protects the railroads, etc.

But a major difficulty is inherent in this notion of capture. Even when an agency regulates a single industry or a few similar industries, the regulated firms are apt to have conflicting interests. For example, the Federal Reserve Board and state banking agencies regulate the commercial banking industry. Yet for many years large banks and small banks have fought a running battle in legislatures and the regulatory agencies over such issues as the extent of branch banking that should be allowed and the permissibility of business arrangements, such as holding companies, that simulate branching.[30] And the banking industry divides still other ways on different issues.

More than any other regulatory agency, the Interstate Commerce Commission has been the source of a widely held view that agencies become captured by regulated interests. Samuel Huntington's notable 1952 article sought to show that the ICC consistently favored railroads in their struggle with motor carriers.[31] Yet others who have analyzed ICC decisions—including W. Z. Ripley, one of the agency's most attentive students—have concluded that the agency is sometimes far more attentive to the needs of shippers—an enormously diverse group—than it is to the needs of carriers.[32] Thus, when truckers better satisfy shipper needs, they win; and when railroads do so, they win. Others have argued that ICC regulatory action has, in the interests of shippers, stifled (if not quite destroyed) the railroad industry.[33] (The same charge of stifling the industry has been made, with considerable evidence mustered, about Federal Power Commission—now FERC—regulation of natural gas rates, another single industry case.[34])

But even if we grant that the capture notion may apply to an agency during a particular period, there is no reason that the agency's approach cannot change. Examples abound of regulatory agencies operating in different styles with different objectives at various times. For example, many agencies, including the ICC and FCC, have recently undertaken to lighten the burden of regulation even if not explicitly commanded to do so under statute. The capture theory cannot explain such inconsistencies or shifts in agency direction.

The fact is that agencies must, first and foremost, always justify their actions under their operating statutes and the general policies underlying these statutes. They must try to explain persuasively the reasons for their actions and frequently for their inactions as well. Second, situations in which an agency is responsive to a single attentive interest, with the rest of the world indifferent or inattentive, are rare. It is far more common in a regulatory proceeding for a number of interests—at least two—to be concerned and to seek different outcomes. And business interests, even within one industry, frequently do not speak with a single voice. In addition, it is not uncommon for courts, legislators, members of the executive branch, and even other regulators to be concerned about the outcomes of particular regulatory proceedings. Obviously, the more important the problem, the more likely it is that others will intervene. At least the possibility of such intervention is often sufficient to compel regulators to consider that possibility and how the agency's decision is defensible. Thus, agency decisionmaking— even when the agency's jurisdiction extends to only one or a few industries—is best characterized as pluralistic and, above all, rational in that it must supply cogent reasons, based on law and policy, for actions taken.

The FCC for a long while upheld AT&T's refusal to allow devices manufactured or distributed by other companies to be attached to AT&T's facilities on the ground that this would impair the quality of telephone service. But in 1968 the important *Carterfone* decision held that such devices were permissible unless AT&T could show that the attachment would have an impairing effect on the telephone system or any part thereof. Again, many diverse interests—the courts, other government agencies, even the petroleum industry, and changing technology—played roles in this transition.[35]

External Influences on the Regulatory Process

As we have noted, many different institutions may play roles in the decisionmaking process: Congress, the executive, other agencies, the courts, and affected groups, firms, or industries. In addition, public interest groups and the agency staff are important. For example, agency staff may conduct an investigation, prepare a report, and release the results, hoping for widespread media coverage prior to the institution of formal proceedings. During the early 1960s, the Securities and Exchange Commission staff conducted an intensive investigation that purported to show a marked deterioration in standards and responsibility on the part of the American Stock Exchange. The well-publicized report, without engaging in extravagant charges, placed the stock exchange on the defensive and facilitated the institution of additional rules and regulations.[36] Often information leaked to the press, an interview, or a speech made before a prominent group can also lead to the institution of a rule or decision.

Similarly, an agency must consider the views of affected groups, industries, and firms. In the most direct sense, such groups participate as a matter of course in formal agency proceedings; and an agency, in making its decisions, must respond to them in a considered statement based on law and the facts. Indeed, this is the very essence of a regulatory proceeding. But two other facets of the relationship are also important. First, the agency must remain on reasonably good terms with the industry or industries that it regulates for information cost reasons. To a large extent, the regulated industry or industries often supply the information required for most agency investigations and proceedings. Their resistance, necessitating resort to compulsory process and procedural hearings, can greatly increase the agency's resource expenditures for each matter.

Second, no agency—whether it regulates practices across industry lines, as the EPA does, or intensively regulates one or a few industries—wishes to use its powers to debilitate those it regulates. Rather, agencies conceive their mission to be either curbing excesses or actually aiding an industry's operations. Of course, an agency might misjudge the impact of its actions, but regulators are usually as concerned as others in government with assuring a thriving economy and therefore with the units that compose it. Consequently, regulators have a strong incentive to be attentive to the complaints of the industries that they regulate. But this does not mean that they simply capitulate to industry groups, which are only one of many groups taken into account in the decisionmaking process.

Relationships between agencies and the courts are considerably less subtle than those that agencies maintain with affected groups, industries, or firms. Since most agency rules, regulations, and orders can be reviewed on appeal to the courts, agencies must constantly be aware of administrative law and constitutional requirements. They must be sure that they can point to provisions of the statutes under which they operate to justify the actions they take and that their findings and conclusions are supported by substantial evidence. The reasoning supporting their decisions and rules must be logical and tight, and they must rigorously follow their own procedures, without any shortcuts or deviations.

Regulators must consider all of these points from the beginning of a matter until the agency's final disposition of it. Failure to do so can result in a matter being reversed by the courts. Not only would a court's adverse disposition of a case be costly and wasteful to an agency, but it would be embarrassing to the agency's personnel as well. Although agency decisions are not infrequently reversed on appeal, the power of a court to reverse or remand provides regulators with a very strong incentive to abide by constitutional, administrative, and other legal requirements.

The executive branch exercises a variety of direct and indirect influences over regulatory agencies. First, the president appoints regulators and, as we noted earlier, may remove or effectively request their resignation, except in the case of members of independent commissions. The president may not remove members of independent commissions who are appointed for a term of years, but usually he may name and replace the chairman with another member.

Equally important, the Office of Management and Budget (OMB), one of the president's staff agencies, must in most cases approve agency budget requests before they are submitted to Congress. This gives the president not only the power to pare down budget requests but also to approve or disapprove specific programs and budget items. For this reason, regulators must be aware of the contours of the president's major programs and attempt to fit the agency's programs into it. For example, if curbing inflation is a presidential priority, an agency should seek to show that its policies aid in this effort or at least do not conflict with it. An agency's frequent disregard of this elementary rule can affect not only its budget and programs for the upcoming fiscal year but also proposals for new legislation and requests for supplementary funds, both of which must also be cleared through the OMB.

But there are even more subtle reasons why an agency should be attentive to the needs, programs, and requests of the president. Obviously, the president's support for appropriations or program approval is invaluable when such requests do reach Congress. Similarly, presidential support is desirable if an agency is under attack in Congress. Furthermore, the president's support can generate considerable public support for the agency, an asset that is particularly valuable if the agency is contemplating undertaking controversial or innovative programs.

The president also can exercise considerable influence in unleashing or restraining another executive branch agency in its relationships with the agency in question. For example, the Antitrust Division of the Justice Department and the Federal Trade Commission have not infrequently commented on or participated in the affairs of other agencies as have other executive branch offices. At times such intervention may prove embarrassing or troublesome to the agency in question. Finally, the president has the power to appoint an advisory group or commission to study the agency in question. The results of such investigations have sometimes been highly critical.[37]

Aware of all of this, policymakers in a regulatory agency should be attentive to the president's programs and how their own either fits in or at least does not conflict with it. Of course, the enormous power of the president and his close associates in the executive branch may also lead regulators *occasionally* to grant undue favors to those people or their friends in the hope of currying support.[38] Finally, as we saw in the last chapter, Congress exercises considerable supervision over regulatory agencies. But supervision or influence is a far cry from decisionmaking. Regulators take many influences into account, but their statutes, rules, and policy dispositions usually loom as most important in their behavior.

CONCLUSION

Administrative agencies are subject to many actual and potential pressures, as this chapter has indicated. But it would be a mistake to conclude that regulatory agencies are nothing more than brokers whose principal function is to provide benefits to those interests that exert the strongest pressures. As we have seen, agencies respond to many factors and actors. They usually seek to *not displease* those with whom they interact to the extent that their budgets, programs, and policies will be threatened; but agencies will usually accommodate those with whom they interact *only to the extent* that such activities do not interfere with budgets, programs, and policies.

Thus, regulatory agencies may expedite matters in which legislators take an interest, but this does not guarantee that the matter will be concluded differently than if no such interest had been expressed. Regulatory agencies usually will not directly challenge the president's program. They typically carry out the program of agency leaders, only being careful not to engage in an open confrontation with the president or Congress. It is not a meaningless nuance to suggest that agencies typically respond to outside groups and institutions not by trying to unduly please but rather by trying not to unduly displease them. Only in this way can regulatory agencies carry out their principal obligation to enforce the laws and policies with which they are charged.

NOTES

1. Richard A. Posner, "Theories of Economic Regulation," *Bell Journal of Economics and Management Science* 5 (Autumn 1974):337, 338.
2. A good case study of the preliminary decisionmaking process in the Antitrust Division of the Justice Department is Suzanne Weaver, *Decision to Prosecute* (Cambridge, Mass.: MIT Press, 1977). As Weaver makes clear, no simple rules can consistently explain Antitrust Division evaluative decisions, no less regulatory decisions generally.
3. See Robert A. Katzmann, *Regulatory Bureaucracy* (Cambridge, Mass.: MIT Press, 1980), chap. 3.
4. See Alan Stone, "The FTC and Advertising Regulation: An Examination of Agency Failure," *Public Policy* 21 (Spring 1975):226, 227.
5. For an excellent detailed study of an FTC investigation, see Joseph Palamountain, "The Dolcin Case and the Federal Trade Commission," in *Government Regulation of Business: A Casebook*, ed. Edwin A. Bock (Englewood Cliffs, N.J.: Prentice-Hall, 1962), pp. 80-86.
6. *Consolidated Edison Co.* v. *NLRB*, 305 U.S. 197, 230 (1938).
7. See William Wardell, "Rx More Regulation or Better Therapies," *Regulation* (September/October 1979):25-33.
8. Details are provided in *Corn Products Refining Co.* v. *Food and Drug Administration*, 427 F.2d 511 (3d Cir., 1970).
9. U.S., Temporary National Economic Committee, *Monograph No. 28: Study of Legal Reserve Life Insurance Companies* (Washington, D.C.: Government Printing Office, 1941), p. 148.
10. *Yick Wo* v. *Hopkins*, 118 U.S. 356, 369-70 (1886).
11. Bruce Owen and Ronald Braeutigam, *The Regulation Game* (Cambridge, Mass.: Ballinger, 1978), p. 23.
12. Howie Kurtz, "The Consumer Product Safety Commission and Asbestos," *The Washington Monthly* (December 1977):29.
13. Jo Thomas, "Performance of Consumer Agency Disappoints its Early Supporters," *New York Times*, January 30, 1978, pp. 1, 14.
14. Cited in *Consumer Protection: Gains and Setbacks* (Washington, D.C.: Congressional Quarterly, 1978), p. 8.

15. See Walter Oi, "Safety at any Price?" *Regulation* (November/December 1977):16-23.

16. Sam Peltzman, *Regulation of Automobile Safety* (Washington, D.C.: American Enterprise Institute, 1975).

17. An excellent graphic study illustrating the many substantive problems involved in developing and promulgating a standard is Milton Z. Kafoglis, "Matchbook Safety," in *Benefit-Cost Analyses of Social Regulation,* ed. James C. Miller III and Bruce Yandle (Washington, D.C.: American Enterprise Institute, 1979), pp. 75-86.

18. See "Lawn Mowers, Matchbooks and Architectural Glass," *Regulation* (November/December 1977):35.

19. The materials that form the basis of this tale are collected in U.S., Congress, House of Representatives, *Consumer Product Safety Commission—Oversight Hearings,* 95th Cong., 1st sess., 1977.

20. Ibid., p. 554.

21. Some of the problems involved in the offeror process are discussed in Larry Kramer, "Safety Standards Process Called Roadblock," *Washington Post,* February 25, 1978, pp. C-1, C-10.

22. See "Aqua Slide 'N' Dive: The CPSC and the Court," *Regulation* (May/June 1978):9, 10.

23. For a thorough discussion of these issues, see Glen O. Robinson, "The Making of Administrative Policy: Another Look at Rulemaking and Adjudication and Administrative Procedure Reform," in *Perspectives on the Administrative Process,* ed. Robert L. Rabin (Boston: Little, Brown & Co., 1979), pp. 273-287.

24. Max Weber, *Economy and Society,* trans. E. Fischoff et al., 3 vols. (New York: Bedminster Press, 1968), pp. 956-959.

25. Juan Cameron, "Nader's Invaders are Inside the Gates," *Fortune* (October 1977):260. An interesting case study of changes at the FTC during Chairman Michael Pertschuk's tenure is Ernest Gellhorn, "The New Gibberish at the FTC," *Regulation* (May/June 1978):37-44.

26. Richard A. Posner, "The Behavior of Administrative Agencies," *Journal of Legal Studies* 1 (June 1972):305-347.

27. On the lottery cases, see Alan Stone, *Economic Regulation and the Public Interest* (Ithaca, N.Y.: Cornell University Press, 1977), pp. 203, 204.

28. John K. Galbraith, *The Great Crash* (Boston: Houghton Mifflin Co., 1955), p. 171. See also Marver H. Bernstein, *Regulating Business by Independent Commission* (Princeton, N.J.: Princeton University Press, 1955), chap. 3.

29. Generally, see A. Lee Fritschler, *Smoking and Politics* (New York: Appleton-Century-Crofts, 1969).

30. For example, see Charles W. Collins, *The Branch Banking Question* (New York: Macmillan, 1926); and Gerald C. Fischer, *American Banking Structure* (New York: Columbia University Press, 1968), chap. 2.

31. Samuel Huntington, "The Marasmus of the ICC: The Commission, the Railroads and the Public Interest," *Yale Law Journal* 61 (April 1952):467-509.

32. William Z. Ripley, *Railroads: Rates and Regulation* (New York: Longman, 1913), p. 118; and Gordon P. MacDougall, "Industry Pricing Practices as a Factor in Regulatory Decisions," in *Transportation Research Forum, Proceedings—Sixth Annual Meeting* (Oxford, Ind.: Richard B. Cross, 1965), pp. 53-58.

33. For example, see Albro Martin, *Enterprise Denied* (New York: Columbia University Press, 1971).
34. Paul MacAvoy, "The Effectiveness of the Federal Power Commission," *Bell Journal of Economics and Management Science* 1 (Autumn 1970):271-303; and Paul MacAvoy, "The Regulation Induced Shortage of Natural Gas," *Journal of Law and Economics* 14 (April 1971):167-199.
35. Alfred E. Kahn, *The Economics of Regulation*, 2 vols. (New York: John Wiley & Sons, 1971), 2:140-145.
36. William L. Cary, *Politics and the Regulatory Agencies* (New York: McGraw-Hill Book Co., 1967), pp. 71, 72.
37. See Erwin G. Krasnow and Lawrence D. Longley, *The Politics of Broadcast Regulation*, 2d ed. (New York: St. Martin's Press, 1978), pp. 56-62.
38. For example, see the case studies in Bernard Schwartz, *The Professor and the Commissions* (New York: Alfred A. Knopf, 1959).

8

Regulatory Reform

A persistent theme in American regulatory history has been a demand for regulatory reform. Nevertheless, there are periods in which the voices of reform reach a fortissimo, while in others they can barely be heard. In the late 1970s, regulatory reform again became a major issue. The first part of this chapter examines the reasons for this upsurge and the critique of contemporary regulation. This discussion will show that there are three principal reform questions—justification, cost-effectiveness, and cost-benefit—as well as three types of regulatory reformer—traditionalist, restrictivist, and populist. Keeping these distinctions in mind will help to illuminate two of the most important terms in the reform debate—deregulation and overregulation, which will be explored in depth.

The remainder of the chapter will focus on specific regulatory reform proposals, of which cost-benefit analysis is the most important. As we will see, cost-benefit analysis actually breaks down into five different techniques, each with its own costs and difficulties. Other reform proposals that we will examine—including greater public participation in agency proceedings, sunset laws, employment restrictions, and agency planning—also pose difficult problems. The central problem of cost, notably information cost, that has pervaded so many issues raised in this book occurs in reform proposals as well. Regulatory reforms may certainly provide improvement, but they are not panaceas.

OLD AND NEW REGULATORY REFORM

The subject of regulatory agency performance is not new. Long before the mid-1970s, investigations of regulatory agency performance had taken place and proposals for reform advanced. Indeed, complaints about the performance of regulatory agencies, the appointments of study commissions, and proposals for reform have been routine recurrences in 20th century American political life. And in many instances important reforms have been instituted that were expected to improve regulatory performance dramatically. The following excerpt from a 1946 issue of *The New York Times* concerning enactment of the Administrative Procedure Act is typical of such reforms and may strike many readers with its contemporary chord:

> Utility, rail and numerous other industries ... are celebrating the recent passage of the Administrative Procedure Act. ... When the ... bill became law last month, corporation counsel and company officials looked back on more than 10 years of continuous effort ... to remove the "onerous" problems that beset companies appearing before these agencies.[1]

Attacks on "red tape," "delay," and "excessive paper work" did not, of course, end with enactment of the 1946 Administrative Procedure Act, nor did previous reforms designed to cure other problems associated with regulation end complaints about these subjects. Many of the principal complaints currently made about regulation have recurred frequently during the last 50 years. Some of these prior proposals additionally have been remarkably comprehensive, such as those made by the 1948 and 1955 Hoover Commissions and regulatory expert James M. Landis's 1960 report to President John F. Kennedy. Nevertheless, there are significant differences between prior criticisms of regulation and the current assault upon it, two of which are paramount: (1) the intensity and widespread public consciousness of regulation as a public problem and (2) the additional layers of criticism captured by such terms as "deregulation" or "overregulation" that supplement (and sometimes contradict) earlier criticisms.

In the past, awareness of alleged regulatory deficiencies was largely confined to select elite groups in American society and did not play a significant role in election campaign discourse. True, in many political campaigns office seekers did expend much energy decrying the size and alleged inefficiency of the federal bureaucracy. But such complaints were not directed to particular sets of public programs such as regulation; rather, they tended to be highly ambiguous with little substantive criticism of programs.

The 1980 presidential election marked a sharp break from prior campaigns, focusing on a set of issues that had been percolating into public consciousness since 1974. Jimmy Carter wasted no effort in proclaiming the regulatory reforms implemented during his presidency, while Ronald Reagan frequently derided the incumbent's reform efforts. For example, in signing the Staggers Rail Act of 1980 (the Railroad Deregulation Act) on October 14, 1980—during the height of the election campaign—President Carter remarked for obvious public consumption:

> We deregulated the airlines, we deregulated the trucking industry, we deregulated financial institutions, we decontrolled oil and natural gas prices and we negotiated lower trade barriers throughout the world for our exports.... We've carried out the most fundamental restructuring of our economy, the relationship between government and the private enterprise system, since Franklin D. Roosevelt's time and the initiation of the New Deal.[2]

Candidate Reagan, in contrast, often asserted that the Carter administration frequently overregulated important industries and did not properly assess the costs and benefits of regulation, so that often costs outweighed benefits.[3] Not only did Reagan hammer hard on the overregulation theme during his campaign in his national addresses, but he emphasized it in many of his local speeches as well, especially in industrial communities. His October 7, 1980, speech in Steubenville, Ohio, contained a typical statement:

> But Mr. Carter acts as if he hasn't been in charge for three and one-half years. He's acting as if he hadn't ignored the crisis of overregulation.... However, in perhaps the most important area—overregulation—Mr. Carter's plan [for the steel industry] is but a pale imitation of my proposal.[4]

The unanimity with which both major presidential candidates attacked "overregulation" and called for "deregulation" and the zeal with which both promised to assure that benefits from regulations would outweigh costs signaled an important change in the public philosophy. Never before had the subject of regulation been so important in a presidential campaign, and not since the Progressive Era had the subject been perceived as so important by ordinary citizens. The candidates were, in part, responding to the concerns of the public and, in part, reflecting a change in the public philosophy toward regulation. The new phrases "deregulation," "overregulation," and "cost-benefit analysis" symbolized not just a continuing trend of regulatory reform but a new approach toward the problems and difficulties of regulation that continued and sometimes supplanted the earlier movements for regulatory reform.

We will look more closely at several distinct orientations toward regulatory reform later, but for the moment it will suffice to note that the new orientation widely and intensively held by the general public seeks important *substantive* changes in regulation and does not merely seek ways to curb delay or red tape or to institute other procedural reforms. The new orientation seeks to compare the extant structure of regulation with other alternatives, especially the (relatively) free market and, more frequently than not, finds the current regulatory structure wanting.

The Context of the New Regulatory Reform

Before examining the various categories of regulatory reform orientation, we need to place the new impetus and awareness of regulation in a wider economic context. Several factors helped to fuel the current generally negative public judgment about regulation. First, regulation was blamed, in part, for declining American competitiveness in world markets; specifically, regulation was held to be one of several causes of sluggish American innovation and capital spending on new plants and equipment as well as of declining productivity.

This simple view begins with the notion of scarce resources and suggests that a firm's resources that must be committed to regulatory compliance cannot be used for other more productive purposes, such as new plant equipment or research and development. Thus, a *Fortune* magazine study asserted in 1978:

> It is no secret by now that in nearly every industry, new requirements by government are putting a significant drag on productivity—by diverting capital expenditures to nonproductive uses, by inhibiting research and development, by channeling R and D toward meeting various government edicts, and by prohibiting use of efficient production processes.[5]

The argument concludes that regulation has had a significant impact on the competitiveness of American-made goods relative to those of principal competitors, especially West Germany and Japan. Regulation is therefore a major contributor to a number of economic ills, including unemployment, a declining standard of living, and high inflation.

The critical question, of course, is how significant an impact recent regulation has had on the decline in American productivity. While no study of this subject purports to be conclusive, a number of estimates have been made, most notably those undertaken under the auspices of the Brookings Institution by economist Edward F. Dennison. While the adjusted growth of national income per person employed (NIPPE) was 2.6 percent a year during the period from 1948 to 1973, it declined to −0.6 percent a year during the 1973 to 1976 period and has not rebounded since. Environmental, safety, and health regulation and crime prevention are "estimated to have retarded the 1973-1976 growth rate of NIPPE by 0.4 percentage points."[6] Dennison concluded that these factors

> contributed importantly to the decline in national income per person employed ....
> ....
> [even excluding other regulatory] programs that impose similar resource costs, and for which requirements are new or have become more stringent. . . .[7]

The technical research of Dennison and other scholars tended to reinforce the view already widely held in the media and popular political rhetoric that regulation is a major contributor to the range of economic problems associated with the productivity decline. The following report from *The Washington Post* is typical:

Many companies put the blame for the research downturn on federal regulations. These companies say the money they would normally spend on exploratory research is being spent to satisfy new regulations.[8]

More generally, the prevailing view has been summarized by *The Wall Street Journal:*

People who prepare government required reports or develop and monitor plans to comply with regulations ... are paid by the companies, but essentially they work for government. Instead of producing tires, hamburgers or revenue generating services, they advance the government's social goals. As their ranks increase, therefore, they tend to reduce the productivity of company work forces.[9]

In short, the first major objection to recent regulation is based on an opportunity-cost argument, contending that in a world of scarce resources "overregulation" shifts their use from activities that would help achieve higher levels of productivity, innovation, capital investment, and greater competitiveness into activities that hinder the attainment of these ends. Moreover, as West Germany and Japan have demonstrated, once these ends are attained, they can act significantly to counteract the effects of inflation.

And because "overregulation" is perceived as inhibiting the attainment of these goals, it also contributes to a higher rate of inflation. Additionally, regulation is viewed as having a very direct effect on inflation by enhancing the price of goods and services. Inflation is the second major factor contributing to the intensively negative public judgment about regulation that began during the second half of the 1970s and played a significant role in the 1980 presidential election.

The Critique of Contemporary Regulation

Murray L. Weidenbaum, an important academic economist and chairman of President Reagan's Council of Economic Advisers, helped to provide the theoretical underpinnings of an argument against regulation that was funneled through the media and political actors to the general public. Weidenbaum's argument—or more accurately, two arguments: "no-benefit" and "cost-benefit"—is that regulations inevitably carry a price tag. Very often, according to the no-benefit argument, regulations serve little purpose and can readily be dispensed with—yet they are still costly. A favorite example of advocates of the no-benefit argument concerns Occupational Safety and Health Administration rules for ladders. As Weidenbaum has illustrated, the definitions and standards for ladders are typically so muddled or involved that few employers can be guided by them effectively. It is obviously not necessary, Weidenbaum implied, to provide so many extremely detailed definitions and rules, including algebraic and trigonometric equations, for so simple a device as a ladder.[10] This situtation is similar to the enormous sums expended and time elapsed before the Food and Drug Administration was able to determine the precise percentage of peanuts required before a product could be labeled peanut butter. Similarly, paper-work requirements imposed upon firms often serve little purpose and are unnecessarily burdensome.

Such unnecessary expenditures, Weidenbaum's argument continues, are not simply imposed upon the affected companies with no rippling effects elsewhere. Rather, many costs are passed on to consumers and are thus inflationary in a direct sense as well as in the indirect sense of resources that might have been employed in more productive endeavors. But, as we observed earlier, there is surprisingly little systematic data compiled on the extent of "silly" regulations. Surely some regulations are unjustified or even harmful, but there is no evidence to indicate that such instances are widespread. Indeed, the principal agencies about which such complaints of inflationary impact have been made—the Environmental Protection Agency and the Occupational Safety and Health Administration—generally perform justifiable tasks.

It is the second branch of the "regulation carries a price tag" argument that has the greater weight. In brief, this argument (which will be examined later in more detail) asserts that the costs of regulation frequently outweigh the admitted benefits. This cost-benefit argument contrasts sharply with the no-benefit argument, which suggests that no benefits flow from many regulations.

The Political Attack on Regulation

Regulation's low standing in the public view stems also from a generally antipathetic attitude toward federal government activity. Denunciation of bureaucracy and bureaucrats and a sense that unrepresentative elites have captured the regulatory process, using it for their own ends, are symptomatic of the political reason for the rejection of regulation. This attitude also embraces the sense that administrative decisionmakers know little about the impact of their regulations on those who must live with them and that they care even less. Interestingly, this view that such elites control our destiny is shared by people on different sides of the political spectrum.

The growth of resentment toward government regulation—characterized by the sharply negative connotation of the word "bureaucrat" in the popular lexicon—probably stems from the breadth of the political forces that allege that regulators work to institute programs promoting some narrow group's selfish economic interest or ideological predisposition. Whether it is the rank paternalism involved in a Federal Trade Commission proceeding that seriously considered a ban on television advertising of candy aimed at children, the intervention by civil rights agencies in numerous employment situations, the frequency with which state utility commissions grant higher rates requested by public utilities, the many instances of corruption or questionable behavior that have occurred when municipalities grant cable television franchises, or a host of other regulatory activities that have deeply impinged upon the public consciousness, considerable evidence *superficially* supports the skepticism about administrators' abilities to regulate properly.

MAJOR REFORM QUESTIONS

It is clear from the foregoing discussion that the demand for regulatory reform ranges throughout the American political spectrum. Yet the underlying reasons for reform and the proposed directions for it vary considerably. Nevertheless, certain key phrases—rich in ambiguity and hyperbole and designed to attract popular support—such as "deregulation" and "overregulation," are used by advocates of every viewpoint.

This manifest ambiguity lumps together not only important ideological differences with respect to regulation but also the major questions about regulation that should be distinguished from each other. These questions that must be considered in examining any set of proposals for regulatory reform are justification, cost-effectiveness, and cost-benefit.

Justification

The first distinct question is: Is regulation warranted under one of the justifications—efficiency, externalities, or equity—that we examined earlier in Part II? And even if regulation was once justified, is it now justifiable? For example, milk minimum price regulation cannot be justified under any of the grounds that we discussed. Regulation in this case has served to shield the dairy industry from the rigors of price competition. In a word, such regulation was instituted not because of market failure but because the market worked too well. To take another example, even if we concede that commercial aviation in its infancy should have been regulated with respect to rates and entry under the promotional category of efficiency regulation, it does not follow that such regulation should persist during the industry's maturity when that justification clearly no longer applies.

Cost-Effectiveness

The justification question, then, concerns ends: Is the end an appropriate one? The second question is the cost-effectiveness one, which assumes that an end is worthy of attainment under one of the justifications that we discussed or under some other one. It then asks what the cheapest and most effective means are to achieve that end. In the simplest possible case, if means A costs $100 and means B costs $200 to attain exactly the same results, then means A is more cost-effective. But, of course, many cost-effectiveness questions are not that simple, since the probabilities of attaining a desirable result can vary considerably. In the same simple example, suppose the probability of attaining the result under means A is .4, and the likelihood is .8 under means B. Which means is more cost-effective under these circumstances?

Actual choices are rarely this simple, but the problem of incorporating both programmatic dollar costs and the probability of attaining ends is always present. As we have noted on many occasions, merely enacting a law hardly assures its successful implementation. Experience, economic theory, and administrative theory are the principal tools that facilitate our ability to answer the cost-effectiveness question. And while these tools do not necessarily guarantee a correct evaluation, they at least permit us to exclude certain alternatives and help us to predict probable outcomes in the remaining cases.

The cost-effectiveness question has both substantive and administrative components and breaks down into a large number of specific questions. At the substantive level, it involves an analysis of whether government intervention or the free market is more cost-effective. If the answer is public intervention, the problem then is to determine which form of intervention will be most cost-effective. This analysis would include comparisons of both regulation and other interventionist techniques as well as alternative forms of regulation.

Assuming that a particular form of regulation is selected as the most cost-effective technique, the next set of cost-effectiveness questions are administrative. These include such major problems as when to use rulemaking rather than litigation techniques and what kind of procedural apparatus to construct as well as technocratic questions such as the minimum number of agency employees needed to attain the goals. In other words, most of the problems raised by the discipline of public administration are embraced under the cost-effectiveness question. And just as in the case of the justification question, alternatives developed in a cost-effectiveness analysis should be evaluated periodically. Indeed, the question of how frequently to undertake cost-effectiveness evaluation is an important cost-effectiveness question.

Cost-Benefit

The third overriding question about regulation is the cost-benefit one. While the first question concerns justifications and the second question calls for an examination of alternative means to a given end, the cost-benefit question requires the weighting of means and ends as well as secondary consequences resulting from regulation.

A simple example will illustrate. Suppose technique A will achieve results worth $20, the means will cost $5, and the costs of the secondary consequences will be $8. Under these circumstances, the net benefit, obtained after incorporating all costs and benefits in our calculations, will be $7. Suppose technique B, an alternative way of attaining results worth $20, will only cost $4, but the costs of the secondary consequences will be $11. Applying cost-benefit analysis, the net benefit under technique B is $5. Technique A is clearly the superior cost-benefit one, although B is apparently the more cost-effective one.

But even though this comparison inexorably leads to the conclusion that we should adopt technique A, this does not mean that cost-effectiveness analysis is useless. It is obviously useful when the means are given and the secondary consequences need not be considered. For example, if we decide to ban a particular pesticide because of the grave dangers it poses to human health, the end is set and secondary consequences need not be considered. Only cost-effectiveness analysis is important in that case.

Cost-benefit analysis is not employed only when the ends are held constant, however. It may be used to address the opportunity-cost problem as well. For example, suppose legislators have $5 that they wish to expend for some regulatory benefit. Their rational response would be to examine a number of possible alternative uses of the funds and ask which of them will yield the greatest net benefit. Thus, given the sums available for consumer protection expenditures, would it be wiser in a cost-benefit sense for Congress to appropriate the available money for the development of a skateboard standard by the Consumer Product Safety Commission or for the institution of an FTC monitoring program that will determine whether high fidelity equipment performs as advertised?

Similarly, in an agency whose budget has already been appropriated, cost-benefit analysis can be employed to rank-order agency priorities and therefore can be an important tool in the agency planning process. Should the CPSC employ its funds in developing a skateboard standard or an electric blanket standard? Oversimplifying what are obviously complex problems, the agency might decide that an expenditure of $5 on standard A will yield results worth $20 but that the cost of the secondary consequences will be $11. On the other hand, the $5 expenditure on standard B will yield results worth $16, but the costs of the secondary consequences will only be $4. Standard B is to be preferred on cost-benefit grounds since its net benefit is $7, while A's is only $4.

Later we will look more closely at the problems associated with cost-effectiveness and cost-benefit analysis. For the moment it is important to appreciate that calls for regulatory reform usually involve one or more of the three major questions that we have touched on here: justification, cost-effectiveness, and cost-benefit. The attention given to these questions depends upon the particular regulatory issue. For example, airline regulation principally raises the justification question; nuclear power regulation principally raises the cost-effectiveness question; and pharmaceutical safety regulation and environmental regulation primarily focus on the cost-benefit issue.

Thus, much of the debate concerning the deregulation of trucking, airlines, and railroads has centered on the question of whether any reasonable justification *currently* exists for the rate and route regulation of these businesses. Criticism of the Nuclear Regulatory Commission concerns the fact that it takes 13 or 14 years to put a nuclear plant on line, largely because of agency procedures that lead to substantially increased costs than what they would be if on-line time were shorter. (In Japan, only 6 years is required.) And the stringent testing requirements imposed by U.S. pharmaceutical regulation *may* be costing more lives, as a result of patients not having access to drugs that are available in other countries, than are saved because of possible adverse side-effects—a cost-benefit problem.[11] Finally, any particular regulatory area may be examined with respect to each of these questions, any two of them, or only one of them.

A TYPOLOGY OF REGULATORY REFORMERS

Posing questions is very different from answering them, and the reader will have surmised by this point that political or social values will play important roles in assigning quantitative values in many cost-effectiveness or cost-benefit evaluations and indeed in the whole area of regulatory reform. This is not to suggest that precise scientific analysis cannot take place but rather that most discussion of economic and social regulation will likely contain a mixture of values, orientations, and scientific analysis. Values and orientations thus have a major impact on the precise prescriptions for reform.

Political scientist David Welborn has provided an excellent framework to help understand three major orientations toward regulatory reform.[12] He pointed out that most regulatory reform proposals considered by government prior to the Nixon administration were largely limited to a few select questions concerning administrative organization, procedure, or the quality of personnel. Of course, many academics and others were critical of regulation from other perspectives before then, but their efforts and recommendations were largely unnoticed in official circles and were not treated seriously by most public officials.

The 1971 Ash Council report to President Nixon was a major breakthrough in its advocacy of more sweeping regulatory reforms than those proposed by any prior official study group. However, it was the Ford administration that first made drastic regulatory reform a central part of the president's program and advanced it as a central political issue. Inflation and energy shortages for which regulation was partly blamed, many complaints about particular regulatory programs, and the Ford administration's impetus combined to place regulatory reform high on the political agenda. The Democratic party, not wishing to allow the Republicans to dominate an increasingly popular issue, launched their own congressional investigations into questions of regulatory reform. In particular, Democratic Senator Edward M. Kennedy of Massachusetts seized upon regulatory reform, most notably in connection with the airline industry, as a major issue with which he sought to be identified.[13]

By 1975 regulatory reform had matured as a political issue. But unlike many political issues, regulatory reform drew its support throughout the political spectrum from left to right. Liberal Democrats, such as Senator Kennedy, joined hands with staunch conservatives who sought market solutions to most economic and social problems. However, in the process that led to regulatory reform becoming as sacred as motherhood, clear differences in reform orientations became obscured. Welborn has identified three distinct orientations in regulatory reform, which he labeled *traditionalist, restrictivist,* and *populist.*

Traditionalists

The traditionalist orientation focuses on the abuse of economic power: the divergence between the narrow self-seeking ends of the unbridled marketplace and "higher" social ends requires government intervention to direct business behavior toward social goals. Regulation is not seen as a perfect instrument but rather one that is at least better than the free market in many instances. But since regulation is admittedly a far from perfect technique, traditionalist reformers emphasize the continual need to improve the regulatory process.

Traditionalists therefore look for and advocate improved procedures, organization, and personnel as well as clearer statutory mandates and additional powers to be given to regulators that will better enable them to carry out their socially benefiting tasks. Substantively, traditionalists call for periodic examination of regulatory goals and agency performance to see whether they are moving toward social goals.

Restrictivists

Those who subscribe to the restrictivist orientation have a distaste for government intervention, generally, and regulation, particularly. While they concede the need for some regulation, restrictivists hold that the burden of proof is upon those who advocate regulation to show that its net benefits exceed those that would prevail under free market conditions. When they do grant the need for regulation, restrictivists opt for the lightest rather than the heaviest burden to be imposed upon those regulated, unless there is a *clear* showing that the net benefits of a lighter regulatory hand are lower than the net benefits of a heavier hand—something they rarely find. Thus, restrictivists generally prefer requirements that information be provided rather than performance standards, which in turn are usually preferred to design standards.

This distaste for controls has both philosophical and economic foundations. Philosophically, any government regulation is seen as an incursion on private freedom, while economic theory is employed to show that the free market will yield better performance than regulation in most situations. The prescriptions of the restrictivist school, then, include deregulation in the sense of a return to market conditions, the substitution of incentives and property rights mechanisms for regulation, and the employment of both cost-effectiveness and cost-benefit analyses.

Populists

The third major reform strand—populist—accepts administrative regulation when it performs socially acceptable goals but rejects it in instances where regulation is viewed as aiding corporate interests. In the populist view, then, regulation of energy prices is accepted because the consumer is better off by paying lower prices. But populists reject airline rate regulation because in that instance consumers pay more for air travel than they would if market conditions prevailed.

Populists view corporate power as both pervasive and mighty in both the legislative and administrative arenas. Civil Aeronautics Board regulation of airline rates and entry is considered as having been brought about through the devious actions of the air carriers that sought to maintain a cartel arrangement. Even if popular pressure initially was responsible for the enactment of regulatory legislation intended to curb business excesses, corporations can concentrate resources at the administrative level in order to influence agencies to move in directions favorable to them. Substantively, the populist orientation is frequently reactive. Its views on particular pieces of legislation, rules, and orders are determined by the regulated firms' reactions to them. If the affected firms approve or feel that a particular governmental action is a reasonable compromise, populists will disapprove or view the action as an unjustifiable compromise of the public interest.

Aside from this substantive orientation, populists have sought certain procedural and organizational reforms designed to reduce corporate influence at the legislative and administrative levels, the most important of which are intended to increase public participation (conceived in this framework as anticorporate participation). Thus, the proliferation of public interest groups that closely scrutinize congressional and administrative activity in many specific policy areas, such as the Center for Auto Safety, is a major part of the populist strategy. But because of the disparity in resources between public interest groups and corporations, one of the populist reform proposals is government funding of public interest group participation in the administrative process.

In addition, populists seek to modify the structure of agency proceedings so that anticorporate viewpoints are afforded an opportunity to participate either through direct group participation or through the establishment of offices within agencies that represent consumers and/or the public interest. Finally, just as it is necessary to expand the influence and participation of the public, so it is also necessary to curb the influence of the regulated firms. Accordingly, populists advocate the prohibition of *ex parte* contacts between public officials and representatives of regulated firms, stringent conflict-of-interest laws, and severe limitations on subsequent private sector employment of agency personnel and their right to participate in agency proceedings.

Thus, while support for regulatory reform *generally* is nearly universal within organized public opinion, the principal direction that reform should take is subject to considerable dispute. From the foregoing discussion and the need in many instances to arrange compromises among various interests, we would expect that some of the slogans employed in regulatory reform would involve a degree of ambiguity. Indeed, as we will see, many of the most important reform proposals are vague phrases behind which the precise regulatory reforms have been and will be carried out. We begin an overview of some significant reform proposals with the most important term in the new reform lexicon: deregulation.

DEREGULATION

The term "deregulation" is usually confined to explicitly economic matters such as rates, routes, or entry barriers, particularly in connection with transportation, communications, or infrastructural services such as banking. In contrast, the term "overregulation" is primarily applied to the areas of health, safety, and consumer affairs. Given the popularity of deregulation, especially with respect to the airline industry, the term has a great deal of ideological value. Unfortunately, deregulation's ideological value exceeds its analytical value, for it may take on three distinctly different meanings.

Different Meanings of Deregulation

Deregulation may mean a *complete* restoration of market mechanisms and withdrawal of government intervention. The airline industry was scheduled to become deregulated gradually in that sense with respect to rates, routes, and entry, but not with respect to safety. Thus, even the airline industry will not achieve deregulation in the sense of having *all* of its activities determined by market mechanisms, even though CAB domestic route authority, under the 1978 Airline Deregulation Act, expired at the end of 1981, fare authority expires at the end of 1983, and the agency itself will terminate on January 1, 1985.

Since some airline activities will continue to be regulated after January 1, 1985, the airline industry is not an example of deregulation in the sense of a *complete* restoration of market mechanisms; nothing is. Airline deregulation provides instead an example of deregulation's second meaning—a reduction in the extent of regulation. When defined in this way, deregulation means an increase in the number of activities over which firms and persons in a subject industry may exercise discretion without fear of government sanction.

This kind of deregulation may be accomplished in several ways. First, regulation may be withdrawn from an activity. For example, regulation may be withdrawn entirely from ratemaking but still govern entry. Second, regulation may be withdrawn from a portion of an activity but continue in the rest. For example, under the Staggers Rail Act of 1980 (the Railroad Deregulation Act) railroads can avoid ICC review of a rate increase as long as the new rate is less than 160 percent of out-of-pocket (or variable) costs, a ceiling that will rise to approximately 175 percent in 1984. Thus, within those ranges railroad firms are free to exercise discretion but are subject to regulation above them. Third, deregulation may mean a measurable decline in a subject firm or person's regulatory burden. The unit of measurement for this deregulation may be costs or employee time. A shift from design to performance standards might save subject companies considerable cost and time necessary to comply with regulation.

It is difficult, if not impossible, in many instances to distinguish the reduction meaning of deregulation from the third one, which is merely changing the regulatory rules from one set to another. The 1980 banking deregulation statute is a good example of this phenomenon. Regulation Q, which sets deposit interest-rate ceilings, will be phased out within six years of the statute's enactment—a clear move toward reduction of regulation. But at the same time, the Federal Reserve Board was granted the right to impose reserve requirements upon a large number of depository institutions over which it previously had no jurisdiction— a clear move toward greater regulation. Other provisions in the statute simply changed the regulatory rules, such as one that limited mutual savings banks' commercial lending authority to 5 percent of an institution's assets but restricted the exercise of the power to a mutual's home state or within 75 miles of its principal office. At the same time, the 1980 statute did not lift any of the severe competitive restrictions upon the ability of commercial banks to enlarge the geographic areas in which they may compete.[14] In short, the Financial Institutions and Monetary Control Act of 1980 contained provisions that reduced regulation, others that increased it, and still others that merely changed the rules.

The Politics of Deregulation

We can make several conclusions about deregulation from the foregoing explication. First and foremost, it is a myth to conceive of deregulation as a synonym for the free market, although most of the deregulatory statutes and proposals do enlarge the area in which market forces may operate. Yet many economic restrictions remain in each case of "deregulation," the principal exception being the 1978 Airline Deregulation Act, which ends economic controls in 1985. Typically, most of the groups involved in the process of enacting deregulatory statutes were neither entirely satisfied nor entirely dissatisfied. The statutes are full of delicately arranged compromises that accord with the marginalist-minimax analysis advanced in our discussion of the regulatory legislative process in Chapter 6. The statutes are incremental, either in time (as in the case of airline deregulation) or subject matter (as in the case of banking). Deregulation does not entail truly drastic market solutions, such as abolishing FCC regulation over television transmission or terminating all banking agency regulation over checking accounts. Its moderate, rather than radical, changes account for the fact that neither the process nor the impetus for deregulation is reflected in sharp party or ideological divisions. Deregulation has been endorsed by

Republicans and Democrats and has drawn fervent support from free market advocates and consumerist organizations as well as from advocates of the traditionalist, restrictivist, and populist reform orientations.

Deregulation is usually concerned with three principal issues: (1) whether there should be freedom to enter an industry or market; (2) whether there should be freedom to exit from a market; and (3) the degree of freedom in price or rate setting. Considerable emphasis is usually placed on the first and third issues, but too little is placed on the second, for regulated firms (especially in transportation) have frequently charged that they are forced to serve low-density routes at a loss. Airline deregulation permitted the subject companies to increase rates or shed low-profit routes, so that within a few months after enactment they had greatly reduced the number of flights in West Virginia—to the chagrin of that state's legislators.[15]

Airline deregulation also greatly expanded the ability of carriers to enter new markets, without CAB approval in some cases and with lower entry requirements in others. Because some airlines (notably United and Continental) felt that lower entry requirements would open up excellent opportunities, they strongly supported this feature of the legislation of which other carriers were wary. But all the airlines favored some degree of price flexibility without continual CAB approval, which obviated the need for time-consuming administrative proceedings—an especially important consideration to them during periods of high inflation.[16]

As the airline case shows, deregulation is neither a simple return to the free market nor is it viewed with unmitigated horror by the affected industries who, indeed, welcome some of its aspects. Deregulatory statutes clearly move in the direction of freer competition, and they are subject to the same rules of compromise as are other statutes dealing with regulatory subjects. Nevertheless, deregulatory statutes do constitute a change from the past—a shift in the public philosophy concerning regulation—and warrant a contextual exploration.

The Economics of Deregulation

One can point to a number of political moves—especially those undertaken by President Ford, Senator Kennedy, and several regulators (notably CAB chairmen in both the Ford and Carter administrations)—as the "causes" of the deregulation movement. But these political moves were reflections of important changes that had been occurring in the American economy and the regulatory response to those changes.

Changing economic conditions and opportunities, particularly those stemming from high and accelerating rates of inflation played an important role. The consumer price index (CPI) rose from an average annual rate of 1.8 percent between 1950 and 1965 to 4.4 percent from 1965 to 1973, and then it skyrocketed to an annual rate of 9.4 percent from 1973 to the first half of 1980. (The annual rate during parts of this last period was frequently well in excess of 9.4 percent.) Since 1976 the *annual* CPI rate has accelerated rapidly, although, of course, rates varied considerably when measured on a monthly basis.[17]

The connection between inflation—uniformly considered the most pressing macroeconomic problem—and deregulation surfaced as a major issue during meetings that led up to President Ford's "economic summit" in late September 1974. The economists invited to those meetings

> agreed that government regulation was a major cause of the high and rising cost of living, and that reforming it was one of the few useful things that could be done to control inflation. The consensus on this point was striking, being shared by economists of every political stripe—a fact not lost on President Ford.[18]

The cost of infrastructural services—particularly transportation, communications, credit provision, and energy—is incorporated in the prices paid by consumers and every industrial and service sector of the economy. In addition, each of these infrastructural services has manifested other serious economic performance problems, including supply problems (especially in energy) and the general deterioration of certain of these industries (most notably rail transportation), and certain wasteful practices under regulation that promoted grossly inefficient resource use (such as rules that prevented regulated truckers from carrying return trip or full loads).[19] But even more important than conspicuous resource misallocation was the widespread view among economists and policymakers that regulation *per se* in transportation inherently led to inefficiency and that a movement toward market mechanisms would lead to greater efficiency and, hence, lower costs for both consumers and corporate purchasers of infrastructural services.

Their message was that regulated infrastructural services tend to be wasteful, excessively costly, and inefficient. The competitive constraints exercised in unregulated markets are absent, and there is a tendency to inflate rather than cut costs, especially fixed ones. This problem is grave enough when consumers and firms subject to these costs can more readily absorb the excessive costs generated by such regulation; but when inflation magnifies each rate increase, regulation-induced inefficiencies are perceived to impose an intolerable burden.

For this reason, the change in the public philosophy toward deregulation of the infrastructural industries drew enormous support from consumer and business interests and, to some extent, from many of the regulated firms themselves who sought to adjust to new economic conditions and changed opportunities. But while deregulation has garnered such great support, the same is not true about another set of regulatory reforms concerning the problem that has come to be known as "overregulation."

OVERREGULATION

The Problem of Overregulation

While the topic of deregulation is largely confined to economic problems in the infrastructural sectors of transportation, communications, and credit, the notion of overregulation is directed toward problems of environmental, safety, health, and consumer affairs (social regulation) across sectoral lines. And while restrictivist and populist reformers generally support deregulation efforts, they bitterly split on the overregulation issue. In general, the restrictivists wish to apply economic theory and cost-benefit analysis to environmental, safety, health, and consumer affairs issues, while the populists either reject its applicability or assert that such analysis produces distorted results that aid corporations but harm the public.

Overregulation, sometimes termed "excessive regulation," is a persistent theme in the business press and was an important issue during the 1980 presidential election campaign. Overregulation has had important policy consequences, most notably in the orders issued by Presidents Ford, Carter, and Reagan directing regulatory agencies to monitor the costs and inflationary impacts of their programs. The cry against overregulation is not an attack on safety, health, and consumer protection regulation *per se* but on the alleged excesses of such programs. The plea to curb excessive regulation draws support from the theoretical studies conducted under the auspices of two conservative "think tanks"—the American Enterprise Institute for Public Policy Research in Washington, D.C., and the Center for the Study of American Business in St. Louis, Missouri.

But how do we recognize overregulation? How does one distinguish it from the proper amount of social regulation? The starting point of the restrictivist argument is the presumption in favor of market arrangements. In other words, anyone proposing a regulation must show market failure or inadequacy. If that can be shown, the next step is to determine whether extending contract, property, or other common law principles cannot solve the problem, as in the case of externalities. Only after a showing that market mechanisms and common law principles cannot be extended to the problem should regulation be considered.

At this point, the restrictivist recipe calls for evaluating the costs and benefits of regulation and other plausible alternatives. If regulation withstands this test, the next step is to design the particular regulations in a manner that yields the highest net benefit and is most cost-effective. This net benefit is to be measured in both the aggregate and marginal senses in designing specific regulations. Overregulation, then, would be defined as those regulations in which aggregate or marginal costs exceed, respectively, aggregate or marginal benefits.

Cancellation and Cumulation

A final point from the restrictivist perspective requiring amplification is that particular regulations should not be considered in isolation from each other but rather in a coordinated way. This problem has two aspects, which we will label "cancellation" and "cumulation."

Cancellation means that different regulations may cancel each other and other government programs, leading to lower net benefits than if just one of the regulatory programs existed. For example, many Americans are aware that while the Environmental Protection Agency seeks to reduce the use of pesticides, the Agriculture Department promotes them; that EPA pushes for stringent air pollution standards, while the Energy Department seeks to promote the use of coal, the dirtiest energy source; and that the Energy Department supports low coal railroad rates to aid utility fuel conversion, while the Department of Transportation favors high rates to aid the beleaguered railroads. Perhaps the most notorious case concerns automobile regulation:

> Federal fuel economy standards increase prices and reduce safety. Federal emissions standards increase prices and reduce fuel economy.[20]

Clearly, given the administrative and compliance costs of regulatory programs at cross-purposes, the outcome is lower net benefits than would be obtained under a coordinated approach. In addition to the coordination problem, it is also possible that the cumulation of regulations applicable to particular industries, even if not in conflict, may have more than merely an additive effect. This is simply another way of observing that the marginal cost imposed by another incremental regulation may rise at more than a linear rate, as Figure 8-1 illustrates.

The Politics of Overregulation

It is apparent that the critics of overregulation rely heavily on cost-benefit analysis to formulate their policy prescriptions. To the extent that such analyses are quantitatively feasible, cost-benefit analysis provides an excellent, neutral scientific tool to evaluate regulation. To that extent, it is no different than computing the production cost of a bar of soap; ideology, values, and politics play no role in the analysis. (Later we will examine the scientific merit of cost-benefit analysis.) But to the extent that such analyses constitute little more than pseudoscien-

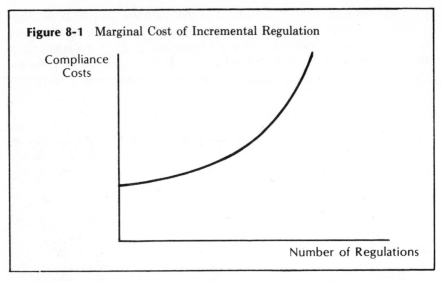

Figure 8-1   Marginal Cost of Incremental Regulation

tific jargon, what is the operational significance of the concept of overregulation?

From our discussion of externalities, we have already seen one of the major difficulties in applying cost-benefit analysis—assigning quantitative values to goods that are not routinely traded. Your valuation of tall trees or beautiful scenery might be very different from mine or many other persons. We observed the extraordinary difficulties that would be involved in polling persons in a quest to ascertain the *precise* point at which marginal cost just begins to exceed marginal benefit. The costs of obtaining such information over a wide variety of issues would be staggering, yet the information would not even be reliable.

Since we can be reasonably confident that the U.S. government is not planning to conduct referenda on such issues, it follows that political processes will determine when overregulation begins to occur. The political process may involve either administrative arbitrariness or bargaining (assuming that administrative discretion exists). During the last year of the Carter administration an obvious movement was initiated to retreat from the extent of health, safety, environmental, and consumer protection regulation that had previously been customary. This retreat was indicative of the gradual change in public philosophy toward regulation, a change occasioned in large part by the crises of several American industries, notably steel and automobiles. At the behest of his Council on Wage and Price Stability, President Carter in 1979 ordered several regulatory agencies to issue economic impact statements assessing the probable economic costs stemming from their actions.

Furthermore, the Carter and Reagan administrations signaled a substantial slowdown in the number of new regulations that would be issued.[21] Additionally, in both administrations, agencies instituted a bargaining process with industry over the appropriate level of regulation, as business-government relations with the steel and automobile industries illustrate. The process begins when the industry complains about some regulations. Their inflationary impact and adverse effect on the domestic industry's competitiveness and employment is then brought to light. The bargaining process leads finally to a reduction in the extent of regulation.

President Carter's moves to accommodate the automobile industry during the last few months of his administration illustrate this bargaining dynamic. In August 1980, the head of the EPA program for controlling mobile-source air pollution notified the automobile industry that a rule requiring "tamper-proof" idlers for 1982 and later model cars was being eliminated. According to a Ford Motor official:

> The government asked us to give them five priorities for regulatory relief. This was one of them. So we feel very pleased by the action.[22]

In September 1980, EPA announced the postponement of several auto emission standards from the 1983 to the 1984 model year. Similarly, as part of a wider aid plan for the steel industry, President Carter offered in October 1980 to request congressional authorization allowing the EPA to permit case-by-case delays of up to three years for meeting air quality standards.[23]

In summary, to the extent that cost-benefit analysis cannot or will not be scientifically employed to determine whether a regulation's costs outweigh its benefits and/or to determine the proper level of regulation, the alternatives are either administrative arbitrariness or bargaining between those regulated and the regulators. Neither of these alternatives is satisfactory in achieving proper regulations or assuring high economic performance. Administrators do not possess magic powers to devise appropriate regulations without the guidance of a rational technique. Many reformers have pinned their hopes on cost-benefit analysis, the technique to which we now turn.

COST-BENEFIT ANALYSIS

The Scope of the Problem

The cost-benefit argument starts out by describing the vast scale of regulation. According to Murray Weidenbaum, the budgets of 56 federal regulatory agencies rose from over $1 billion in 1970 to more than $6 billion in 1980, while the number of pages in the *Code of Federal Regulations* covered by regulatory rules climbed from approximately

60,000 in 1975 to almost 85,000 by 1980. But the direct governmental costs, according to Weidenbaum, are only a small part of the total costs of regulation. The costs that business firms must sustain to comply with (or contest) these regulations—much of which is passed on to consumers—far exceed the direct governmental costs. The annual compliance costs of meeting federal regulations for consumer product safety, job safety, environmental protection, and other regulatory requirements were estimated to be about $97.9 billion in 1979. The total administrative and compliance costs rose, according to Weidenbaum, from $79.1 billion in fiscal 1977 to $102.7 billion in 1979—or about 4 percent of gross national product (GNP).[24]

These estimates, it should be added, include only the first-order (administrative costs) and second-order (compliance costs) effects of regulation, and not what Weidenbaum has termed the induced costs, or third-order effects. Induced costs include the costs imposed because of opportunities lost, such as the cost of cutting back on productive investment and the "adverse effects on capital formation by introducing uncertainty about the future of regulations governing the introduction of new processes and products." [25]

Other aggregate studies of the costs of government regulation also tend to indicate that administrative and compliance costs are very high, although the estimates vary from the Weidenbaum study. One of the most respected of these, which surveyed 48 major firms, was conducted for the Business Roundtable by Arthur Andersen & Co., a major auditing firm.[26] Among the findings was that the firms' costs of complying with the requirements of six regulatory agencies in 1977 were approximately $2.6 billion. In comparison, the firms' total research and development costs were $6.0 billion, while net income after taxes was about $16.6 billion.

One of the most important lessons revealed by the Arthur Andersen study was that regulatory compliance costs fall very unevenly among different industries but are most burdensome to the manufacturing sector: their regulatory costs were about $2.3 billion compared with $10.9 billion net income after taxes. Furthermore, many firms in the manufacturing sector revealed that the effects described by Weidenbaum as third-order (induced costs) were often very high. In any event, the study concluded that the second-order effects (compliance costs) caused by these six regulatory agencies resulted in

> a price level increase of more than 1 percent—an addition to costs that
> aggravated the pressures of inflation on their operations and on their
> competitiveness in domestic and foreign markets.[27]

It should be remembered that this conclusion is based on the impact of just six agencies and does not take into account the costs associated with third-order effects. Finally, the Andersen study compared its results with those of four other studies (two of which were conducted by the government) and concluded that its results were "in line with earlier studies in concluding that the cost of regulation is high." [28]

It is a mistake, however, to think that regulation solely affects big business. To the contrary, a large part of the resentment of overregulation stems from its widespread impact on smaller firms. Indeed, some observers claim that the proportional impact is much greater on smaller firms than on larger ones.[29] For example, if firms in an industry must install new equipment to meet an EPA standard, a bigger firm can average this fixed cost over a much larger number of units sold than a smaller one can.

The first step, then, in the "regulation is inflation" argument delineates the costs of regulation and the impacts upon particular important economic sectors. Thus far nothing has been said about the benefits of regulation and the possibility that in many, perhaps most, instances the benefits outweigh the costs. But the second step of this argument is not that overall benefits outweigh overall costs or that overall costs outweigh overall benefits; it is instead that before particular regulations are instituted, the agency should conduct cost-effectiveness and cost-benefit analyses. Can such analyses be undertaken on a precise scientific basis in most regulatory problems?

The Costs and Benefits of Cost-Benefit Analysis

Do costs outweigh benefits? Like many simple questions and concepts, further exploration tends to reveal problems of extraordinary complexity and a latent value structure. Moreover, as we will see, cost-benefit analysis is a phrase with a certain degree of ambiguity that embraces several distinct types of analysis.

Our conclusion—to state it at the outset of the discussion—must be that cost-benefit analysis is useful in virtually every regulatory case. This technique is more useful in some cases than in others; its range of utility can extend on a continuum from extremely useful to trivial. Sometimes cost-benefit analysis can answer questions, while at other times it cannot lead to the "right answer"; but it will at least exclude certain options from serious consideration. Certainly, in a world rife with substantial gaps in information and judgment, this is a valuable attribute. Nevertheless, when the costs and benefits of cost-benefit analysis are tallied, we must conclude that it is a useful technique when employed carefully but certainly not *the* magic answer to the question of what direction regulatory reform should take.

The first problem that must be considered is what cost-benefit analysis, at its best, cannot do. And the simple answer is that, assuming we are capable of tallying costs and benefits exactly, cost-benefit analysis still cannot make decisions for us. Ezra Mishan, a leading student of the cost-benefit technique, has explained why:

> A project that is adjudged feasible by reference to a cost-benefit analysis is . . . quite consistent with an economic arrangement that makes the rich richer and the poor poorer. It is also consistent with manifest inequity, for an enterprise that is an attractive proposition by the lights of a cost-benefit calculation may be one that offers opportunities for greater profits and pleasure to one group, in the pursuit of which substantial damages and suffering may be endured by other groups. . . . [T]he quantitative outcome of a cost-benefit calculation itself carries no distributional weight, it shows that the total of gains exceeds the total of losses, *no more*.[30] (Emphasis supplied)

This point is an extremely important one and is the source of a great deal of the bitter dispute concerning cost-benefit analysis. Proponents of the technique sometimes seem to imply that because it is scientific at its best, it is the sole tool that should be used in determining whether a policy would be socially approved. Many populist regulatory reformers bitterly reject any use of the cost-benefit technique because they suspect that its application almost always helps the rich and advantaged at the expense of the poor and disadvantaged.

But both of these views fail to put cost-benefit analysis in proper perspective. It is only *one* tool that can be used to reach a decision concerning socially desirable action; it is hardly the sole consideration in arriving at many (perhaps most) regulatory decisions. The effects of regulatory decisions are distributed unevenly, which inevitably involves the imposition of values and ideology. Obviously, then, to the extent that equitable considerations can be held constant over the range of options, cost-benefit analysis becomes more important in reaching social decisions.

Values play a role together with cost-benefit analysis not only in arriving at appropriate social decisions but in the process of engaging in cost-benefit analysis itself. The problem is illustrated by the experience of a researcher seeking to employ cost-benefit analysis to a concrete problem:

> After arriving at OSHA, I engaged in an in-depth consideration of cost-benefit analysis, applying the methodology to the coke-oven standard. There were more data available for coke-oven effects on a population at risk than in any other area of standards setting. . . . The range in values arrived at, based on the different assumptions, was so wide as to be virtually useless. The conclusion I reached after this exercise was that the methodology of cost-benefit analysis for disease and death effects is very preliminary, and one can almost derive any desired answer.[31]

Perhaps the conclusion is overstated, but the author does point out one of the great difficulties faced in cost-benefit analysis—placing a dollar-cost value on untraded goods (in this case life, health, injury). It can be done and, indeed, often is done in personal injury and wrongful death awards in private litigation. But the enormous differences in awards in private cases involving approximately the same injuries indicate that an exact formula is not even remotely at hand. Only when we can compare the same things (dollars lost versus dollars gained or lives lost versus lives saved) can a value-free cost-benefit analysis be undertaken. Once we are required to translate the value of one thing that is not ordinarily traded into a medium of exchange (lives saved converted into dollars), our personal predilections will enter into the calculations.

Of course one must not erroneously reject cost-benefit analysis simply because judgment must be used in such translations, for the cost-benefit technique at least compels us to frame a more precise question than would be the case without it. We can ask: How much additional cost would I be willing to incur to save a certain number of additional lives? Posing a question this way would allow most of us to conclude (albeit based in part on personal values) that the additional cost involved in requiring cars to be built as sturdily as army tanks is too costly relative to the additional lives that would be saved in automobile collisions.

Regulators, even those hostile to cost-benefit analysis, inevitably use the technique, although frequently in a crude form. Not even the most zealous EPA administrator wants to reduce industrial emissions to zero, for that would mean the elimination of production as well. Nor would the most fanatic OSHA regulator want to eliminate all risk in manufacturing plants, which would also bring activity to a standstill. In practice, regulators must consider costs and benefits. Why not do it in a precise, consciously conceived manner?

The Development of Government Cost-Benefit Analysis

Cost-benefit analysis was used as early as the 19th century in evaluating public works projects, but its modern refinements occurred during the 1960s when the Defense Department began using the technique to evaluate alternative weapons systems. In 1974 President Ford issued an executive order requiring regulatory agencies to evaluate the effects of their actions on inflation, a first step in the application of cost-benefit analysis to regulatory decisions.

President Carter continued President Ford's initiative and in March 1978 issued a new executive order renaming the pertinent documents "regulatory analyses." He also created the Regulatory Analysis Review Group (RARG), chaired by a member of the Council of Economic Advisers and charged with reviewing rules and regulations issued by executive branch agencies that had potential cost impacts of more than $100 million. Notwithstanding these good intentions, the number of pages in the *Federal Register* continued to increase, while RARG had studied only eight regulations in the first eighteen months of its existence. Few observers felt that RARG's work and either the Ford administration's requirement of economic impact analyses or President Carter's requirement of regulatory analyses had been effective in moderating cost pressures on industry.[32] It remains to be seen whether President Reagan's Task Force on Regulatory Relief, charged with analyzing existing and proposed regulations' impacts on the economy, will fare any better.

One reason for this result has been the failure of regulatory agencies to translate the general guidelines of Ford's and Carter's executive orders into rigorous cost-benefit analyses. Rather, agencies have used these documents, as well as the environmental impact statements that agencies have also been required to prepare, in a self-serving manner designed to support agency action.[33]

Types of Cost-Benefit Analysis

Cost-benefit analysis can entail five different types of analysis, and agencies have not consistently or rigorously applied these particular frameworks. The first framework is termed *no-risk analysis,* where the only question is whether some activity constitutes a risk.[34] If it does, it is prohibited.

The 1958 Delaney Amendment to the Food and Drug Act, which requires the banning of any food additive for which there is evidence of a carcinogenic effect, is probably the best known example of the no-risk framework. As the much-publicized FDA ban on the sale of saccharin—about which the agency had no choice under the amendment—illustrates, the no-risk framework simply *assumes* that costs outweigh benefits and does not permit further examination. Its defect, as the saccharin case illustrates, is obvious: a blind assumption is no substitute for assessment. More lives might be prolonged through the use of saccharin than would be saved through its ban.

The second cost-benefit framework is termed *risk-risk analysis* and may be viewed as a response to the rigidities of the no-risk framework. Risk-risk analysis attempts to compare the risks of one alternative with other risks. For example, according to several scientific tests, sodium nitrite, which is used in preserving meats, may cause cancer; but its absence in cured meats may also lead to botulism, which also causes death. Obviously it would be foolish to save the lives of a small number who might die of cancer at the expense of a larger number who might die of botulism. Risk-risk analysis provides the framework for attempting to compare risks under different alternatives.

But as the following example will show, risk-risk analysis leaves much to be desired. Assume that the only alternatives are sodium nitrite or no preservatives and that the only risk about which we are concerned is death (D) and not injury, discomfort, aesthetic displeasure, etc. Assume further that we are dealing with a stable population (P) of 100 people under both alternatives (an assumption that is often unrealistic since changes in a product or service can affect the number of consumers). Now assume that the probability of death from cancer (R_c) in the nitrite case is .05 and that from botulism (R_b) in the non-nitrite case is .04, but that the margin of error in the first case (M_c) is $\pm$ .01 and in the second case is $\pm$ .02. Then the probable death formulae are:

$$(1)\ D_c = P(R_c \pm M_c)$$
$$(2)\ D_b = P(R_b \pm M_b)$$

As we can determine from even this extremely simple example, the better course of action is far from clear. The range of deaths under case 1 is 4 to 6, and under case 2 it is 2 to 6. Thus, while case 2 appears to be better public policy, there is a possibility that in fact it is not. In other words, under the simplest assumptions that can be made, risk-risk analysis does not guarantee an unambiguous guide to action in which choices are clearly defined. When the data and choices become more complex and numerous, the limitations of risk-risk analysis become even sharper.

However, the most serious problem with risk-risk analysis, succinctly described by William R. Havender, an eminent researcher on health problems, is that scientific judgments are not always clear. It is not uncommon for equally well-performed experiments and investigations to give widely varying or even contradictory results. The two most careful studies of the relationship between saccharin and cancer, for example, gave conflicting results:

> One [study] completed ... in Baltimore on some 500 bladder cancer patients and a matched cancer-free group found no significant difference in saccharin use between the two groups, while the other carried out in Canada, found less usage of saccharin among women with bladder cancer than among women without it, and a small excess of use in men with bladder cancer compared with men without it.[35]

Risk-benefit analysis, the third framework, might almost be considered a reaction to the difficulties just elaborated in risk-risk analysis. The risk-benefit framework consists of an informal attempt to consider both the positive and negative effects of an activity without straining to place quantitative measures on such effects as the cost in lives or the impacts on future generations. The risk-benefit framework, then, is an informal type of cost-benefit analysis that does not rigorously attempt to determine the choice to be made.

By simply focusing on the lists of probable costs and benefits and looking at who will benefit and who will suffer without attempting to quantify each rigorously, risk-benefit analysis, its advocates argue, allows the analyst to consider distributional impacts—which groups will benefit and which will suffer. But the advocates of formal cost-benefit analysis assert that ultimately risk-benefit analysis provides no canons that can guide agencies in making their decisions; it is an invitation to administrative arbitrariness. Second, the critics of risk-benefit analysis assert that it provides no guidelines that would separate trivial from nontrivial effects, one consequence of which is that agency proceedings could include interminable consideration of numerous trivial effects. In other words, unnecessary procedural delay is practically built into risk-benefit analysis. Finally, critics of risk-benefit analysis argue that direct redistributional policies, and not regulation, should be used to redress situations in which distributional impacts are subject to criticism.

The fourth framework of cost-benefit analysis is termed the *regulatory budget*.[36] This concept, associated with economist Robert Crandall, calls for regulatory agencies to be guided by two budgets. The first budget is based on the usual congressional appropriation of agency funds. The second, the regulatory budget, would assign an upper limit of dollar-value costs that would arise *as a result* of any particular agency's actions. Once the limit is reached, an agency would be unable to issue new regulations unless it canceled earlier ones in an amount that would permit the agency to remain within its regulatory budget. If the agency felt the need for the expenditure of a sum above its upper limit, it could argue for a supplementary budget before the Office of Management and Budget and before Congress in the same manner that agencies now request supplemental appropriations.

What is more, administrators would be instructed to maximize the benefits of their regulations within the confines of their regulatory budgets. Thus, if the regulatory budget does not quite provide an efficiency incentive to regulators, it would at least compel them to think in regulatory efficiency terms. Of course, the regulatory budget is faced with the same difficulties faced by other cost and benefit estimating techniques, among which is the difficulty of quantification. But it does compel those advocating and those opposing a particular regulation to join issue and argue with specificity about particular costs that will flow from a course of action. The dialectic of reasoned debate between adversaries is presumed to bring about better results than other methods.

In order to implement the regulatory budget, two institutional mechanisms are necessary. First, an independent office in government would be required to review agencies' final calculations of costs, impose standardized accounting rules, and certify results. Second, a system of retrospective accounting would have to be devised that would periodically determine whether the actual costs flowing from a regulation were in line with the costs projected under the regulatory budget procedure. Under the most prominent variant of the regulatory budget scheme, the costs to be measured would include only out-of-pocket expenditures by complying firms (Weidenbaum's second-order effects) and would exclude third-order effects (those flowing from the opportunity costs of complying rather than employing resources elsewhere, such as building new plant and equipment or for research and development).

In addition, the regulatory budget concept excludes the calculation and estimation of benefits; it is only concerned with costs in the restrictive sense just set forth. The reason for the exclusion of benefits in the administrative process is that these would be taken into account earlier in the process. When the amount of an agency's appropriations is considered at the presidential and congressional levels, it would also be determined that major agency programs would indeed yield significant benefits, although they would not be precisely quantifiable. One facet of this aspect of the regulatory budget process is that actual benefits also would be compared with prospective benefits contemplated before a regulation (or set of regulations) was instituted. In this way, an opportunity to determine whether a regulation accomplished what it was intended to do would become a routine executive and legislative activity.

Like the other cost-benefit techniques described, the regulatory budget would have certain inherent practical difficulties, the paramount one being the problem of collecting and analyzing the vast amount of information needed to make it operational—itself a costly process. The second major problem is the development of reasonable accounting rules to be employed where precise information is not available and estimates must be made. This kind of cost accounting is a very expensive process involving considerable judgment. Third, as in the case of risk-benefit analysis, a wide area of nonquantifiable judgment remains. Consequently, agencies as well as the executive and legislative branches *might* opt for the politically sound, rather than the economically best, regulatory programs.

While *formal cost-benefit analysis,* the fifth framework, would *theoretically* avoid this problem of quantification, the first two problems would involve even greater difficulty than under the regulatory budget process—indeed, much more difficulty. Formal cost-benefit analysis requires, first, the enumeration of all negative and positive effects associated with a proposed action:

> For example, if you were talking about abating air pollution, these effects would include the kinds of control devices you put on smoke-

stacks, any possible unemployment that might result, any increases in prices, and so on.[37]

At the outset, then, the task of data collection in formal cost-benefit analysis is much more formidable than that involved in the regulatory budget. One must include not only Weidenbaum's first- and second-order effects (administrative and compliance costs) but the third-order ones (induced costs) as well.

But this is only the first step. The second consists of classifying each effect as a cost or benefit. The third step is to relate each effect quantitatively to the specific action. That is, in the case of air pollution abatement, one would have to determine the extent to which air quality is improved and the extent to which human health is improved by *that* action abstracted from many others.

Fourth, one must translate these very different effects into a common metric. For example, health improvement and the prolongation of life would have to be translated into a metric that allows quantitative comparison between them and the dollar cost of installing new equipment. It should be emphasized that this translation does not have to be into dollars; any common metric will do. There are, of course, methods of calculating nontraded goods such as human lives, but the theories are not easy to apply and involve the imposition of value judgments; the economic worth of a life, for example, is more than anticipated future earnings discounted to the present since few of us would trade our lives for that sum.[38]

The fifth step is to take the effects that occur over time and bring them back to a common period since with inflation a dollar now is worth more than a dollar five years hence. After performing all of these operations, the sixth and final step is to compare the costs and benefits of an action. And even if one arrives at a figure showing a net benefit, one would want to find out whether some alternative way of doing the same thing might yield a greater net benefit.

Little elaboration is required to show the immense effort that would be needed to perform each of these operations—assuming that the data is available. And, of course, such data is often not available or involves estimating procedures that are apt (given varying assumptions) to lead to differing quantitative values. Finally, how does one deal with problems in which long-run effects are not known or understood? Of course, there are some cases, especially in the regulation of rate, route, or entry matters, when formal cost-benefit analysis might be easier to apply. For example, a reasonable amount of evidence was available to compare the costs and benefits of unregulated and regulated passenger air travel. Nevertheless, even though it is clear that formal cost-benefit analysis is not the panacea that some of its advocates suggest, it still can be valuable in excluding some possible courses of action, even if it does not necessarily lead to *the* correct one. In a word, formal cost-benefit analyis can exercise *some* discipline upon regulatory decisionmakers in place of the arbitrariness with which they have been charged.

All of these techniques embraced under the aegis of cost-benefit analysis may be valuable in regulatory reform, although they may also be abused. The regulatory budget is probably the most useful, but even that technique, as we saw, has its limitations. Since regulators inevitably must make cost-benefit judgments, it is better to do so using explicitly designed frameworks that utilize economic analysis than to do so on an ad hoc basis without understanding what is being done. Because of the limitations of the various forms of cost-benefit analysis, many traditionalist regulatory reformers prefer to place greater weight on procedural reforms that they surmise will lead to greater regulatory cost-effectiveness. In addition, populist and restrictivist reformers have proposed procedural reforms based on their perspectives of regulatory reform.

COST-EFFECTIVENESS AND PROCEDURAL REFORM

Cost-effectiveness, it will be recalled, assumes that the ends are given and attempts to determine the cheapest means of attaining them. It embraces not only the cost of each means that might achieve a result but also the probability of attainment. Consequently, rational cost-effectiveness analysis may lead to selecting a more expensive means of attaining a given result if the probability of attainment is significantly higher than a cheaper means.

Experience, economic theory, and administrative theory are the major tools employed in answering the cost-effectiveness question. Consequently, cost-effectiveness analysis has both substantive and procedural or administrative components. During the course of this book, we have looked at some of these substantive issues, such as the problem of whether property rights, taxation, or regulation is apt to be the cheapest way to achieve a given level of environmental purity. In this final section, we will look at some administrative and procedural reforms that have been proposed to make agencies more cost-effective.

The Problem of Delay and Administrative Reform

The first point to be noted is that the cost-effectiveness concept, like the cost-benefit notion, contains an underlying set of values. Implicit in cost-effectiveness is the value that the cheapest means is the best way to attain given regulatory results; yet one need not accept this value as the highest priority. For example, one may believe that public and interest group participation in administrative proceedings should be encouraged for its own sake, even though as a general rule this will delay proceedings and raise costs not only for the agency but also for those who will be affected by the outcome.

Consider Nuclear Regulatory Commission construction permit regulation, where proceedings are very open and groups as well as interested individuals can readily participate. Not only are the administrative costs obviously increased, but the costs of building plants are also raised because of increases in real costs of components over time, interest charges on components purchased at the outset of proceedings, the amortized cost of goods lying around and doing nothing, the greater costs involved in attracting investor capital because of the additional time needed to realize any profits, etc.[39]

Procedural delay can, of course, be costly for groups other than business firms. Delay in Consumer Product Safety Commission proceedings can increase accident costs for consumers who purchase products, and Civil Aeronautics Board delay in permitting another airline to enter a market can cost travelers substantial sums they might save from additional competition. Delay can adversely affect any group, although, of course, particular interests (especially lawyers drawing handsome fees) can profit from delay in particular cases. And these particular interests, aware of this, often make strategic use of delay possibilities.[40]

Notwithstanding that delay can be costly in many ways, populist regulatory reformers still often favor the delay that might be caused by wide participation in hearings because, in their view, without it agencies are usually dominated by corporate influence. To reduce this influence, populists are willing to incur the costs resulting from wide public participation and have advocated other reforms to guard against corporate influence as well. These include setting up offices of public counsel within agencies to represent consumers, government funds being made available to subsidize interest group and public participation in administrative proceedings, and the establishment of a government-wide consumer counsel with the power to intervene in the proceedings of virtually any agency. Other proposals include restrictions on ex parte communications between regulators and those regulated, limitations on the future employment opportunities of regulators in the sectors or fields that they regulate (an ICC lawyer, for example, would be precluded from being employed by a firm that represented common carriers for five years), and more stringent conflict-of-interest laws.[41]

While restrictivists and traditionalists usually concur with at least part of the populist agenda—the reduction of ex parte communications and the required commitment of such discussions to a public record through sunshine laws—they otherwise believe that the populist proposals have limited utility. In their view, agencies are usually the best judges of who can supply useful information and who cannot, promulgating participation rules accordingly. But more important, rules regarding wider public participation would further delay proceedings, which are already notoriously slow, without any compensating benefit.

According to the restrictivists and traditionalists, public interest groups and allied individuals arrogantly assume that they represent the public and know the public interest. Yet these groups operate not on scientific or economic principles but rather on a deep emotional bias against business corporations. More often than not, their political preferences are not realized (as witness the 1980 elections), indicating that these groups cannot truthfully claim to represent the public. Finally, the view that regulators are beholden to corporations is not supported by the evidence. Certainly, the Environmental Protection Agency and most of the newer regulatory agencies as well as older ones, such as the Securities and Exchange Commission and the Federal Trade Commission, often make decisions and rules that corporations abhor. Consequently, according to the restrictivists and traditionalists, restrictions on the activities and employment opportunities of government personnel serve no purpose and are counterproductive in that they deter more talented persons with alternative opportunities from applying for government positions.

Agency Planning

The traditionalists instead have argued for the adoption of many reforms designed, in their view, to improve regulatory performance. The most important of these is the development of agency planning processes and guidelines that seek to maximize agency benefits. For example, traditionalists would approve of the FTC project that developed measures to determine which of the numerous advertising messages to examine for deception or falsity. Instead of using instinct or a "mailbag" approach to determine which industries and firms to monitor most closely, the FTC has devised a complex formula that weighs such variables as total industry sales, profit margins, price trends, consumer demographics (who buys the product), consumer complaints, advertising expenditures, and accidents caused by products.[42]

While one can argue that such a mechanistic formula is no replacement for the more complex processes involved in human judgment, an even more difficult problem remains, notwithstanding such agency planning. Performance can improve very marginally or can get even worse because of faulty value judgments programmed into such a formula. For example, suppose that in these calculations the FTC accorded greater weight to high total industry sales and profit margins than to lower figures but that in fact smaller firms are more likely to engage in deceptive advertising. Under these circumstances, success in thwarting falsity and deception could actually decline.

And the FTC has been charged with building false staff predispositions into its model without actually expending the substantial costs required to weight and scale factors properly. Several years after the institution of the FTC model, two separate investigations concluded that the agency's effectiveness against false advertising had not improved; indeed, it was generally worse, notwithstanding the bringing of several important advertising matters.[43]

Agency planning, then, is not a panacea for improved agency performance. It may or may not improve it, depending on the human judgments and on the extent and reliability of information supplied in the planning process. Obviously, limited and relatively unreliable information employed in agency planning is more dangerous than no planning at all, since rigidity invariably sets in when a comprehensive plan is devised; it is much easier to change course and requires a much lower expenditure of resources when the basis of decision is judgment.

On the other hand, planning may improve agency performance but, even if it does, its extent may be marginal; it is possible that the costs of devising and implementing a plan may exceed the difference in benefits between planning and not planning. Improvements in performance through planning may be very slight, especially when: (1) information costs necessary to discover wrongdoing are high; (2) regulatory goals are very broad; and (3) the number of units subject to regulation is large. Thus, in the case of FTC advertising regulation: (1) the discovery of false or misleading claims is often very difficult and costly; (2) the goals—control of *all* deceptive practices—are very broad; and (3) the number of units covered—virtually every company that sells goods and services except those explicitly not covered, such as banks or railroads— is very large. Conversely, of course, as goals narrow, information costs are reduced, and the number of units subject to regulation is narrowed, the likelihood of successful agency planning increases.

Planning may occur not only within an agency but across agency lines as well. Clearly, it makes little sense for agency officials to pursue their missions blindly without regard to the efforts of other agencies or broader governmental goals. It is good sense, for example, for rate-setting agencies to be aware of the overriding public goal to control inflation. Conversely, it is not very logical for industries to be subject to conflicting and duplicative regulatory requirements, examples of which were noted earlier.[44]

Accordingly, recent presidential administrations have required agencies to prepare statements indicating the impact of particular regulatory decisions on the environment, inflation, small business, etc. Few observers have waxed enthusiastic about these requirements, however, because these statements are either perfunctory or self-seeking in supporting agency conclusions reached on other grounds. Finally, many agencies lack the capacity to make reasonable judgments on the environmental or inflationary consequences of their actions; their areas of expertise lie elsewhere, and such forecasting is little more than guesswork.[45]

Attempts at centralized regulatory coordination, also undertaken in recent administrations, have not generally been considered successful. Regulatory coordination, like so many other ideas advanced by the traditionalists, has an obvious surface appeal and would be very laudable if it could be made to work. But the principal problem with such coordination is one that has occurred with respect to so many regulatory problems—information costs. A coordinating agency must first develop a large amount of information in order to produce a comprehensive regulatory plan. Second, it would be required to review an enormous number of individual agency rules, regulations, and proposals. Third, in order to do its job effectively, the coordinating agency frequently would have to obtain facts and estimates independently, checking them against facts and estimates developed by other agencies. Since regulatory agencies often deal with highly complex matters requiring considerable expertise, a coordinating agency would have to hire experts to undertake such specific agency reviews.

Aggregating these tasks over the vast regulatory apparatus would involve enormous expenditures of time and money by the coordinating agency. Accordingly, it is not surprising that President Carter's Regulatory Analysis Review Group only studied eight regulations in its first eighteen months of operations, while his Regulatory Council, designed to keep agencies from working at cross-purposes, did little more than publish a calendar of regulations that were under consideration at various agencies.[46] Finally, as economist Roger Noll has observed, a regulatory coordinating agency has an

> inherent potential for disaster. An administration . . . not only could promulgate regulatory policies that were uniformly disastrous, but could also coordinate its disastrous policies effectively.[47]

Legislative Reform

Some traditionalists concede that executive branch coordination is not likely to be a successful road to reform and instead call for relying on a series of reforms centered on Congress. Initially, we should recall from our examination of Congress and regulation that we cannot necessarily expect any greater wisdom from legislators than we can from administrators in assuring effective, efficient, or sensible regulatory performance. At best, legislators are confronted with so many concerns other than regulation to which they must be attentive that in most instances we can reasonably anticipate a less probing analysis from them than those who administer programs. The political model involving adjustments among competing interests, which was described in Chapter 7, is quite different from a rational policymaking model (although both may at times reach the same or a similar result).

Nevertheless, congressional involvement—not domination—in the regulatory process is important for a number of reasons. First, this involvement can act as a corrective for an agency's inbred approach to a regulatory problem. For example, Congress's dissatisfaction with the many rules OSHA promulgated during its early years compelled that agency to retreat and cancel many regulations. Second, because legislators must be concerned with a wide variety of issues, they are in a better position to connect a particular regulatory problem with other issues. In other words, Congress can be the coordinating mechanism, not only between regulations but also between regulatory and other issues. Finally, Congress is the branch of government closest to both public opinion and interest groups. Consequently, it may be able to check regulatory agencies when they adopt positions sharply dissonant with public opinion or the reasonable concerns of interest groups.

As we discussed in Chapter 6, the traditional ways in which Congress has attempted to supervise regulatory behavior are through appropriations, oversight hearings, and investigations. But several new reform developments have occurred in recent years. The first is sunset legislation. Under the sunset concept, agencies and programs go out of existence automatically at a pre-established expiration date unless they are renewed by the legislature. More than half of the states have adopted some kind of sunset law, and several federal regulatory statutes contain sunset provisions.

The intention of the sunset concept is to assure that legislatures and regulators make periodic systematic and in-depth studies of each major agency responsibility, instead of the perfunctory examination of specific rules and regulations that the traditional legislative supervisory processes usually involve. Those agencies that cannot stand up to such critical scrutiny presumably will disappear. Proponents of the sunset idea argue that the CAB would have gone out of existence much earlier than under the current schedule had sunset examinations of the agency taken place. But opponents of the sunset idea suggest that, first, it ignores political realities:

> The Appropriations committees routinely examine agency budgets and policy; and if there is political pressure for these political units not to decrease the funds of a particular agency, then the same pressure is likely to sustain agencies through the sunset process.[48]

While this observation might appear to be a bit mechanistic, experience does reveal that sunset laws have failed to live up to their promise. Colorado, one of the first states enthusiastically to employ sunset review, eliminated only 3 of 39 state regulatory agencies covered by the statute in its first review. Eliminating these agencies—which regulated boxing, licensed sanitarians, and certified shorthand reporters—saved $11,000 a year, but auditing the first 13 agencies (including those 3 eliminated) under the initial review cost $212,000. Furthermore, legislative sunset review of more important agencies, notably those regulating insurance and public utilities, consumed a great deal more money and time than had been originally contemplated. Finally, some agencies used the sunset process as a means to increase staffs and budgets and expand jurisdiction. Other states with sunset laws have reported that their experiences are similar to Colorado's.[49]

The crucial problem in sunset review once again is information costs. Regulators, who most of the time firmly believe in their missions, are in better control of information than are legislators, who must expend considerable resources to ascertain independently agencies' arguments for continued existence. Multiplied over the entire federal regulatory apparatus, the sunset task becomes an enormous one. This suggests that sunset review is perhaps most useful in eliminating relatively minor regulatory programs and agencies whose missions are simply—and cheaply—understood and that it is not a particularly useful way to examine and eliminate major, complex problems.

Many of these same difficulties are associated with another recent congressional reform mechanism—the legislative veto. Under this proposal, either one or both houses of Congress (depending upon the specific proposal) would have the right to cancel a regulation of which it disapproved or to send the regulation back to the agency for reconsideration in light of the legislative veto message. The first application of the legislative veto concept to a federal regulatory agency occurred when Congress in May 1980 enacted a bill permitting veto of certain types of FTC rules if *both* houses of Congress approved. The merit of this reform is that it allows Congress to correct agency actions that are politically out of line with the popular or congressional mood or that are inconsistent with broader public goals.

But the legislative veto also may be used for the rankest political motives or in an unscientific manner. And once again Congress, even when well-intentioned, is faced with the difficult information cost problem when it seeks to evaluate regulations independently and to second-guess the expertise of regulatory agencies. Finally, given the nature of the congressional calendar-setting process, there is no assurance that the objectively most pressing regulatory rulings, under any reasonable criteria, would be among the few that Congress would in fact select for review under the legislative veto process.

NONCONCLUSION

It is tempting to become an ideologue who can provide simple reductionist answers to the problems posed by regulation and regulatory reform. It is easy to assume uncritically that the free market, regulation, or some other governmental technique is the ready answer to all of these problems. But whereas a presumption should be made in favor of free markets (as we saw in Chapter 2), that presumption often may be rebuttable. Ultimately, each individual case must be examined on its own merits, measured against economic and social performance goals. Ultimately, as R. H. Coase has urged, an opportunity-cost approach must be employed to determine the best solution to each public problem.

The law-and-economics approach, coupled with experience, provides the basic tools to be employed not only in examining the economic ramifications of each possible governmental arrangement but in understanding political behavior as well. We saw in our survey of regulatory policies, politics, and reform proposals that costs—notably information costs—as well as risks and ignorance are associated with every policy alternative. And frequently the magnitudes of these costs, risks, and ignorance are not—and cannot be—known.

For this reason, categorical answers to the problems raised by regulation and its alternatives will always elude us; beware of the self-righteous ideologue who spouts certainties. The best for which we can hope is that theory, experience, and reasoned debate will continually move us closer to attaining the goals that regulation is intended to meet. For these reasons, this book ends not with a definitive conclusion but with a nonconclusion.

NOTES

1. John P. Callahan, "Industries Hail Curb on Agencies," *New York Times,* July 21, 1946, Sec. 3, p. 1.
2. Jimmy Carter, "Remarks on Signing S. 1946 (Staggers Rail Act of 1980) into Law," *Presidential Documents* (October 14, 1980):2226.
3. Quoted from the text reprinted in *The New York Times,* October 25, 1980.
4. Ronald Reagan, "Excerpts from Remarks—Steubenville, Ohio," *Reagan-Bush Committee News Release,* October 7, 1980, p. 2.
5. Edward Meadows, "A Close-up Look at the Productivity Lag," *Fortune* (December 4, 1978):83.
6. Edward F. Dennison, *Accounting for Slower Economic Growth: The United States in the 1970s* (Washington, D.C.: Brookings Institution, 1979), pp. 2, 3. For a review of the recent productivity literature and the high standing of Dennison's work in it, see Mark Perlman, "One Man's Baedeker to Productivity Growth Discussions," in *Contemporary Economic Problems,*

ed. William Fellner (Washington, D.C.: American Enterprise Institute, 1979), pp. 79-113.

7. Dennison, *Accounting for Slower Economic Growth,* pp. 74, 128.
8. Thomas A. O'Toole, "U.S. Industry Cutting Basic Research," *Washington Post,* November 28, 1977, p. 1.
9. Ralph E. Winter, "Many Businesses Blame Government Policies for Productivity Lag," *Wall Street Journal,* October 28, 1980, p. 1.
10. Murray L. Weidenbaum, *Business, Government and the Public* (Englewood Cliffs, N.J.: Prentice-Hall, 1977), pp. 63-65.
11. See, for example, William Wardell, "Rx: More Regulation or Better Therapies," *Regulation* (September/October 1979):25-33.
12. David Welborn, "Taking Stock of Regulatory Reform" (Paper presented at the annual meeting of the American Political Science Association, Washington, D.C., September 1, 1977).
13. See Paul Weaver, "Unlocking the Gilded Cage of Regulatory Reform," *Fortune* (February 1977):179-188; John R. Meyer, "Transportation Deregulation: Possibilities and Prospects," *Journal of Contemporary Business* 9 (1980):69-71; and Stephen Breyer, "Analyzing Regulatory Failure: Mismatches, Less Restrictive Alternatives and Reform," *Harvard Law Review* 92 (January 1979):604-608.
14. See Harry Guenther, "Deregulation—Is it Happening in Banking?" *Regulation* (November/December 1980):42-49.
15. "How West Virginia has the CAB up in the Air," *Business Week* (June 23, 1980):63.
16. Rush Loving, Jr., "The Pros and Cons of Airline Deregulation," *Fortune* (August 1977):209-217; and Rush Loving, Jr., "How the Airlines will Cope with Deregulation," *Fortune* (November 20, 1978):38-41.
17. See the summary in Harry Brandt, "Inflation: Still Our Number One Problem," *Federal Reserve Bank of Atlanta Economic Review* (September/October 1980):16, 17.
18. Paul Weaver, "Unlocking the Gilded Cage," p. 180.
19. On varying empty backhaul estimates, see "Freedom from Regulation?" *Business Week* (May 12, 1975):80.
20. William Niskanen, "Auto Regulation," *Regulation* (November/December 1980):24. See also U.S., Congress, Joint Economic Committee, *An Inquiry into Conflicting and Duplicative Regulatory Requirements Affecting Selected Industries and Sectors,* 96th Cong., 2d sess., 1980.
21. For example, see "Regulation," *Business Week* (October 13, 1980):177; and Gene G. Marcial, "Reagan Expected Pollution-Curb Changes, EPA Rules Seen Lift to Waste Disposal Issues," *Wall Street Journal,* November 24, 1980, p. 45.
22. Quoted in Reginald Stuart, "Auto Makers Benefit as EPA Cancels Rule," *New York Times,* August 27, 1980, p. D-6. See also Ernest Holsendolph, "Pollution Limits Deferred to Help Auto Industry," *New York Times,* September 18, 1980, pp. D-1, D-6.
23. Edward Cowan, "White House Seeks Delay in Pollution Rules," *New York Times,* October 1, 1980, pp. D-1, D-5.
24. Murray L. Weidenbaum, *The Future of Business Regulation* (New York: Amacom, 1979), pp. 11-23.
25. Ibid., p. 24. See also Murray L. Weidenbaum, "Mr. Weidenbaum Answers his Critics," *New York Times,* November 4, 1979, p. F-18; and Murray L. Weidenbaum, "How Much Regulation is too Much?" *New York Times,* December 17, 1978, p. F-16.

26. Arthur Andersen & Co., *Cost of Government Regulation Study: Executive Summary* (New York: The Business Roundtable, 1979). For background on the study, see "Cost of U.S. Rules Said to Spur Prices," *New York Times*, March 15, 1979.

27. *Cost of Government Regulation Study*, p. ii.

28. Ibid., p. 21. For reports of impact on individual firms, see "Costly Regulations," *Journal of Commerce*, June 12, 1980, p. 4; "Complying with Government Regulations can be Costly, Corporations Find," *Wall Street Journal*, March 19, 1979, p. 1; "Excessive Regulation Costing Dow Many Millions of Dollars," *Journal of Commerce*, April 5, 1977, p. 3; and "Goodyear Chief Hits Regulation," *New York Times*, Nov. 11, 1975, p. 45.

29. William Lilley III and James C. Miller III, "The New Social Regulation," *Public Interest* (Spring 1977):51. See also Ann Crittenden, "Big Burden for Small Business: Government Rules," *New York Times*, July 2, 1977, pp. 23, 27; and Bernard Wysocki, Jr., "Mr. Newton's Foundry Spends Time, Money Coping with Red Tape," *Wall Street Journal*, November 21, 1977, pp. 1, 33.

30. E. J. Mishan, *Economics for Social Decisions* (New York: Praeger Publishers, 1973), pp. 13, 15.

31. Jacqueline Karnell Corn and Morton Corn, "The Myth and the Reality," in *Economic Effects of Government Mandated Costs*, ed. Robert F. Lanzillotti (Gainesville: University Presses of Florida, 1977), p. 106.

32. Jerry Flint, "A System that has Run Wild," *Forbes* (November 12, 1979):38, 39; and "A Hit List of Regulatory Reforms," *Business Week* (June 11, 1979):139.

33. "Inflation Fighters Draw A Bead on the Regulators," *U.S. News & World Report* (September 18, 1978): 27, 28; and Gay Sands Miller, "Environmental Report may have Little Value in Predicting Impact," *Wall Street Journal*, June 1, 1978, pp. 1, 17.

34. This discussion of cost-benefit analysis relies heavily on the presentation of Lester B. Lave in U.S., Congress, House, Committee on Interstate and Foreign Commerce, *Use of Cost-Benefit Analysis by Regulatory Agencies, Hearings*, 96th Cong., 1st sess., 1979, pp. 5-23.

35. See William R. Havender, "Ruminations on a Rat: Saccharin and Human Risk," *Regulation* (March/April 1979):20, 21.

36. See the excellent discussion in Christopher D. De Muth, "Constraining Regulatory Costs—Part II," *Regulation* (March/April 1980):29-39, 42-44.

37. Lave in *Cost-Benefit, Hearings*, p. 7.

38. On this topic, see especially, Guido Calabresi, *The Cost of Accidents: A Legal and Economic Analysis* (New Haven, Conn.: Yale University Press, 1970).

39. See U.S., Congress, Senate, Committee on Governmental Affairs, *Study on Federal Regulation, Volume IV: Delay in the Regulatory Process*, 95th Cong., 1st sess., 1977, pp. 8-10.

40. See especially Bruce M. Owen and Reginald Braeutigam, *The Regulation Game* (Cambridge, Mass.: Ballinger, 1978), pp. 2-9.

41. Generally, see Simon Lazarus, *The Genteel Populists* (New York: Holt, Rinehart & Winston, 1974).

42. "The FTC Builds a Model Informer," *Business Week* (March 11, 1972):94.

43. See the General Accounting Office's report in U.S., Congress, House, Committee on Appropriations, *Agricultural, Environmental and Consumer Protection Appropriations for 1975, Hearings*, Pt. 6, 93rd Cong., 2d sess., 1974, p. 665; and ibid., Committee on Interstate and Foreign Commerce,

Staff Report: The Federal Trade Commission, 93d Cong., 2d sess., 1974, pp. 1, 14.

44. See U.S, Congress, Joint Economic Committee, *An Inquiry into Conflicting and Duplicative Regulatory Requirements Affecting Selected Industries and Sectors,* 96th Cong., 2d sess, 1980.

45. See the Congressional Research Service's pessimistic report reprinted in U.S., Congress, Senate, Committee on the Judiciary, *Administrative Procedure Act Amendments of 1978, Hearings,* 95th Cong., 2d sess., 1978, pp. 922-926.

46. Jerry Flint, "A System that has Run Wild," *Forbes* (November 12, 1979):38, 39.

47. Roger Noll, *Reforming Regulation* (Washington, D.C.: Brookings Institution, 1971), p. 90.

48. Randall L. Calvert and Barry R. Weingast, "Six Myths of Regulation: Congress and the Failure of Regulatory Reform" (Unpublished paper delivered at Conference on Regulatory Reform, Chicago, Ill., December 3, 1979), p. 32.

49. "Sunset Laws: One More Brave Idea that's Gone Awry?" *U.S. News & World Report* (May 29, 1978):45, 46.

Bibliographic Note
and Research Guide

The literature on the topic of regulation is immense, embracing contributions from the disciplines of economics, history, law, and political science. Articles and books range from general overviews of the subject to meticulous examinations of specific decisions and rules. What follows is not a bibliography or even a bibliographic essay but rather a guide to assist students who wish to conduct research or inquire further into the subject of regulation.

Regulation is an ongoing activity with events occurring daily. Fortunately, three newspapers cover many of these activities quite well: *The Wall Street Journal, The New York Times,* and, most important, *The Journal of Commerce.* Several periodicals are also valuable sources of information: *Business Week,* Congressional Quarterly *Weekly Report, Fortune, Industry Week, National Journal,* and *Science. Regulation,* published under the auspices of the American Enterprise Institute for Public Policy Research in Washington, D.C., specializes in the subject; each issue contains abstracts of important books and articles published elsewhere.

In addition to these more general sources, a great deal of valuable information and analysis can be obtained from specialized trade and business journals. For example, for research on FCC telecommunications policy, journals such as *Telephony, Interconnection, Telephone Engineer and Management, Telephone News, Sound & Communications,* and *Communications News* are indispensible. The *Index of Business Periodicals* can direct the researcher to the best trade journals under each topic.

Congressional Quarterly's periodically revised *Federal Regulatory Directory* is a gold mine of information on the particular areas of regulation. The heart of each volume compiles an enormous amount of information on the organization and processes of each regulatory agency, including bibliographic material about agency rules and regulations, data and statistics, publications, and additional references.

Many scholarly journals contain important articles about regulatory topics. These include journals in the fields of law, economics, business, and public policy. However, several are particularly valuable: *Bell Journal of Economics, Business History Review, Journal of Economic History, Journal of Legal Studies, Journal of Political Economy, Public Interest,* and, most important, *Journal of Law & Economics.* Additionally, there are important scholarly and semischolarly journals that specialize in particular topics, such as *Federal Communications Law Journal, ICC Practitioners Journal,* and *Public Utilities Fortnightly.*

Government materials, of course, constitute the primary source of information about regulation. At the national level, congressional materials—including committee hearings, reports and prints, and executive and administrative agency reports—are listed in the *Monthly Catalog of Government Publications,* which contains an excellent annual index in its December issue. But this is only the tip of the iceberg, for each regulatory agency issues numerous decisions, orders, rules, proposed regulations, etc. *The Code of Federal Regulations* and the *Federal Register* compile some of this information, but much of the information about the output of particular agencies must be obtained from more specialized sources. Commerce Clearing House (CCH) and the Bureau of National Affairs (BNA) produce loose-leaf reporting services in many of these areas and are usually available in law school libraries. Finally, other periodicals provide current information about specific topics. *Traffic World,* for example, is exemplary in its weekly coverage of the activities of transportation regulatory agencies.

Most books on regulatory topics contain useful bibliographies, but two recent ones are outstanding in this respect: Barry Mitnick, *The Political Economy of Regulation* (New York: Columbia University Press, 1980); and Paul Quirk, *Industry Influence in Federal Regulatory Agencies* (Princeton, N.J.: Princeton University Press, 1981).

At this point the reader will probably be overwhelmed by the avalanche of material on regulation, but this book has sought to provide some ordering to it. At the risk of ignoring many valuable articles and books, I feel obligated to enumerate some works that intended to accomplish that same task. A list of some of the most important follows.

Breyer, Stephen. *Regulation and its Reform.* Cambridge, Mass.: Harvard University Press, 1982.
Coase, R. H. "The Problem of Social Cost." *Journal of Law & Economics* 3 (October 1960):1-44.

Cushman, Robert. *The Independent Regulatory Commissions*. New York: Oxford University Press, 1941.

Kahn, Alfred. *The Economics of Regulation: Principles and Institutions*. 2 vols. New York: John Wiley & Sons, 1971.

Kohlmeier, Louis, Jr. *The Regulators*. New York: Harper & Row, 1969.

Kolko, Gabriel. *The Triumph of Conservatism*. New York: Free Press, 1963.

Lowi, Theodore. *The End of Liberalism*. New York: W. W. Norton & Co., 1969.

Peltzman, Sam. "Toward a More General Theory of Regulation." *Journal of Law & Economics* 19 (August 1976):211-240.

Posner, Richard. "Theories of Economic Regulation." *Bell Journal of Economics and Management Science* 5 (Autumn 1974):335-358.

Stigler, George. "The Theory of Economic Regulation." *Bell Journal of Economics and Management Science* 2 (Spring 1971):3-21.

Wilson, James Q. "The Politics of Regulation." In *The Politics of Regulation*, edited by James Q. Wilson. New York: Basic Books, 1980.

Index

Act to Regulate Commerce. *See* Interstate Commerce Act of 1887.

Adjudication - 29, 197, 203, 205-211, 222
administrative trial - 209-211
appeals - 211
proactive approach - 206-207
reactive approach - 206-207

Administrative Procedure Act of 1946 - 199, 210, 214, 238

Advertising - 205-207. *See also* Federal Trade Commission (FTC).
children's - 7, 243
drug - 20, 151-152, 181
false and misleading - 14-15, 22, 24, 153, 158-160

Affirmative action programs - 14, 144-145

Affirmative language - 19

Agriculture Department
Agricultural Marketing Service - 200
Agricultural Stabilization and Conservation Service - 200
Animal and Plant Health Inspection Service - 200
Federal Grain Inspection Service - 200
Food Safety and Quality Service - 200

Air pollution. *See* Emissions, Environmental regulation.

Airline Deregulation Act of 1978 - 250-251

Airline regulation - 8, 78, 87-88, 134, 160, 239, 243-244, 246-248, 252. *See also* Civil Aeronautics Board (CAB).
Airline Deregulation Act of 1978 - 250-251
Civil Aeronautics Act of 1938 - 13, 41, 65, 86
History - 13, 32, 86

Alexander, Tom - 194n

American Enterprise Institute for Public Policy Research - 254

American College of Physicians - 181

American Stock Exchange - 231

American Telephone and Telegraph Company (AT&T) - 224, 230-231

American War of Independence - 44

Antimonopoly - 76-77

Antitrust regulation - 65, 74-78. *See also* Justice Department.

Architectural glass - 219-221

Arthur Andersen & Co. - 258

Ash Council - 247

Atomic Energy Commission (AEC) - 32

Automobile industry - 24, 91, 93, 102, 114-115, 187, 190, 257

Automobile safety - 53, 158-159, 163

Bain, Joe S. - 37, 39, 60n

Banking regulation - 30-32, 47, 85, 182-183, 229
Depository Institutions and Monetary Control Act of 1980 - 183, 251
Emergency Banking Act of 1933 - 182
Federal Reserve Act of 1913 - 182
Regulation Q - 251

Bargaining power disparity - 133-134, 146-151

Baumol, William J. - 106-107, 109

Becker, Gary - 192

Bell System - 229

Berger, Curtis J. - 123n

Bethlehem Steel - 50

Black lung disease - 150

Bonbright, James - 72

Boston Red Sox - 130

Braeutigam, Ronald - 27, 216

Broadcasting regulation - 25, 67, 80-83, 229. *See also* Federal Communications Commission (FCC).

Brookings Institution - 240

Bubble concept - 116-117, 119

Buchanan, James M. - 98-99

Burton, Phillip - 150

Business Roundtable - 258

Cable television - 139

Callahan, John P. - 274n

Calvert, Randall L. - 277n

Cameron, Juan - 235n

Campbell, Rita Ricardo - 166n

Capitalism - 44, 130-131

Capture theory - 229-231

Carter, Jimmy - 224, 238, 252, 254, 256-257, 261
Caterfone (1968) - 231
Cary, William L. - 236n
Caveat emptor - 54
Center for Auto Safety - 249
Center for the Study of American Business - 254
Certificate of public convenience and necessity (CPCN) - 136-139
Certificates of deposit - 183
Certification - 156-158
Chesterfield, Earl of - 147
Chrysler Corporation - 180
Civil Aeronautics Act of 1938 - 13, 32, 41, 65, 86
Civil Aeronautics Board (CAB) - 32, 86, 200, 202, 224, 248, 252, 268, 272
Civil rights regulation - 141-145
    affirmative action programs - 14, 144-145
Civil sanctions - 26
Civil Service Commission (CSC) - 198
Clark, J. M. - 40
Clean Air Amendments - 41
Coal mining industry - 150-151
Coase, R. H. - 80-82, 110, 113, 115, 122, 274
Code of Federal Regulations - 257-258
Collective bargaining - 127, 149-150
Commerce Department
    National Bureau of Standards - 200
Commodity Futures Trading Commission - 200
Commodity Futures Trading Commission Act of 1974 - 15-17
Common calling - 139-140
Communications regulation. *See* Federal Communications Commission (FCC).
Competition - 44-55, 76-77
    economic performance - 48-52
    efficiency - 66
    equilibrium - 51-52
    free market - 45-55
    social performance goals - 52-55
    unfair methods - 18
    workable - 40
Conditional language - 19
Congress, U.S.
    investigative functions - 174
    legislative rulemaking - 216
    legislative veto - 174-175
    oversight functions - 174
    regulatory legislation - 172-177
Constitution, U.S. - 135, 214
Consumer price index (CPI) - 252-253
Consumer Product Safety Act - 41
Consumer Product Safety Commission

(CPSC) - 32, 158-159, 200, 203, 207, 245, 268
    architectural glass - 219-221
    Bureau of Epidemiology - 220
    rulemaking - 216-222
Consumer Reports - 54
Consumer safety - 217-221
Consumer Safety Glazing Committee (CSGC) - 219
Consumer sovereignty - 49, 129
Consumerism - 32, 174, 189
Consumers Union - 53
Continental Airlines - 252
Contract system - 10, 54, 127-133
    bargaining power disparity - 133-134, 146-151
    discriminatory contracts - 133-134, 139-146
    duress - 134, 147-149
    employment - 143-144
    government agreements - 133-139
    information disparity - 133-134, 151-163
    labor contracts- 149-151
Coordination regulation - 65, 78-83
Corn, Jacqueline Karnell - 276n
Corn, Morton - 276n
Corporate charter - 135
Cost-benefit analysis - 10, 42-43, 63, 121, 239, 241-242, 245-246, 256-262
    formal cost-benefit analysis - 265-266
    no-risk analysis - 262
    regulatory budget - 264-266
    risk-benefit analysis - 263-264
    risk-risk analysis - 262-263
Cost-effectiveness - 244-246, 267-268
Council of Economic Advisers - 241, 261
Council on Wage and Price Stability - 256
Court of Appeals, U.S. - 201
Cowan, Edward - 275n
Crandall, Robert - 264
Criminal sanctions - 26
Crisis - 179-184
Cuban missile crisis - 180
Cullom Report (1886) - 145

Dahlman, Carl - 115, 123n
Dairy industry - 243
Dales, J. H. - 123n
Davis, Kenneth Culp - 34n
Decision rules - 214-216
Defense Department
    Army Corps of Engineers - 200
    cost-benefit analysis - 261
Delaney Amendment (1958) - 162-163, 262
Demsetz, Harold - 73
Dennison, Edward F. - 240-241

Depository Institutions and Monetary Control Act of 1980 - 183, 251
Deregulation - 10, 13, 237, 239, 243, 249-254. *See also* Regulatory reform.
 economics - 252
 politics - 251-252
Dioxin - 92
Discrimination - 126, 141-145. *See also* Civil rights regulation.
Discriminatory contracts - 133-134, 139-146
Distribution - 11
Due, John F. - 165n
Duress - 134, 147-149

Economic performance goals - 5, 35, 37-40, 48-52
Economic Regulatory Administration - 200
Edelman, Murray - 186
Efficiency
 technical - 65-68
 welfare - 65-68
Efficiency regulation - 9, 65
 antitrust - 65, 74-78
 coordination - 65, 78-83
 market failure - 9, 63, 66-68
 natural monopoly - 65, 68-78, 86
 promotional - 65, 83-86
Effluent fees. *See* Tax-subsidy policy.
Emergency Banking Act of 1933 - 182
Emissions - 32, 93, 95, 105, 109, 120-121, 227, 255
 automobile - 24, 91, 93, 102, 114-115, 118
 bubble concept - 116-117, 119
Energy and Commerce Committee (House) - 176
Energy Department - 200, 255
Environmental Protection Agency (EPA) - 3, 32, 172-173, 198-200, 224, 229, 231, 242, 255, 269. *See also* Emissions, Environmental regulation.
 air pollution regulation - 95, 227, 255
 banked pollution rights - 110
 bubble concept - 116-117, 119
 information gathering - 21-22
 Love Canal - 92-93
 tax-subsidy policy - 104-105
Environmental regulation - 37, 42-43, 47, 240. *See also* Environmental Protection Agency (EPA).
 property rights - 111-115
Epstein, Richard A. - 164n
Equal Employment Opportunity Commission (EEOC) - 144, 200, 224
Equilibrium - 51-52
Equitable sanctions - 26-27

Equity regulation - 9, 125-127
 bargaining power disparity - 133-134, 146-151
 discriminatory contracts - 133-134, 139-146
 government agreements - 133-139
 information disparity - 133-134, 151-163
Evins, Joe - 175
Externalities - 9-10, 91, 92-121
 actual and potential - 99-100, 121
 marginal and inframarginal - 98
 positive and negative - 94, 104-106
 relevant and irrelevant - 98-99
 separable and nonseparable - 107-108
 symmetrical and asymmetrical - 112-113

Fair Labor Standards Act of 1938 - 149
Farris, Martin T. - 60n
Federal Aviation Administration (FAA) - 7, 32, 78-80, 160, 200
Federal Communications Commission (FCC) - 78, 111, 200, 216, 224, 230, 251
 certificate of public convenience and necessity - 138
 history - 31, 82
 industry protection - 229-231
 licensing - 25, 67-68
Federal Deposit Insurance Corporation (FDIC) - 32, 200
Federal Energy Regulatory Commission (FERC) - 200, 230
Federal Home Loan Bank Board (FHLBB) - 32, 200
Federal Maritime Commission - 200
Federal Mediation and Conciliation Service - 200
Federal Power Commission - 230
Federal Radio Commission - 82
Federal Register - 219, 221, 262
Federal Reserve Act of 1913 - 182
Federal Reserve Board - 31, 200, 229, 251
Federal Trade Commission (FTC) - 18, 29, 173-175, 187, 198, 200, 214-215, 224, 226, 229, 245, 269
 adjudication - 204-211
 advertising - 7, 14-15, 24, 127, 153, 158-159, 243, 270
 antitrust - 78, 233
 Bureau of Consumer Protection - 207-208
 history - 31, 33
 price discrimination - 223-224
Federal Trade Commission Act of 1914 - 14-15, 21, 28, 173, 205
Fenno, Richard - 190
Fifth Amendment - 20

Firestone Tire and Rubber Company - 126
Flammability standards - 217
Flint, Jerry - 276n, 277n
Food and Drug Act of 1906 - 31, 181
Food and Drug Administration (FDA) - 7, 176, 205, 214, 242
  peanut butter - 29, 212, 242
  pharmaceutical licensing - 28, 126
  pharmaceutical test information - 22, 153, 159, 212, 214
  rulemaking - 29
  saccharin - 262
Food, Drug and Cosmetic Act - 58
  Delaney Amendment (1958) - 162-163, 262
Ford, Gerald - 247, 252-254, 261
Fortune - 240
Fourth Amendment - 20
Fraud - 132, 153
Free market - 3-4, 10
  competition - 45-55
  contract system - 164
  economic performance goals - 48-52
  market failure - 63-64
  Smith, Adam - 4, 9, 35, 43-46, 48, 55, 59
  social performance goals - 52-55
Friedman, Milton - 44, 157

Galbraith, John Kenneth - 228
General Accounting Office (GAO) - 95, 217
General Motors - 41, 77
Gerschenkron, Alexander - 89n
Government agreements - 134-139
Government-imposed monopoly - 129, 134-139
Governmental Affairs Committee (Senate) - 27
Graebner, William - 151
Great Depression - 30-31, 178, 182-183
Guilds - 135

Havender, William R. - 263
Hawley, E. W. - 194n
Hayek, Friedrich - 44, 48
Hazardous waste disposal - 92-93
Health and Human Services Department
  Food and Drug Administration. *See* Food and Drug Administration (FDA).
Health and safety regulation. *See* Safety and health regulation.
Highway traffic safety. *See* National Highway Traffic Safety Administration (NHTSA).
Hilton, George W. - 165n
Hite, James C. - 123n
Hjalte, Krister - 123n
Holmes, Oliver Wendell - 149

Hooker Chemical Corporation - 7, 22, 92-93
Hoover, Herbert - 81-82
Hoover Commission - 238
Housing and Urban Development Department
  Office of Interstate Land Sales Registration - 200
Houthhaker, Hendrik - 12
Huntington, Samuel - 230

IBM - 50
Illinois Supreme Court - 157
Inflation - 106, 241-242, 247, 253, 258-259
Informal procedures - 204-205, 207
Informal sanctions - 26-27
Information costs - 176, 186, 207-208, 212-214
Information regulation - 20-23, 133-134, 151-163, 217
Infrastructure - 85-86
Interest groups - 186-188
Interior Department
  Office of Surface Mining Reclamation and Enforcement - 200
Interstate Commerce Act of 1887 - 19, 41, 145, 147
Interstate Commerce Commission (ICC) - 19, 25, 29, 125, 139, 176, 187, 199-200, 215, 224, 229-230
  history - 30-31
  railroad regulation - 145-146, 198, 230, 250
Interurban railways - 137
Isaacson, Marc - 165n

Japan - 240-241, 246
Johns Hopkins University - 181
Johnson, Lyndon - 189
Joint costs - 113-114
Justice Department
  Antitrust Division - 78, 200, 227, 233
  Drug Enforcement Administration - 200
  regulatory jurisdiction - 23

Kahn, Alfred - 72, 85, 88n, 136, 235n
Kasper, Daniel - 165n
Kaysen, Carl - 89n
Kefauver, Estes - 181-182
Kennedy, Edward M. - 247, 252
Kennedy, John F. - 181, 238
Keyes, Lucille S. - 86
Keynes, John Maynard - 178
Kingdon, John - 189-191
Kitch, Edmund W. - 165n
Kolko, Gabriel - 13
Kurtz, Howie - 234n

Labor contract - 149-151
Labor Department - 149
  Mine Safety and Health Administra-
    tion - 200
  Occupational Safety and Health Ad-
    ministration. *See* Occupational Safety
    and Health Administration (OSHA).
  Office of Federal Contract Compliance
    Programs (OFCCP) - 126, 144, 200
  Wage and Hour Division - 200
Labor regulation
  collective bargaining - 127, 149-150
  history - 32
  minimum wage - 14, 127, 146, 149
Labor Relations Act of 1935 - 149
Laissez-faire - 55
Landis, James M. - 238
Landrum-Griffin Act - 150
Lave, Lester B. - 276n
Law
  litigation - 102-103
  nuisance - 101-102
  private - 54, 91, 100-104, 132
Law-and-economics approach - 4-6, 125,
  171, 274
Leffler, Keith B. - 166n
Licensing - 154-157
  broadcast - 25, 67
  drugs - 28, 126
  medical profession - 126, 153-154
  nuclear reactors - 28, 216
  real estate brokers - 166
Life cycle theory - 228-231
Life insurance industry - 213
Lilley, William, III - 276n
Lindgren, Karl - 123n
Loan guarantees - 12
Love Canal - 92-93
Loving, Rush, Jr. - 275n
Lowi, Theodore J. - 11-12, 187

MacAvoy, Paul - 236n
McGee, John S. - 89n
McNeil, Donald G. Jr. - 34n
Macroeconomics - 37
Makielski, S. J., Jr. - 123n
Marcus, Alfred - 112
Margolis, Howard - 187
Maritime industry - 11
Market failure - 9, 63-64, 66-68, 87, 91-97
Marshall, Alfred - 93
Marshall, John - 135
Marshall, Ray - 126
Market-property rights system - 116
Mayhew, David - 190
Meadows, Edward - 274n
Medical licensing - 126, 153-154
Mendeloff, John - 165n

Mercantilism - 8
Mergers - 76-78
Meyer, Peter - 165n
Microeconomics - 37
Miller, James C., III - 276n
Mills, Edwin S. - 123n
Minimax marginalism - 191-192
Minimum wage - 14, 127, 146, 149
Minimum winning coalition - 191-192
Mises, Ludwig Von - 44
Mishan, Ezra J. - 123n, 260
Monopoly - 31, 44, 178
  government-imposed - 129, 134-139
  natural - 65, 68-78, 86-87, 129, 134
Monopoly rent - 157
Motor Carrier Act of 1980 - 41
Multiple-dwelling regulation - 148
Munn v. *Illinois* - 74, 140
Muskie, Edmund - 187

Nader, Ralph - 32, 53, 179, 203, 224
National Highway Traffic Safety Admin-
  istration (NHTSA) - 32, 158-159, 224
National Industrial Recovery Act - 31
National Labor Relations Board (NLRB)
  - 32, 149, 200
National Mediation Board - 200
National Transportation Safety Board -
  200
Natural gas regulation - 230
Natural monopoly regulation - 65, 68-78,
  86-87, 129, 134
Nebbia v. *New York* (1934) - 140
Negotiable-order-of-withdrawal (NOW)
  accounts - 183
New Deal - 30-32, 177-179, 239
New York Times - 7, 217, 238
New York Yankees - 130
Ng, Yew-Kwang - 122n
Nijkamp, Peter - 94, 123n
Niskanen, William - 275n
Nixon, Richard - 187, 247
No-benefit argument - 241-242
No-risk analysis - 262
Noise pollution - 32, 93
Noll, Roger - 271
Nuclear Regulatory Commission (NRC) -
  7, 200, 214, 246
  history - 32
  licensing - 28, 212, 216, 268
  standards - 118
Nuisance - 101-102

Occupational Safety and Health Act of
  1970 - 41, 150
Occupational Safety and Health Administration (OSHA) - 7, 32, 127, 146, 150, 173,
  200-201, 224, 242, 260, 272

Office of Management and Budget (OMB) - 199, 232-233, 264
Oi, Walter - 235n
Oil crisis - 180
Okun, Arthur - 66
Organic statute - 15-19, 173
Organization of Petroleum Exporting Countries (OPEC) - 180
O'Toole, Thomas A. - 60n, 275n
Overregulation - 237, 239-243, 254-257
    cancellation - 255
    cumulation - 255
    politics - 255-257
Owen, Bruce - 27, 216

Paretian optimality - 128-129
Pareto, Vilfredo - 128
Parisi, Anthony J. - 122n
Peanut butter - 29, 212, 242
Peltzman, Sam - 235n
Pennsylvania Supreme Court - 102
Performance goals. *See* Economic performance goals, Social performance goals.
Performance standards
    person - 154-155
    activity - 161, 163
Pesticides - 117
Pharmaceutical regulation
    advertising - 20, 151-152, 181
    information - 151-154, 160, 162
    licensing - 28, 126
    testing - 22, 23, 153, 159, 181, 205, 212
    thalidomide - 180-184
Pigou, A. C. - 89n, 93-94, 104-106, 108
Policy techniques - 9
    distribution - 11
    redistribution - 11-12
Pollution. *See* Emissions, Environmental regulation, Noise pollution, Water pollution.
Pollution control equipment - 112
Pollution rights - 91, 110-111, 114-115
Posner, Richard - 160, 202-203, 225-226
Postal Service, U.S. - 58
Price controls - 55, 68
Price discrimination - 19, 223-224
Private law - 91, 100-104, 132
Product safety - 158-159
Prohibition - 117, 119
Progressive Era - 31, 151, 239
Promotional regulation - 65, 67, 83-87
Property rights system - 91, 101, 110-111, 113, 115, 121-122
    joint costs - 113-114
    pollution - 111-115
    transaction costs - 114-115
Public goods - 85

Racial Discrimination - 126, 141-145
Radio Act of 1927 - 81-82
Radio regulation - 25, 67, 80-81. *See also* Federal Communications Commission (FCC).
Railroad Deregulation Act. *See* Staggers Rail Act of 1980.
Railroad regulation - 8, 19, 30-31, 85, 125-126, 145-147, 198, 230
    certificate of public convenience and necessity (CPCN) - 136-137
    Staggers Rail Act of 1980 - 238-239, 250
Randall, Alan - 123n
Reagan, Ronald - 33, 238-239, 254
Redistribution - 11-12
Registration - 156-157
Regulation over the activity - 158-163
Regulation over thè person - 154-158
    certification - 156-158
    licensing - 154-157
    registration - 156-157
Regulation Q - 251
Regulatory agencies
    Executive department bureaus - 173, 198-201
    decision rules - 214-216
    independent agencies - 173, 198-200
    independent commissions - 173, 198-200
Regulatory Analysis Review Group (RARG) - 261-262, 271
Regulatory budget - 264-266
Regulatory history - 30-33
Regulatory justifications - 9, 243-244. *See also* Efficiency regulation, Equity regulation, Externalities.
Regulatory legislation - 171-194
    minimax marginalism - 191-193, 251
    minimum winning coalition - 191-193
    motivation - 189-193
    public philosophy - 177-179, 193
Regulatory politics
    capture theory - 229-231
    life cycle theory - 228-229
Regulatory reform - 169, 237-247. *See also* Deregulation, Overregulation.
    Ash Council - 247
    populists - 248-249
    restrictivists - 248, 255, 269
    Task Force on Regulatory Relief - 262
    traditionalists - 247-248, 269
Regulatory statute - 15-19, 23-27
Remedies - 24-26
Residuum rule - 210
Resource Conservation and Recovery Act of 1976 - 93
Ripley, W. Z. - 230
Risk-benefit analysis - 263-264

Risk-risk analysis - 262-263
Robinson, Jackie - 141-142
Robinson-Patman Act - 19, 139, 178
Roosevelt, Franklin D. - 199
Ruff, Larry E. - 42, 97
Rulemaking - 29, 197, 204, 216-222
Russia Company - 135
Ruth, Babe - 130

Saccharin - 262-263
Safety and health regulation - 43, 53-55, 240
    consumer - 217-221
    environmental - 37, 42-43, 47
    occupational - 32, 127, 150-151
Sanctions - 23, 26-27
Savings and loan associations - 32. *See also* Banking regulation.
Schmalensee, Richard - 69-70, 72-73, 88n
Securities and Exchange Commission (SEC) - 32, 153, 158, 176, 200, 231, 269
Seidman, David - 165n
Separation - 117-118
Sexual discrimination - 126
Sherman Antitrust Act of 1890 - 31, 75-76
Smith, Adam
    competition - 50-51
    free contract - 131
    free market - 4, 9, 35, 43-46, 48, 55, 59
    natural monopolies - 75
    regulation - 46-48, 98
    The Wealth of Nations - 4, 9, 35, 44, 47
Social costs - 212-214
Social performance goals - 5, 35, 40-44, 92
    competition - 52-54
    costs - 41-44
Soviet Union - 39, 180
Specification standards - 161, 163
Staggers Rail Act of 1980 - 238-239, 250
Stahl, Ingemar - 123n
Standard Oil Company - 76
Standards - 118-119, 161, 163, 217-221
    performance - 161, 163
    specification - 161, 163
Stigler, George - 40, 44, 129
Stock exchanges - 32, 158, 231
Stubblebine, W. C. - 98-99
Subpoena - 20-22
Subsidies - 8, 11-12, 58, 87, 107-109
    Baumol approach - 106-107
    Pigouvian approach - 104-106
    positive externalities - 91-101
Sulfur dioxide - 105
Sunset provisions - 272-273
Supreme Court
    appeals - 211
    contracts - 147
    corporate charter - 135

Munn v. *Illinois* (1877) - 74, 140
Nebbia v. *New York* (1934) - 140
subpoenas - 22
Yick Wo v. *Hopkins* (1886) - 215
Symbolic politics - 186-188

Task Force on Regulatory Relief - 262
Tax-subsidy policy - 5, 91, 101, 107-109
    Baumol approach - 106-107, 109
    Pigouvian approach - 104-106, 108
Technical efficiency - 65-68
Television regulation - 25, 67, 80-81, 83, 216
Temporary National Economic Committee (TNEC) - 213
Tennessee Valley Authority - 58
Textile Fibers Identification Act - 18-19
Textile industry - 180
Thalidomide - 180-184
Thomas, Jo - 234n
Thompson, Arthur A. - 60n
Tobacco industry - 190
Toxic substances - 32
Transaction costs - 114-115, 121-122
Transportation Department - 255
    Federal Aviation Administration - 7, 32, 78-80, 160, 200
    Federal Railroad Administration - 200
    National Highway Traffic Safety Administration (NHTSA) - 32, 158-159, 200, 224
Treasury Department
    Bureau of Alcohol, Tobacco, and Firearms - 200
    Comptroller of the Currency - 30, 200
    U.S. Customs Service - 200
Truth in Lending Act - 148
Turner, Donald F. - 89n

U.S. Steel - 50
United Airlines - 252
United Mine Workers (UMW) - 150
Utilities regulation - 23, 68-70, 74-76. *See also* Antitrust regulation, Natural monopoly regulation.

Vehicle Safety Act of 1966 - 163
Vietnam war - 189
Vinyl chloride - 103
Volkswagen - 49

Wall Street Journal - 241
Wardell, William - 60n, 212
Warranties - 133, 161
Washington Post - 241
Water pollution - 21, 32
Water Pollution Control Act - 21
Waverman, Leonard - 88n

The Wealth of Nations - 4, 9, 35, 44, 47
Weaver, Paul - 275n
Weber, Max - 15, 164n, 222-223
Weidenbaum, Murray L. - 41, 241-242, 257-258, 265
Weingast, Barry R. - 277n
Welborn, David - 12
Welfare economics - 94-95
Welfare efficiency - 65-68

Wellisz, Stanislaw - 122n
West Germany - 240-241
Williams, Walter E. - 143-144
Wilson, James Q. - 179, 184-185
Winter, Ralph E. - 275n

Yick Wo v. *Hopkins* (1886) - 215

Zoning - 107, 117-118